SOCCER
Winning Through Technique and Tactics
Revised Edition

*To my wife Mira and children Rudy,
Mitchell and Elizabeth*

*To my parents Rudolph and Millie,
and to my sister Nancy*

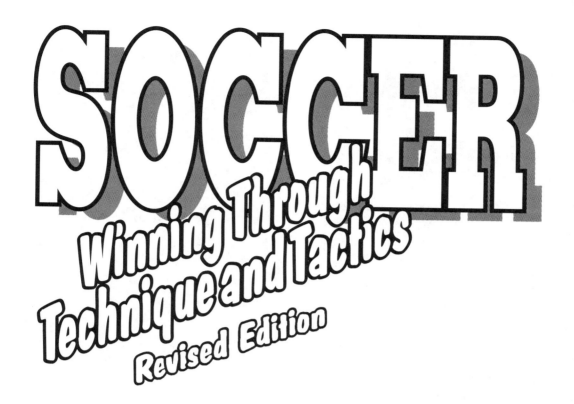

SOCCER
Winning Through Technique and Tactics
Revised Edition

Richard Alagich

McGRAW-HILL BOOK COMPANY Sydney
New York   San Francisco   Auckland   Bogotá
Caracas   Lisbon   London   Madrid   Mexico City
Milan   Montreal   New Delhi   San Juan
Singapore   Tokyo   Toronto

First published 1995
Revised edition 1996

National Library of Australia Cataloguing-in-Publication data:
    Alagich, Richard.
    Soccer: winning through technique and tactics.

        Rev. ed.
        Includes index.
        ISBN 0 07 470366 8.

1. Soccer - Coaching. 2. Soccer for children - Coaching.
I. Title.

796. 334077

Published in Australia by
McGraw-Hill Book Company Australia Pty Limited
4 Barcoo Street, Roseville NSW 2069, Australia
Acquisitions Editor   Robert McLeod
Production Editors   Sybil Kesteven, Sarah Baker
Designer   George Sirett, Asymmetric Typography Pty Ltd
Illustrator   Diane Booth
Photographer   David Basioli
Typeset in Palatino in Australia by Craftsmen Type & Art
Printed in Australia by McPherson's Printing Group

Foreword

Ernst Happel, the world-class coach who sadly died all too early, would probably describe this book by saying, 'Don't let yourself be led by the nose — unless you see this book, which makes fascinating reading and contains invaluable information for football, the world's leading sport!'

The football connoisseur, in this case the author of this book, does not belong to that group of people who hound junior players around the 400 m racing track to enhance their fitness or to warm them up during their training session, or who know nothing about 'individual capacity' and 'steady state', or who boast about peak form or even use it to pressure players. He knows for certain that fitness means more than physical capacity or the player's mental and physical state. If sensibly and specifically graded, whether in team practice or alone, with or without the ball, a player's standard of performance is more important than a sportsman's fitness during training.

Our friend has skilfully transformed his vast experience into words, logically and sensibly incorporating topics such as technique and tactics for up-and-coming players, as well as for amateurs and professionals, into words and in pictures.

FIFA, the world governing body of football, has no doubt that this well thought out and illustrated handbook will prove to be a great help for theoretical and practical training. We have to congratulate the author on his work and thank him for the service he has rendered football and his continent with this book. We warmly recommend it to every football fan, whether young or old, or theoretically or practically biased.

J. S. BLATTER
FIFA General Secretary

Les Murray, from Australia's SBS Television, recommends...

We all have visions of the complete footballer: superbly skilled, able to be the master of the ball with both feet, the chest, the head. Sharp as a razor, intelligent, innovative, calm, tactically disciplined, fit to last for two games, explosive on takeoff, fearless in the tackle and always fully motivated.

And we would all readily take to the training field to teach him or her all these qualities if any of them were seen to be lacking. Trouble is once we get there we don't know where to start. Little do we know that players vary enormously in age and responsiveness, not to say physical attributes. And that developing or training soccer players is a simple but systematic, often scientific business.

How dearly I would have loved to have a method to call on when, some years ago, I took to the business of junior coaching. They were a bunch of 11 year olds, all willing learners and I a willing teacher. But our minds rarely met.

This book is the one most such coaches, and even the more educated ones, ought to be looking for. It tells you, in a simple and easy-to-follow yet analytical way, how a footballer is fashioned — from a raw minor who has never kicked a ball in his life to a young adult, fully equipped and ready to play at the highest professional level.

Soccer the world game, with all its vastness, the teeming millions who play and follow it, has been remarkably short on a book such as this, a tool suitable and common to all who want the complete and comprehensive guide to football coaching.

It fills, and is destined to fill for a very long time, a huge void indeed.

Letter from FIFA

Comment on your teaching manual *Soccer: Winning Techniques and Tactics* by Richard Alagich

We refer to the above-mentioned document and would like to take the opportunity to thank you for your efforts for the publication of this teaching manual. We utterly appreciate your engagement in this respect and would like to congratulate you on the realisation of this project.

We have studied this publication with great interest and are pleased to say that the author deserves praise for his work. The contents are clearly divided and the texts accompanied by photographs are excellent. This teaching manual can be recommended especially to active youth coaches, be it professionals or amateurs.

Thanking you for your valuable co-operation, we remain with best regards.

Sincerely yours,
FEDERATION INTERNATIONALE
DE FOOTBALL ASSOCIATION

Walter Gagg
Head of Technical Dept.

Preface

Soccer: Winning Techniques and Tactics has been written for youth coaches developing players from 5 to 17 years.

This manual will be of great benefit, not only to soccer coaches and players, but also to school teachers, parents and soccer administrators participating in the organising and educating of youth soccer players.

Soccer is the result of many years of research, using a youth development program to analyse the major technical–tactical elements and structuring them to meet the demands of youth development.

The 111 training sessions, 222 technical–tactical coaching drills, 111 shooting exercises, over 1000 photographs, 126 drawings, 22 introductory helpful tactical games, 24 playing patterns and 26 set play situations provide a comprehensive aid to soccer coaching.

This coaching manual is divided into 6 levels, covering the ages of 5 to 17 plus years.

Level 1 (5 to 8 years) represents the fun phase, where the players are involved in small pitch soccer, gymnastics and playing soccer without the competitive technical–tactical and physical pressures of being an instant success.

Levels 2 and 3 (9 to 12 years) represent the technical period in which elements are taught for the sole purpose of creating a basis for tactical development. Tactical development is not taught at this level at the expense of techniques.

Levels 4, 5 and 6 (13 to 17 plus years) represent the tactical period. The successful transition to tactical elements is made possible by the development of a solid technical basis.

As coaches progress from one level of development to another, provisions are made in the program for reinforcement of the technical–tactical elements learnt in previous levels.

The questions that usually puzzle coaches are: at what age should systematic specialisation start? What technical–tactical elements should be taught? What are the common faults and corrections? How should a coaching session be organised?

This coaching manual will provide the answers to these questions.

Acknowledgments

The author wishes to thank the following people for their co-operation and assistance in turning a huge and complicated manuscript into a useful coaching manual.

Editorial consultant: Les Murray
Diagrams: Fred Wall
Youth players: Anthony Barbalace, Anthony Surace, Nicholas Femia, Frank Chirillo, David Pascuzzo, Roland Weber, Malcolm Stewart, Elizabeth Alagich, Adrien Janssen, Neil Martin, Sandro Teghini, Glen Butcher, David Osmond, Iain Church, Chris Murace, Matthew Turner, Wade Mitford, Luke Mitchell, Bobby Durdevic, Nathon Foti, Tom Pears, Andrew Barton and Lal MacAllan.

Special thanks are due to Paul Raxworthy and John Rowe at McGraw-Hill for making this project a reality.

Contents

Explanation of symbols

Movement of the player when not in possession

Movement of the player when in possession

Movement of the ball

Shot at goal

Players

Ball thrown by hand

Coach

Rotation of players when not in possession

Rotation of players when in possession

Posts

Markers

Net

Kicking boards

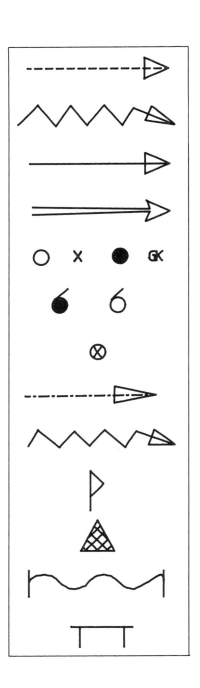

Introduction

The period of soccer specialisation

The quality and demands of today's modern game require early specialisation and a controlled systematic development of players.

The eventual success or result in soccer will be determined by many factors. These factors need to be considered in the following equation and in the overall youth development program.

$$R = F1A + F2F + F3P + F4C1 + F5C2 + F6M + F7S + F8C3 + F9O + F10E$$

where:

R	=	result
F1A (factor 1A)	=	anthropometric factor
F2F (factor 2F)	=	functional factor
F3P (factor 3P)	=	psychomotor factor
F4C1 (factor 4C1)	=	cognitive factor
F5C2 (factor 5C2)	=	conative factor
F6M (factor 6M)	=	motivation factor
F7S (factor 7S)	=	sociological factor
F8C3 (factor 8C3)	=	coaching factor
F9O (factor 9O)	=	objective factor
F10E (factor 10E)	=	error factor

The problems and questions that will arise with early specialisation of players are:

- At what age should specialisation start?
- How much should the players exercise?
- What technical–tactical elements should be taught?
- What is the coaching session structure for different age groups?

It is intended that these questions be answered in the soccer development program.

Soccer can be played at any age but systematic coaching should start around the age of 9 to 10 years. At this age the psychomotor and intellectual functions are well balanced. In other words the players are physically and mentally well balanced for starting to learn soccer.

There are anatomical, physiological, psychological and sociological changes that occur in human development. There are biological differences between players even though they are of the same calendar age. For example, in a junior team, you will always have players that look older and behave much older than others even though they are of the same calendar age. This is why there is no definite age when to start on the program, just around 9 to 10 years.

This period of 9 to 10 years does not necessarily apply to other sports.

It takes almost a decade to develop a player so coaches should be patient with the development process and not try to 'feed' too much information in too short a time. They should get away from the winning emphasis, where concentration is on tactical development, and spend more time in the early phases in creating a solid technical basis.

The period of systematic preparation lasts on the average approximately 8 to 9 years.

In coaching, success and accomplishment will be greater the more stable the habit. If a person develops a habit in certain specific movements, then he or she will with greater ease and success execute the movement. In understanding this it is necessary in the coaching sessions for the coach to conduct and create movements that the player will experience in the game. The coach should control these movements with or without the ball so that the correct habits are adopted.

This modern tendency is called situational coaching.

The program of development in the soccer development program is made up of 6 levels or 3 phases:

- *Level 1:* 5 to 8 years — fun phase
- *Levels 2 and 3:* 9 to 12 years — technical phase
- *Levels 4, 5 and 6:* 13 to 17 years — tactical phase

Fun phase

Technical phase

Tactical phase

First phase of development — fun phase

Level 1: 5 to 8 years

The 'ripe' age to start with systematic coaching is around the age of 9 to 10 years.

Many will no doubt agree with this but will then ask the question — what do we do with players that have yet to reach this ripe age? If these youngsters want to play soccer then we should let them play.

Players at this level should not be subjected to the technical, tactical, physical and competitive pressures. This is their fun period; training and playing should be for fun.

The competition should be small-sided and informal — small-sided simply because there is more touch of the ball, less distance to cover between the two goals and all players are able to defend their goal and attack to score goals. In this way there is total freedom in the game, and this is what the players enjoy most.

It has to be understood that players at this early age are not motivated to learn the repetitious technical elements, have limited concentration spans and are very easily distracted.

At this level children should be encouraged to play soccer without the pressure of trying to win and of being an instant success.

Children playing small pitch soccer for fun, without the pressure of trying to win

Second phase of development — technical phase

Levels 2 and 3: 9 to 12 years

The second phase is regarded as the technical phase, when the player is taught the basic technical elements of the game correctly. This phase, with its technical emphasis, will establish a solid basis for later tactical development.

Tactics must not be taught at this early age at the expense of techniques; however, parallel with the teaching of techniques, progression is maintained with the implementation of basic tactical elements. This implementation is secondary.

There is no value in teaching a player support in attack or defence if she is unable to control the ball in the simplest of situations. As long as a player has difficulty in controlling the ball she will not be able to realise her tactical ideas.

The gradual progression in coaching techniques is as follows:

1. player with the ball — without pressure
2. player with the ball — token pressure
3. player with the ball — full pressure

From an early age players must develop correct technical–tactical habits

Third phase of development — tactical phase
Levels 4, 5 and 6: 13 to 17+ years

The third phase of development is represented by an increase in the tactical and physical demands on the player.

Tactics decide how the physical qualities and advantages and technical skills of the player should be used for the benefit of the team in the actual match situation.

Having established a solid technical basis, the coach now is able to progress on to the more complex exercises of combining the technical knowledge in given specific match situations.

With coaching tactics, as with techniques, it is important to ensure that there is a gradual progression and move from the central (basic) to the peripheral (complex) elements.

The coaching of tactics is represented by 3 stages:

1. individual tactics
2. group tactics
3. team tactics

The gradual progression in coaching tactics is as follows:

1. player without the ball — without pressure
2. player with the ball — without pressure
3. player with the ball — token pressure
4. player with the ball — full pressure

All exercises given are to be situational, that is, situations that the player is going to experience in the game.

In the third phase of development the objectives differ from the objectives in the second phase. Coaches during this phase of development should primarily be concerned with:

1. increasing the general and specific physical development of the player;
2. the technical improvement of the player moving with or without the ball; teaching the fine technical points combined with speed and explosive player movement;
3. the tactical improvement of the individual, group and team. The coach should show a greater interest in the player in regard to his attacking and defensive function. For example, how effective is the player in moving and creating space in attack and closing down space in defence;

4. flexibility in relation to the player specialising in a particular position or playing role. Even during this phase players should be encouraged to play different roles or positions. This way the player will establish a better understanding of how players play, react and think in different situations;

5. forming a positive relationship within the group. To achieve this it is important to arrange cultural/social activities. These activities will further improve the harmony within the squad and at the same time allow the coach to reach a better understanding of his players. Such activities could be dinners, picnics, film nights, trips, camping, etc.

The greatest player of all time — Pele — with a young admirer and the author

Teaching methods in the soccer development program

The teaching methods in the soccer development program are:

1. the situational method
2. the analytic method
3. the combined method

The modern way of coaching is dominated by the *situational method*. This is teaching elements as a complete movement that meets the conditions of the game. The disadvantage of the situational method is that some players are unable to complete the technical–tactical movements as a whole. If this occurs then the *analytic method* is applied.

The analytic method is where the movement is broken up and 1 particular phase is executed. For example, the player does not have his ankle joint locked and hard when kicking with the full instep. With this method the player stands beside the ball and executes the kick, concentrating only on the ankle joint.

When the coach is satisfied with the movement, he or she then goes back to the situational method of coaching.

The *combined method* is a combination of the situational and analytic methods. Here the movement is executed as a whole but where the technical fault occurs, then that part is frozen and the analytic method applied.

The situational method, however, must dominate the coaching sessions and coaches are only to apply other methods if there are technical–tactical difficulties.

Three points that are important for the coach to observe are:

1. when coaching move from the *central* (basic) to the *peripheral* (complex) technical–tactical elements;
2. when progressing on to new subject matter in the program it is necessary to have repetition and reinforcement of the elements already exercised in the program;
3. when teaching the technical–tactical elements it is necessary for the coach to progress in a certain order.

The order is as follows:

1. Talk to the players about the element you are going to introduce and its role in the game.

2. Demonstrate the element, explaining the correct and incorrect executions. The demonstration should be from 3 angles: front, back and side.

3. The players then execute the element with correction from you.

4. Link and combine several elements of technique (such as receiving, dribbling and kicking for goal) with increased demand on the psychomotor ability (such as moving quickly to control the ball, speed in changing direction and accuracy in shooting). Emphasis is on deception and change of rhythm in moving with or without the ball. The technical–tactical execution is to be done without defensive pressure.

5. Execution of the exercises with token and then progressing to full pressure.

6. Play a game to examine to what degree the players are solving the technical–tactical problems, and to what degree you have been successful in exercises of correction.

The basic direction in coaching you should take is: exercise, game, correction.

Order of teaching technical–tactical elements

A very important aspect of coaching soccer is in what order the technical–tactical elements should be taught.

An order has to be established, moving from the central (basic) to the peripheral (complex) elements.

The soccer development program has been designed to satisfy an order in the complete development of the player:

- level 1: 5 to 8 years of age
- level 2: 9 to 10 years of age
- level 3: 11 to 12 years of age
- level 4: 13 to 14 years of age
- level 5: 15 to 16 years of age
- level 6: 17+ years of age

Level 1 is a fun period, so training and playing should simply be for the sole purpose of having fun.

Levels 2 and 3 are regarded as the technical periods of development where emphasis is placed on teaching the technical elements. Parallel with the technical elements, tactical elements are introduced, bringing the exercises closer to situations the player will find in the game. However, this is secondary during levels 2 and 3.

Levels 4, 5 and 6 are the tactical periods of development. We are now able to progress into a more complex period of development, as a solid technical basis has been established in levels 2 and 3.

In each level new elements are introduced; however, provisions in the program allow for reinforcement with progression on to the more complex elements.

This balanced systematic program guarantees that during the course of education, the major technical–tactical elements are taught, moving from the central (basic) to the peripheral (complex) elements.

Structure of a practical coaching session

The structure of a practical coaching session comprises an introduction, main and concluding part, explained in detail at each level in the soccer development program.

Within the coaching structure there are also physiological, intellectual and emotional loads that have to be satisfied.

The physiological load is achieved through the various exercises. The load gradually increases to a maximum in the middle of the main part of the coaching session with a reduction towards the concluding part.

The intellectual load is at its maximum during the main part of the session when new elements are being taught or old ones are reinforced.

In the introductory and concluding parts the intellectual loading is at a minimum.

The emotional loading is high at the start of the session with an interesting helpful tactical game and again in the main part of the session with the game. Here the emotions are running high with the desire to defend or score a goal.

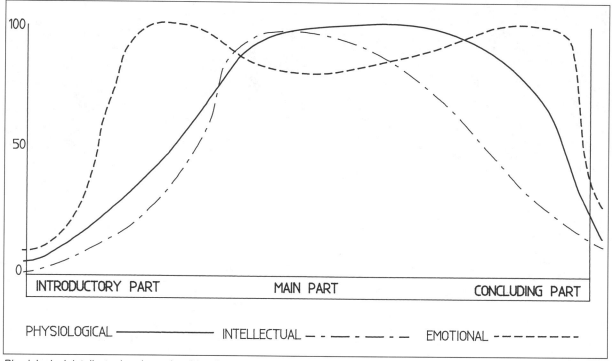

Physiological, intellectual and emotional loading during a practical coaching session

1958 World Cup champions Brazil with 17-year-old superstar Pele (fifth from right) in Sweden

Superstar Pele competes for the ball in the 1958 World Cup final

LEVEL 1: 5 TO 8 YEARS

technical–tactical development program

Core learning areas in the soccer development program

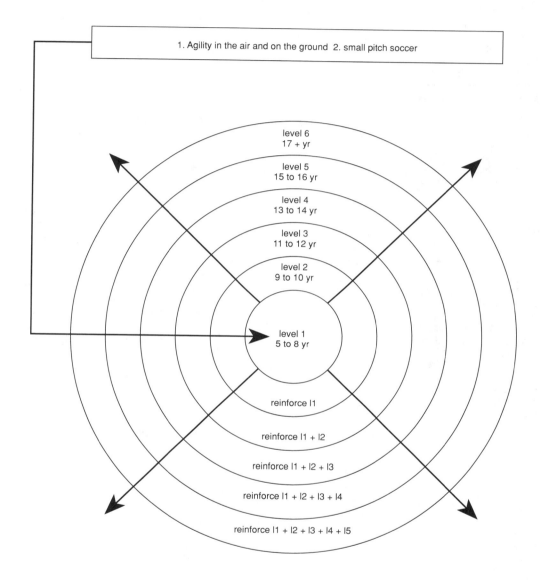

1. Agility in the air and on the ground   2. small pitch soccer

level 6
17 + yr

level 5
15 to 16 yr

level 4
13 to 14 yr

level 3
11 to 12 yr

level 2
9 to 10 yr

level 1
5 to 8 yr

reinforce l1

reinforce l1 + l2

reinforce l1 + l2 + l3

reinforce l1 + l2 + l3 + l4

reinforce l1 + l2 + l3 + l4 + l5

Technical–tactical program

Element	Level 1 (5–8 yr)	Level 2 (9–10 yr)	Level 3 (11–12 yr)	Level 4 (13–14 yr)	Level 5 (15–16 yr)	Level 6 (17+ yr)
Agility in the air and on the ground	1	Reinforce	Reinforce	Reinforce	Reinforce	Reinforce
Basic running and sprinting technique		1	Reinforce	Reinforce	Reinforce	Reinforce
The start technique (forward side)		2	Reinforce	Reinforce	Reinforce	Reinforce
Jumping with 1 and 2 feet			1	Reinforce	Reinforce	Reinforce
Changing direction and speed				1	Reinforce	Reinforce
Dribbling with the full instep		3	Reinforce	Reinforce	Reinforce	Reinforce
Dribbling with the sole of the foot		4	Reinforce	Reinforce	Reinforce	Reinforce
Dribbling with the outside of the instep			2	Reinforce	Reinforce	Reinforce
Dribbling with the inside of the instep			3	Reinforce	Reinforce	Reinforce
Deceptive dribbling and feinting (15 tricks)		5	Reinforce	Reinforce	Reinforce	Reinforce
Deceptive dribbling and feinting (10 tricks)			4	Reinforce	Reinforce	Reinforce
Deceptive dribbling and feinting (5 tricks)				2	Reinforce	Reinforce
Juggling the ball (individual)		6	Reinforce	Reinforce	Reinforce	Reinforce
Juggling the ball (partner)			5	Reinforce	Reinforce	Reinforce
Juggling the ball (group)				3	Reinforce	Reinforce
Kicking the ball with the full instep		7	Reinforce	Reinforce	Reinforce	Reinforce
Kicking the ball with the inside of the foot		8	Reinforce	Reinforce	Reinforce	Reinforce
Kicking the ball with the inside of the instep			6	Reinforce	Reinforce	Reinforce
Kicking the ball with the outside of the instep			7	Reinforce	Reinforce	Reinforce
The wall pass — 1–2 pass			8	Reinforce	Reinforce	Reinforce
Chipping the ball				4	Reinforce	Reinforce
Full volley kick (front side)				5	Reinforce	Reinforce
Half volley kick (front side)				6	Reinforce	Reinforce
Overhead (scissors) volley kick					1	Reinforce
Kicking with the toe, heel and knee					2	Reinforce
Receiving (amortisation) — inside of the foot		9	Reinforce	Reinforce	Reinforce	Reinforce
Receiving (amortisation) with the full instep		10	Reinforce	Reinforce	Reinforce	Reinforce
Receiving (amortisation) with the thigh			9	Reinforce	Reinforce	Reinforce
Receiving (amortisation) with the chest			10	Reinforce	Reinforce	Reinforce
Receiving (amortisation) with the head				7	Reinforce	Reinforce
Receiving (trapping) — inside of the foot		11	Reinforce	Reinforce	Reinforce	Reinforce
Receiving (trapping) with the sole of the foot		12	Reinforce	Reinforce	Reinforce	Reinforce
Receiving (trapping) with the outside of the instep			11	Reinforce	Reinforce	Reinforce
Receiving (trapping) with the stomach/chest				8	Reinforce	Reinforce
Heading with the middle zone of the forehead			12	Reinforce	Reinforce	Reinforce
Heading with the side zone of the forehead				9	Reinforce	Reinforce
The diving header					3	Reinforce
The delay and basic block tackle		13	Reinforce	Reinforce	Reinforce	Reinforce
The sliding–straddle tackle			13	Reinforce	Reinforce	Reinforce
The shoulder charge				10	Reinforce	Reinforce
Intercepting the pass					4	Reinforce
Basic combinations — 1:1		14	Reinforce	Reinforce	Reinforce	Reinforce
Basic combinations — 2:0			14	Reinforce	Reinforce	Reinforce
Basic combinations — 2:1			15	Reinforce	Reinforce	Reinforce
Basic combinations — 2:2				11	Reinforce	Reinforce
Basic combinations — 3:0					5	Reinforce
Basic combinations — 3:2					6	Reinforce
Helpful tactical games		15	Reinforce	Reinforce	Reinforce	Reinforce
Kicking at goal		16	Reinforce	Reinforce	Reinforce	Reinforce
Heading at goal			16	Reinforce	Reinforce	Reinforce
Team technical–tactical playing patterns — attack					7	Reinforce
Team technical–tactical playing patterns — defence					8	Reinforce
Set play — attacking situations					9	Reinforce
Set play — defending situations					10	Reinforce
Small pitch soccer — TE–TA elements	2	Reinforce	Reinforce	Reinforce	Reinforce	Reinforce
Full pitch soccer — TE–TA elements				12	Reinforce	Reinforce
	2	16	16	12	10	0

Total soccer development program elements = 56 elements

Technical–tactical elements to be coached

1. Agility in the air and on the ground
2. Small pitch soccer
   Total elements = 2

Time allocation for the 60 minute coaching session

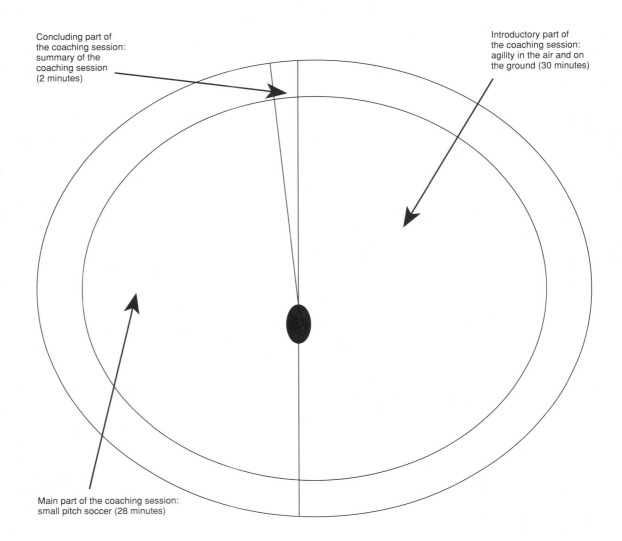

Concluding part of the coaching session: summary of the coaching session (2 minutes)

Introductory part of the coaching session: agility in the air and on the ground (30 minutes)

Main part of the coaching session: small pitch soccer (28 minutes)

Structure of the practical coaching session — 60 minutes

1. Introductory part of the coaching session
2. Main part of the coaching session
3. Concluding part of the coaching session
    3.1 Summary of the coaching session (2 minutes)

Total practical coaching time = 60 minutes

1. Introductory part of the coaching session

1.1 AGILITY IN THE AIR AND ON THE GROUND

Agility refers to the ability to move the whole body quickly and efficiently while maintaining body balance. In other words, agility is needed for quick changes of direction.

The agile and balanced players will quickly bounce up to their feet from the ground and keep playing, while the less agile player will push up with both hands in an unco-ordinated manner to regain balance.

The development of agility in the air and on the ground is necessary for creating a solid basis for the structured movements of soccer players with or without the ball.

The following basic elements of gymnastics will serve as an introduction to the soccer development program. These elements should only be conducted under the guidance of a qualified gymnastics coach.

However, if a club does not have such facilities available then the introductory part of the coaching session should be made up of helpful tactical fun games.

Some examples of introductory helpful tactical games are explained on page 28.

The elements of gymnastics are structured in 2 phases:

- *Phase 1:* 5 to 6 years
- *Phase 2:* 7 to 8 years

Phase 1: 5 to 6 years

TRAMPOLINE

The basic bounce: *can be used as a warm-up activity. The body and arms should be straight with head erect. At the top of the bounce keep the legs straight with toes pointing down. On the downward bounce flex the legs, hitting the mat with flat feet shoulder width*

The seat drop: *from the basic bounce position raise the legs to a horizontal position, moving arms forward and upwards. From here drop back on to the mat into the seat position and bounce back to vertical*

The tuck jump: *at the top of the bounce clasp the shins bringing the knees to the chest. Tuck the elbows in with eyes fixed on the centre end of the trampoline. The heels are against the seat while the toes are pointing downward*

The closed pike jump: *from the basic bounce bring the legs straight with toes pointing to a horizontal position. Bend the body forward at the hips with the hands straight with the legs*

The half pirouette: *on the bounce, raise 1 arm above the head while bending the other at 90° across the chest. Twist the body 180° around its vertical axis*

The split pike jump: *the split pike is similar to the closed pike jump except that both legs and arms are stretched apart during the bounce*

The pirouette: *this is similar to the half pirouette but twist a full 360° instead of 180°*

FLOOR

The forward roll: *crouch on the toes with hands on the mat shoulder width apart. Place the chin to the chest, lift the hips and kick off the mat and overbalance. Roll over to the crouch position*

  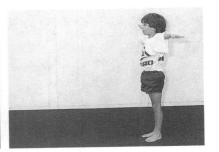

The backward roll: *squat on the mat with elbows bent and palms facing up. Curl the body and rock back, lowering the seat to the mat. Roll back and swing the feet over the head, rolling into a squat*

The mule kick: *place the hands on the mat shoulder width apart. All the weight is taken by the hands with a kick of 1 leg followed by the other high in the air*

The crouch balance: *place the hands on the mat shoulder width apart, palms down. Kick both legs high in the air, bent together while balancing on the hands in the crouch position*

The twist crouch: the player stands with 1 foot forward, bends and places hands flat on the mat. Travelling sideways, the legs are bent and together, twisting at the hips

BALANCE BEAM

Walking forward   *Walking backwards*

Walking through hoops   *Bouncing a ball*

   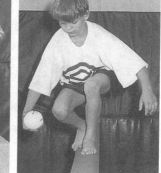

Balancing objects   *Picking up objects*

UMBRO

Catching a ball

Walking over objects

Hopping

MINI-TRAMPOLINE / VAULTING BOX

The basic bounce: *on hitting the trampoline mat swing the arms down and bend the legs with the feet flat. To get the upward bounce, push hard on the heels with the forward and upward swing of the hands*

The tuck jump: *the same technique as with the basic bounce but bring the knees to the chest, clasping the shins. Land softly on the mat*

The closed pike jump: *following the bounce bring the legs straight and to a horizontal position. Bend the body at the hips with the hands pointing down the shins*

The split pike jump: *the technique with this element is the same as with the closed pike jump, only the legs and arms are stretched apart*

The side vault: *from the mini-trampoline bounce place the hands on either side of the box. Twist the body to 1 side with a soft landing side-on to the box*

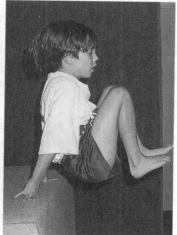

The bent leg squat vault: *following the bounce the stretched out arms touch the box while the legs are bent and close to the chest. The upper extremity is leaning forward. The legs straighten for a soft landing*

Phase 2: 7 to 8 years

TRAMPOLINE — Reinforce basic elements: 5 to 6 years

Swivel hips: *from a basic bounce, go into a seat drop. At the top of the bounce do a half twist and drop into another seat drop*

FLOOR — Reinforce basic elements: 5 to 6 years

The dive roll: *dive forward, stretching the body to land on the hands. Tuck the chin to the chest. Roll over the shoulders and on to the back*

BALANCE BEAM — Reinforce basic elements: 5 to 6 years

Inclined bench balances   See-saw   Passing over arms

MINI-TRAMPOLINE/VAULTING BOX — Reinforce basic elements: 5 to 6 years

Straddle vault: *following the bounce, lean forward and straighten the legs, keeping them apart with toes pointed. Extend the hands quickly so that they make contact with the apparatus and the body can straddle over it. Land on 2 feet, hands wide*

Forward dive roll: *leap forward with the body and arms stretched. The hands make contact first with the mat, softening the fall, the chin tucked into the chest and knees likewise. Staying curled, roll to your feet*

Forward somersault: *from the forward bounce clasp the shins by the hands with the chin tucked into the chest. With the quick rotation spin into the somersault, opening out before coming to the vertical axis*

1.2 Helpful tactical games

As explained earlier in this chapter, these games are applied only during the introductory part of the coaching session, instead of agility in the air and on the ground, if a qualified gymnastics coach and suitable gymnastic facilities are not available.

Two different helpful tactical games would be sufficient before the start of the main part of the coaching session.

1. Soccer marbles

Every player on the edge of the grid has a ball. A player has to dribble the ball up and down the grid. See how many laps the player can dribble without the ball being struck.

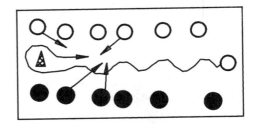

2. Last person in

All players in the grid dribble their ball, keeping possession, and trying to kick another player's ball out. A player must leave the grid when their ball is kicked out. The last player with a ball in the grid wins.

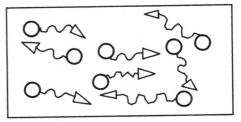

3. Shooting at the target

Players are divided into 2 teams. All players have a ball to the side of the grid. Each player shoots at the target. Each time the target is hit that team gains a point.

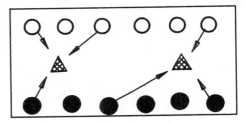

4. Lost ball

All players, except one, have a ball and dribble in the grid. The player without a ball must try and get a ball from 1 of the other players. The game continues with the player without a ball.

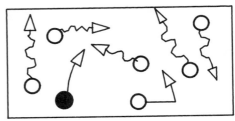

5. Dribbling across the grid

All players stand opposite each other with a ball. On a given signal they dribble the ball across to the other side and place it on the line. The team that first has all the balls on the line gains a point.

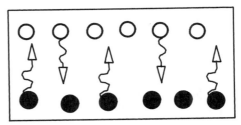

6. Dribbling relay races

Groups have dribbling relay competitions around stakes or markers.

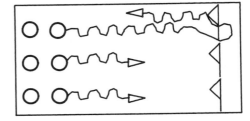

2. Main part of the coaching session

2.1 SMALL PITCH SOCCER

Every coaching session, at this level, should end with a small-sided game on a small pitch. It is these small-sided situations that the young players enjoy most. They are in constant contact with the ball, enabling the technical-tactical and physical skills to be put into practice.

The aim when playing small-sided games is simply to attack the opponent's goal in the phase of attack and defend your goal in the phase of defence. The phase of attack is the moment that your team gains possession, while the phase of defence is the moment that the team has lost possession.

This is called soccer tactics — the art by which the player's technical and physical qualities are used to achieve the best possible result.

Tactics can be divided into 3 distinct categories:

1. *Individual tactics:* pressing the player, pressing the ball, creating space, dribbling, feinting, receiving, heading, passing, shooting, etc.
2. *Group tactics:* the mobility and interchange of players, the recovery behind the ball of the front attacking line, defending the goal, counter attacking, offside tactics, co-operation with the goalkeeper, play wide or through the middle, etc.
3. *Team tactics:* keeping possession, slow build up, long direct penetrating passes, playing the high ball, keeping the ball low, switch of play, recovering behind the ball into a zone, pressing on all parts of the field, etc.

Team tactics used by the coach will also be determined by many factors that may include the way the opponents play, state of the playing surface, the team's position in the competition, phase of the game, the weather, etc.

The technical–tactical elements in the phase of attack are:

1. *Mobility:* the ability to move with or without the ball to create playing space.
2. *Penetration:* the ability to get past or behind defenders, with or without the ball.
3. *Width and depth:* the ability to create playing space across and along the field of play.
4. *Switch of play:* the ability to draw defenders out of position and exploit space on the opposite side.

The technical–tactical elements in the phase of defence are:

1. *Balance:* the ability to limit the creation of space, penetration and passing angles.
2. *Pressing the player without the ball:* the ability to reduce the time and playing space an attacking player will have when receiving the ball.
3. *Pressing the ball*: the ability to reduce the time and space the attacking player will have to receive, pass, dribble or shoot at goal.
4. *Zone and combined zone formations:* the ability to recover goal side of the ball, cover an area, and press any player entering that zone.

Note: It is necessary for coaches, coaching at all levels, to understand the technical–tactical elements in the phases of attack and defence. However, in level 1 emphasis is on agility and playing soccer to have fun.

Order of coaching technical–tactical elements in attack and defence

The following technical–tactical elements in attack and defence are to be applied and reinforced at each level.

TE–TA *elements in attack*				**TE–TA** *elements in defence*			
Number 1	*Number 2*	*Number 3*	*Number 4*	*Number 1*	*Number 2*	*Number 3*	*Number 4*
Level 1 (5 to 8 years) — Unlimited touches with the ball Playing for fun				Unlimited touches with the ball Playing for fun			
Level 2 (9 to 10 years) — Mobility Maximum 3 touches Reinforce level 1				Balance Reinforce level 1			
Level 3 (11 to 12 years) — Mobility Maximum 2 touches Reinforce levels 1 and 2	Penetration			Balance Reinforce levels 1 and 2	Pressing the player without the ball		
Level 4 (13 to 14 years) — Mobility Maximum 1 touch Reinforce levels 1 to 3	Penetration Reinforce level 3	Width and depth		Balance Reinforce levels 1 to 3	Pressing the player without the ball Reinforce level 3	Pressing the ball	
Level 5 (15 to 16 years) — Mobility Maximum 1 touch Reinforce levels 1 to 4	Penetration Reinforce levels 3 and 4	Width and depth Reinforce level 4	Switch of play	Balance Reinforce levels 1 to 4	Pressing the player without the ball Reinforce levels 3 and 4	Pressing the ball Reinforce level 4	Zone and combined zone defence
Level 6 (17+ years) — Mobility Maximum 1 touch Reinforce levels 1 to 5	Penetration Reinforce levels 3 to 5	Width and depth Reinforce levels 4 and 5	Switch of play Reinforce level 5	Balance Reinforce levels 1 to 5	Pressing the player without the ball Reinforce levels 3 to 5	Pressing the ball Reinforce levels 4 and 5	Zone and combined zone defence Reinforce level 5

The laws of the game

1. *The field of play*
   Length — 32 to 47 yards
   Width — 21 to 46 yards
   The goal area — no goal area required at this level
   The penalty area — 16 × 6 yards
   The corner area — no corner area required at this level
   The goals — shall be 4 yards apart joined by a horizontal cross-bar 4 feet high
   The centre circle — shall have a radius of 4 yards

2. *The ball* — shall be a size 3 and of leather

3. *Number of players* — a match shall be played by 2 teams consisting of not more than 6 players each; in each team there is a goalkeeper

4. *Referees and linesmen* — the coach shall officiate at each game

5. *Duration* — 12 minutes each way with 4 minutes for half-time (following the 30 minutes of agility elements)

6. *The start of play* — before or after goals are scored, play is started by a player taking a place kick at the centre. All defending players must be in their half and outside the circle

7. *The ball out of play* — when it has wholly crossed the goal line or touch line, when in the air or on the ground

8. *Offside* — there are no offsides at this level

9. *Fouls and misconduct* — the player is penalised by awarding a free kick

10. *Free kicks* — all free kicks can result in a direct shot at goal. All opposing players shall be at least 4 yards from the ball

11. *Penalty kicks* — the penalty kick is taken 6 yards from the goal line

12. *Throw-in* — at the point where the ball crossed the line, the throw is taken with both hands behind the head and with both feet on the ground

13. *Goal kick* — at the side where the ball crossed the line, the ball is placed in the goal area and kicked into play

14. *Corner kick* — if the ball passes over the goal line, excluding the goals, and is last played by the defending team, then a player from the attacking team takes a free kick from the corner of the field

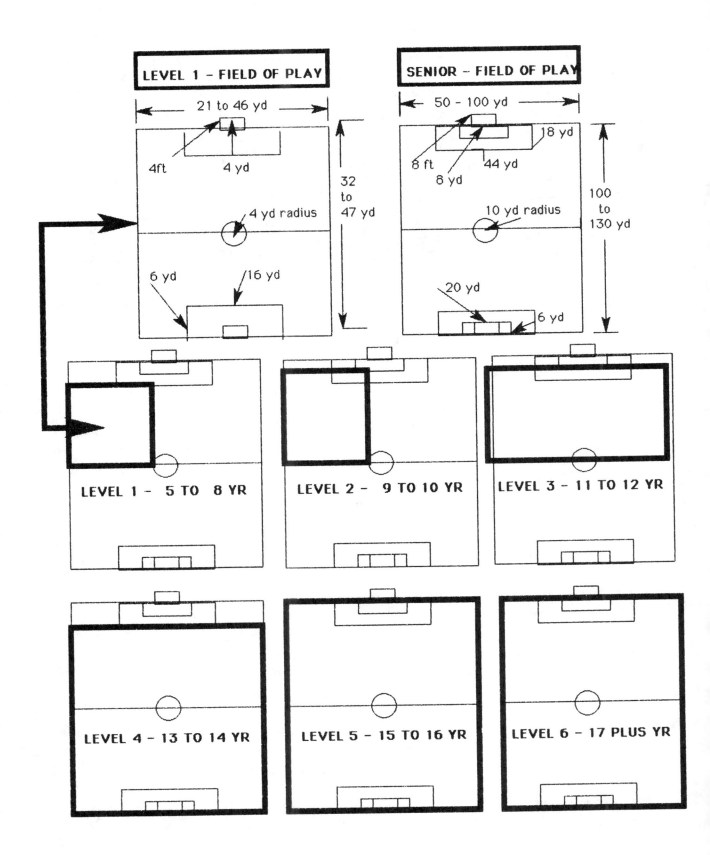

LEVEL 1 – FIELD OF PLAY

21 to 46 yd

4ft   4 yd

4 yd radius

6 yd   16 yd

32 to 47 yd

SENIOR – FIELD OF PLAY

50 – 100 yd

18 yd

8 ft   44 yd

8 yd

10 yd radius

20 yd   6 yd

100 to 130 yd

LEVEL 1 – 5 TO 8 YR

LEVEL 2 – 9 TO 10 YR

LEVEL 3 – 11 TO 12 YR

LEVEL 4 – 13 TO 14 YR

LEVEL 5 – 15 TO 16 YR

LEVEL 6 – 17 PLUS YR

technical–tactical development program

Core learning areas in the soccer development program

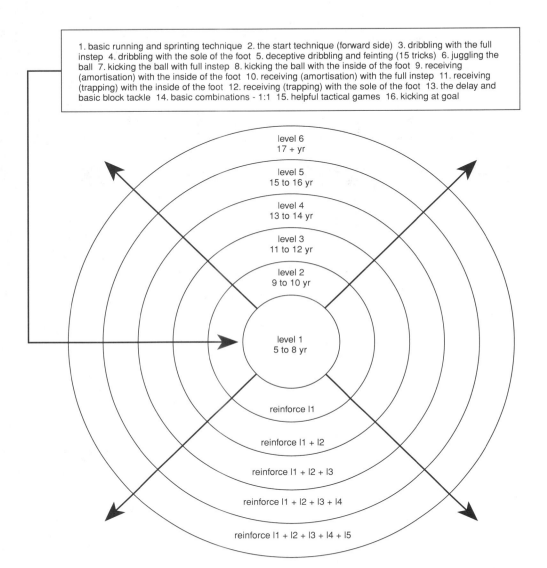

1. basic running and sprinting technique 2. the start technique (forward side) 3. dribbling with the full instep 4. dribbling with the sole of the foot 5. deceptive dribbling and feinting (15 tricks) 6. juggling the ball 7. kicking the ball with full instep 8. kicking the ball with the inside of the foot 9. receiving (amortisation) with the inside of the foot 10. receiving (amortisation) with the full instep 11. receiving (trapping) with the inside of the foot 12. receiving (trapping) with the sole of the foot 13. the delay and basic block tackle 14. basic combinations - 1:1 15. helpful tactical games 16. kicking at goal

level 6
17 + yr

level 5
15 to 16 yr

level 4
13 to 14 yr

level 3
11 to 12 yr

level 2
9 to 10 yr

level 1
5 to 8 yr

reinforce l1

reinforce l1 + l2

reinforce l1 + l2 + l3

reinforce l1 + l2 + l3 + l4

reinforce l1 + l2 + l3 + l4 + l5

Technical–tactical program

Element	Level 1 (5–8 yr)	Level 2 (9–10 yr)	Level 3 (11–12 yr)	Level 4 (13–14 yr)	Level 5 (15–16 yr)	Level 6 (17+ yr)
Agility in the air and on the ground	1	Reinforce	Reinforce	Reinforce	Reinforce	Reinforce
Basic running and sprinting technique		1	Reinforce	Reinforce	Reinforce	Reinforce
The start technique (forward side)		2	Reinforce	Reinforce	Reinforce	Reinforce
Jumping with 1 and 2 feet			1	Reinforce	Reinforce	Reinforce
Changing direction and speed				1	Reinforce	Reinforce
Dribbling with the full instep		3	Reinforce	Reinforce	Reinforce	Reinforce
Dribbling with the sole of the foot		4	Reinforce	Reinforce	Reinforce	Reinforce
Dribbling with the outside of the instep			2	Reinforce	Reinforce	Reinforce
Dribbling with the inside of the instep			3	Reinforce	Reinforce	Reinforce
Deceptive dribbling and feinting (15 tricks)		5	Reinforce	Reinforce	Reinforce	Reinforce
Deceptive dribbling and feinting (10 tricks)			4	Reinforce	Reinforce	Reinforce
Deceptive dribbling and feinting (5 tricks)				2	Reinforce	Reinforce
Juggling the ball (individual)		6	Reinforce	Reinforce	Reinforce	Reinforce
Juggling the ball (partner)			5	Reinforce	Reinforce	Reinforce
Juggling the ball (group)				3	Reinforce	Reinforce
Kicking the ball with the full instep		7	Reinforce	Reinforce	Reinforce	Reinforce
Kicking the ball with the inside of the foot		8	Reinforce	Reinforce	Reinforce	Reinforce
Kicking the ball with the inside of the instep			6	Reinforce	Reinforce	Reinforce
Kicking the ball with the outside of the instep			7	Reinforce	Reinforce	Reinforce
The wall pass — 1–2 pass			8	Reinforce	Reinforce	Reinforce
Chipping the ball				4	Reinforce	Reinforce
Full volley kick (front side)				5	Reinforce	Reinforce
Half volley kick (front side)				6	Reinforce	Reinforce
Overhead (scissors) volley kick					1	Reinforce
Kicking with the toe, heel and knee					2	Reinforce
Receiving (amortisation) — inside of the foot		9	Reinforce	Reinforce	Reinforce	Reinforce
Receiving (amortisation) with the full instep		10	Reinforce	Reinforce	Reinforce	Reinforce
Receiving (amortisation) with the thigh			9	Reinforce	Reinforce	Reinforce
Receiving (amortisation) with the chest			10	Reinforce	Reinforce	Reinforce
Receiving (amortisation) with the head				7	Reinforce	Reinforce
Receiving (trapping) — inside of the foot		11	Reinforce	Reinforce	Reinforce	Reinforce
Receiving (trapping) with the sole of the foot		12	Reinforce	Reinforce	Reinforce	Reinforce
Receiving (trapping) with the outside of the instep			11	Reinforce	Reinforce	Reinforce
Receiving (trapping) with the stomach/chest				8	Reinforce	Reinforce
Heading with the middle zone of the forehead			12	Reinforce	Reinforce	Reinforce
Heading with the side zone of the forehead				9	Reinforce	Reinforce
The diving header					3	Reinforce
The delay and basic block tackle		13	Reinforce	Reinforce	Reinforce	Reinforce
The sliding–straddle tackle			13	Reinforce	Reinforce	Reinforce
The shoulder charge				10	Reinforce	Reinforce
Intercepting the pass					4	Reinforce
Basic combinations — 1:1		14	Reinforce	Reinforce	Reinforce	Reinforce
Basic combinations — 2:0			14	Reinforce	Reinforce	Reinforce
Basic combinations — 2:1			15	Reinforce	Reinforce	Reinforce
Basic combinations — 2:2				11	Reinforce	Reinforce
Basic combinations — 3:0					5	Reinforce
Basic combinations — 3:2					6	Reinforce
Helpful tactical games		15	Reinforce	Reinforce	Reinforce	Reinforce
Kicking at goal		16	Reinforce	Reinforce	Reinforce	Reinforce
Heading at goal			16	Reinforce	Reinforce	Reinforce
Team technical–tactical playing patterns — attack					7	Reinforce
Team technical–tactical playing patterns — defence					8	Reinforce
Set play — attacking situations					9	Reinforce
Set play — defending situations					10	Reinforce
Small pitch soccer — TE–TA elements	2	Reinforce	Reinforce	Reinforce	Reinforce	Reinforce
Full pitch soccer — TE–TA elements				12	Reinforce	Reinforce
	2	16	16	12	10	0

Total soccer development program elements = 56 elements

Technical–tactical elements to be coached

1. Basic running and sprinting technique
2. The start technique (forward side)
3. Dribbling with the full instep
4. Dribbling with the sole of the foot
5. Deceptive dribbling and feinting (15 tricks)
6. Juggling the ball
7. Kicking the ball with the full instep
8. Kicking the ball with the inside of the foot
9. Receiving (amortisation) with the inside of the foot
10. Receiving (amortisation) with the full instep
11. Receiving (trapping) with the inside of the foot
12. Receiving (trapping) with the sole of the foot
13. The delay and basic block tackle
14. Basic combinations — 1:1
15. Helpful tactical games
16. Kicking at goal

Total elements = 16

Time allocation for the 70 minute coaching session

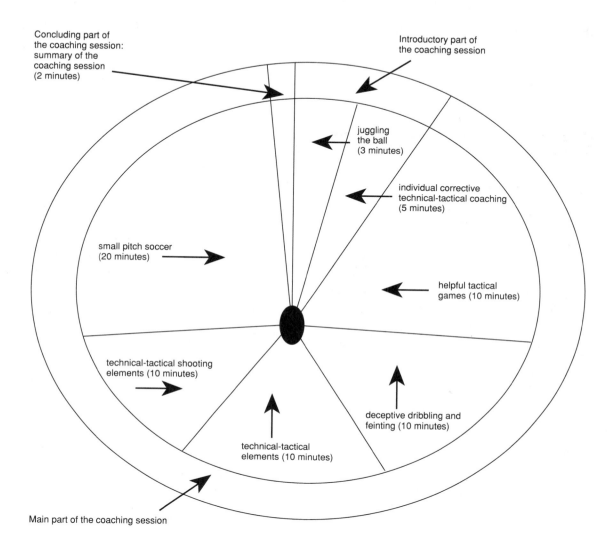

Concluding part of the coaching session: summary of the coaching session (2 minutes)

Introductory part of the coaching session

juggling the ball (3 minutes)

individual corrective technical-tactical coaching (5 minutes)

small pitch soccer (20 minutes)

helpful tactical games (10 minutes)

technical-tactical shooting elements (10 minutes)

deceptive dribbling and feinting (10 minutes)

technical-tactical elements (10 minutes)

Main part of the coaching session

Structure of the practical coaching session — 70 minutes

Total practical coaching time = 70 minutes

1. Introductory part of the coaching session

1.1 JUGGLING THE BALL

Juggling the ball is simply keeping the ball off the ground, playing it with all parts of the body except from the arms to the hands.

There is no better exercise for young players than juggling the ball to get universal feeling and confidence with the ball.

When juggling, it is necessary to be relaxed and have good body balance.

Juggling the ball is an important introductory part of each coaching session.

1. Juggling with the use of the instep

2. Juggling with the use of the thigh

3. Juggling with the use of the inside of the foot

2. Main part of the coaching session

2.1 HELPFUL TACTICAL GAMES

1. Soccer handball

1 team attacks and 1 team defends until a goal is scored or possession lost. Players interpass by throwing the ball with the hand with a maximum of 1 step with the ball. The attacking player with the ball must play a 1–2 pass and switch to another team player. Goals can only be scored by throwing the ball through the small goals. There are no outs or offside.

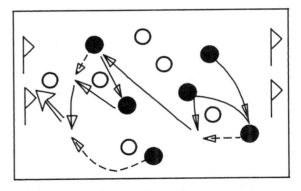

2. Piggy in the middle — 3:1

Three players, in a marked grid, keep possession of the ball away from the defending player in the middle. The defending player in the middle tries to intercept the ball being passed. If the ball is intercepted the defending player changes places with the attacking player who lost possession.

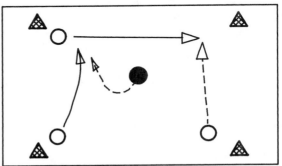

3. Soccer with 4 goals

Each team has 2 goals to attack and 2 goals to defend. There are no goalkeepers, no offside and no outs. Goals can only be scored from shooting from inside the grid.

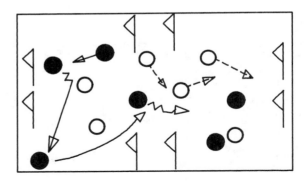

4. Hit your coloured marker

The playing area is covered with 2 different types of coloured markers, evenly distributed. The players must hit any 1 of their markers to score a goal. There are no outs and offside. Teams must defend their coloured marker.

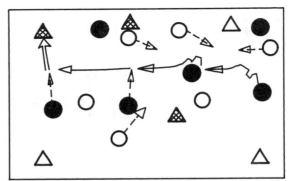

 UMBRO

2.2 DECEPTIVE DRIBBLING AND FEINTING

Dribbling is running with the ball under close control, using any part of the foot.

Feinting is the art of making deceptive body movements to delude the opponent.

Dribbling is movement with the ball while feinting is movement without the ball.

So we could describe both dribbling and feinting as deception, where we use the body or ball or both to throw the defenders off balance to get past them.

In today's modern game every player must be able to master the art of dribbling and feinting.

No technique in the game of soccer causes greater pleasure than a good piece of dribbling and feinting.

As players progress through the soccer development program they will discover the dribbling and feinting techniques that suit them best.

Superstar Pele celebrates scoring for Brazil in the 1970 World Cup final

Methods of progress

The following exercises represent the methods of progress when coaching deceptive dribbling and feinting techniques.

1. No pressure — 1 player

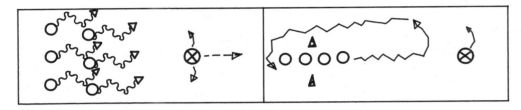

2. Token pressure — 2 players

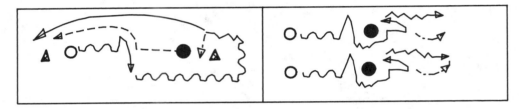

3. Token pressure — 3 players

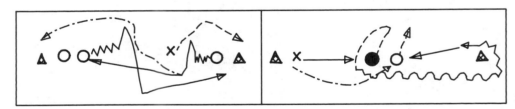

4. Token pressure — 4 players

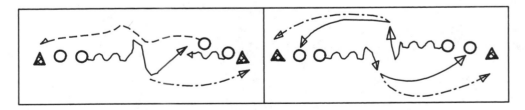

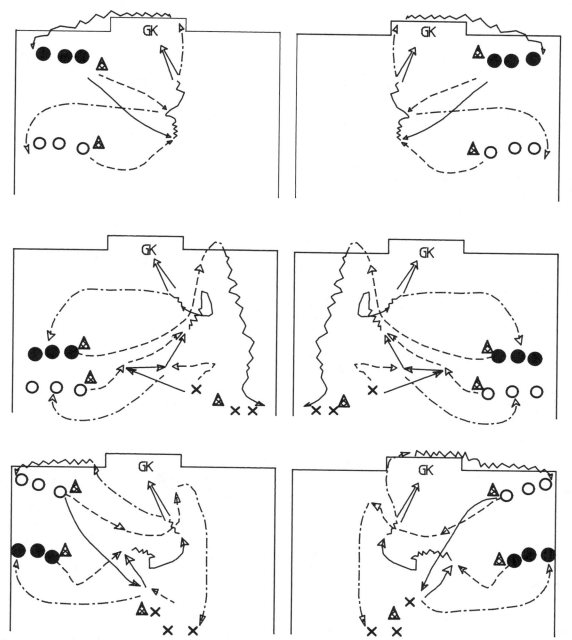

5. Full pressure — 1:1 combinations: combine the full pressure situations with goalscoring opportunities. This develops both the attacking and defending functions of players

Deceptive dribbling and feinting techniques

The following represent the 15 deceptive dribbling and feinting techniques to be executed in level 2.

1. *Cutting the ball back inside*

2. *Cutting the ball back under the bottom*

3. *Scissors 1 way and go the other way*

4. *Dipping the shoulder 1 way and go the other*

5. *The shuffle*

6. *Inside and outside the instep*

7. *Run over the ball and go the other way*

8. *Roll out and cut back*

9. *Scissors 1 way and go the same way*

10. Dummy kick and roll back

11. Placing the ball between the legs

12. Dummy heel pass

13. *Cross over heel pass*

14. *Roll under the bottom and change direction*

15. *Overhead heel of the ball*

Superstar Stanley Matthews, one of England's best ever players in the 1950s

2.3 TECHNICAL–TACTICAL PROGRAM ELEMENTS

Basic running and sprinting technique

Running is brought about by a combination of *internal* and *external* forces. The internal forces are muscles, ligaments and tendons while the external forces are gravity, air and the forces exerted by the ground.

Good running calls for a co-ordinated action of the entire body and can be divided into the *phase of recovery* and the *phase of drive*.

The recovery phase starts the moment the toes leave the ground, with the leg flexing at the hip, knee and ankle joints. The movement of the thigh is forward and upward, increasing the reaction from the ground and the speed with which the centre of gravity moves away from the supporting leg.

The driving phase starts the moment the outside edge of the foot lands with the toes pointing slightly outwards. The body passes over the foot with the heel slightly touching the ground. The knee and ankle joints are flexed to take the landing impact. As the body passes over the standing foot there is complete extension in the hip, knee and ankle joints.

In sprinting the leg thrust results in twisting along the vertical axis which can only be countered with good arm and shoulder movement. During the swings, the arms are kept flexed and at an angle of 90°, absorbing the forward twist.

The backward swing is of equal importance as the swing tends to thrust the corresponding shoulder forward, countering the vertical axis twist. Here the arm straightens at the elbow but at the end of the backward swing, the arm bends again and speeds up to match the final fast stages of leg drive.

The hands are not completely closed, with the swing no higher than shoulder level to the front and hip level to the back.

COMMON FAULTS — CORRECTIONS

1. The leading foot is stretched too long.
2. The hands are not at 90° at the elbow joint and not moving to the side of the body.
3. The body angle is not forward but vertical.
4. The sprinting movement is too tense and not relaxed and co-ordinated.
5. The initial steps are too high and give the appearance of jumps.
6. The player is running flat-footed and coming down too heavy on the feet.
7. The heels and toes are not moving in a straight line.
8. The hands are not coming high enough at the front and back.

1. Introductory part of the coaching session
1.2 Individual corrective technical–tactical coaching

2. Main part of the coaching session
2.3 Technical–tactical program element

 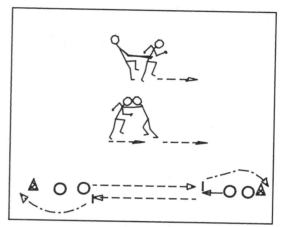

2.4 Technical–tactical shooting element

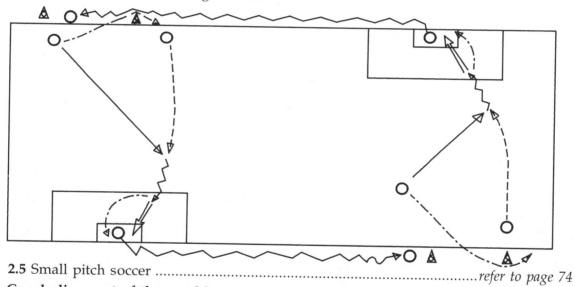

3. Concluding part of the coaching session
3.1 Summary of the coaching session

The start technique (forward side)

The start technique involves a player moving from a relatively stationary position or basic running position into maximum speed. The basic movement should comprise small short relaxed steps with the feet raised only slightly off the ground. This frequent contact with the ground allows maximum speed reaction to any impulse and in return a more effective start.

To achieve maximum speed players should always be moving to have a flying start.

Starting from an upright and static position should be avoided. The technique involves the player leaning to the intended direction, lowering the centre of gravity and taking the body weight on the front half of each bent foot.

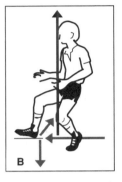

The first strides are quite short, with the back foot driving to complete extension well behind the vertical axis. The front thigh moves forward and upward, increasing the reaction from the ground. This thrust results in twisting the body which is countered and absorbed by the vigorous moving of the arms flexed at an angle of 90°. The hands are not completely closed and swing no higher than the shoulder level to the front and straighten slightly to swing to hip level to the back. The head is raised with the neck muscles relaxed and loose.

The correct starting technique could mean the difference between which player gets to the ball first.

COMMON FAULTS — CORRECTIONS

1. The first step is too long with the foot stretched out, resulting in counter movement.
2. The hands are not at 90° and to the side of the body. No vigorous arm swing.
3. There is no extension of the rear leg with weight on the front half of the foot.
4. The body is too much in the vertical position and not leaning to the intended direction.
5. The upper extremity is too tight and not relaxed.
6. The body is bent too far over the hip joint, reducing the forward side drive.

1. Introductory part of the coaching session
1.1 Juggling the ball ....*refer to page 39*
1.2 Individual corrective technical–tactical coaching

2. Main part of the coaching session
2.1 Helpful tactical games ....*refer to page 40*
2.2 Deceptive dribbling and feinting techniques ....*refer to page 44*
2.3 Technical–tactical program element

 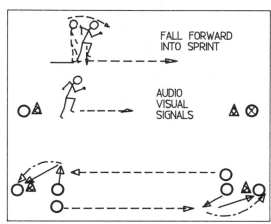

2.4 Technical–tactical shooting element

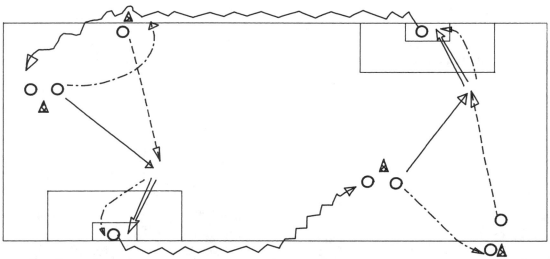

2.5 Small pitch soccer ....*refer to page 74*

3. Concluding part of the coaching session
3.1 Summary of the coaching session

Dribbling with the full instep

The laces part of the soccer boot represents the area used when dribbling with the full instep.

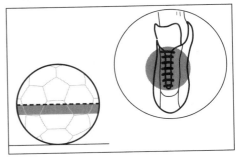

When dribbling with the full instep the leg striking the ball is extended and stretched, with the instep making contact with the ball below the line of the horizontal axis.

Using this extended technique, the player creates a slight backspin on the ball which prevents it from running too far in front and out of control. However, striking the ball too low below the horizontal line will give the ball too much backspin and make it difficult for the player to control. At the same time if the ball is hit above the horizontal line the chances are the player will lose balance, falling over the ball. The ideal spot to strike the ball is just below the line. The hands and elbows are raised and wide for balance with the eyes on the ball at the moment of contact. The head is then raised and kept high, viewing the field of play looking for possible solutions.

The player should be able to push the ball comfortably over a distance in a running rhythm, playing the ball with the left and right foot in every stride.

COMMON FAULTS — CORRECTIONS

1. There is no extended stretch of the instep when striking the ball.
2. Contact is not made below the horizontal axis of the ball.
3. The ankle joint is not relaxed but hard and locked when striking the ball.
4. The head is continually fixed on the ball and not raised to view the playing field.
5. The toes may be hitting into the ground because of the instep length. This can be corrected by not having the instep vertical but at an angle to the vertical axis of the ball.
6. The hands are not at 90° while the player is dribbling the ball and not high enough in front or at the back.
7. The body angle is not leaning forward but more in the vertical position.
8. The ball is struck too high or too low above or below the horizontal axis. In both instances the player will not be in complete control of the ball.

1. Introductory part of the coaching session
1.1 Juggling the ball ....*refer to page 39*
1.2 Individual corrective technical–tactical coaching

2. Main part of the coaching session
2.1 Helpful tactical games ....*refer to page 40*
2.2 Deceptive dribbling and feinting techniques ....*refer to page 44*
2.3 Technical–tactical program element

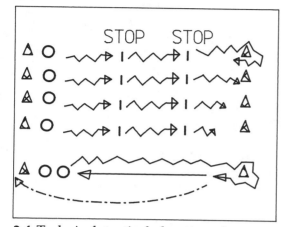 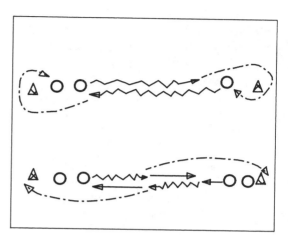

2.4 Technical–tactical shooting element

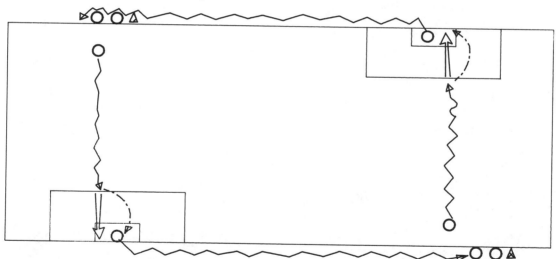

2.5 Small pitch soccer ....*refer to page 74*

3. Concluding part of the coaching session
3.1 Summary of the coaching session

Dribbling with the sole of the foot

A player should only adopt the dribbling and feinting techniques if there is no other solution. If he is able to pass to a supporting player in a better position or have a shot at goal then that's the solution, otherwise he should dribble and take a chance.

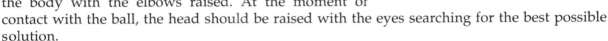

In today's modern game the space and time that a player has with the ball is very restricted. It may be necessary to use this technique of dribbling, in pressure situations, to maintain possession and keep the ball rolling close to the body and under control away from the defender. This way the attacking player can gain extra time and space before releasing the pass or shooting at goal.

With this technique the hands should be away from the body with the elbows raised. At the moment of contact with the ball, the head should be raised with the eyes searching for the best possible solution.

All body weight should be supported by the flexed standing leg with the other controlling the ball. The foot on the ball is to be relaxed and loose.

The great advantage of this technique is that a player is able to quickly turn 180° with the ball and get his body between the ball and the defender.

COMMON FAULTS — CORRECTIONS

1. The player is continually focusing on the ball and not holding the head up at any time while in control.
2. Poor body balance with all the weight not on the supporting leg but also on the ball. This will usually result in the player slipping over.
3. The player controls and dribbles the ball, moving it too far from behind the vertical axis resulting in the ball running away and out of control.
4. The hands are relaxed and close to the side of the body instead of being raised and wide to assist in balance.
5. The ball is dribbled too far in front of the vertical axis, resulting in the player missing the ball altogether.
6. When pressurised the attacking player does not roll or dribble the ball, getting his body between the ball and the defender.

1. Introductory part of the coaching session
1.2 Individual corrective technical–tactical coaching

2. Main part of the coaching session
2.3 Technical–tactical program element

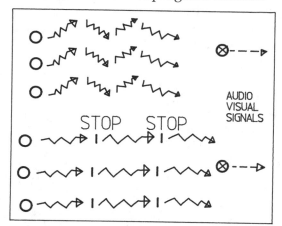
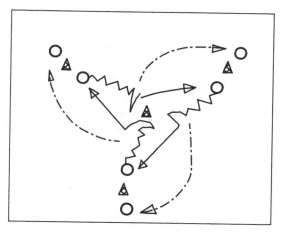

2.4 Technical–tactical shooting element

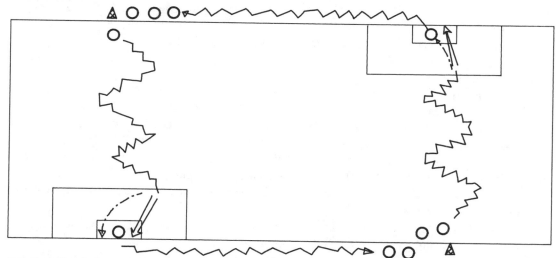

3. Concluding part of the coaching session
3.1 Summary of the coaching session

Kicking the ball with the full instep

This technique is the most natural and most often used in the game. This element allows the player to kick the ball short, long, soft, hard, high and low without disrupting to any great extent his running technique. As a result of this the full instep element should be given high priority at training.

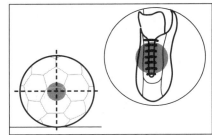

The full instep is the area that corresponds exactly to the laces part of the boot. When kicking with this technique the toes are pointed down, the heel raised and the ankle joint locked and hard.

The hands should be out wide for balance and the eyes fixed on the ball. The movement always starts from the hip, ending with the snap of the knee and complete extension of the instep. The ball should be kicked through the horizontal and vertical axis to enable it to travel low with accuracy. If the ball is kicked below the horizontal axis it will go high; if kicked above the horizontal axis it will bounce and have very little power.

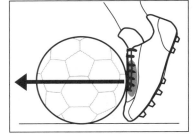

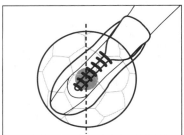

COMMON FAULTS — CORRECTIONS

1. The ankle joint is not locked and hard at the moment of contact.
2. There is no snap of the knee before contact with the ball; the movement just continues from the hip.
3. The instep is not extended with toes pointing down and there is no follow through.
4. The hands are not relaxed and wide but held to the side of the body.
5. The player may continually kick the ground. This is because the instep is too long for the ball diameter. This can be corrected by the player having a sharper approach to the ball and striking it across the vertical axis.
6. The kicking foot goes straight to the ground, with the sole, after the kick. This is the result of poor body balance where the player needs the kicking foot for support.
7. The eyes are not looking at the ball at the moment of contact.
8. The standing foot is too close to the ball which does not allow for the free co-ordinated complete movement when kicking.
9. Before kicking the player looks up and bends the body back. This results in a high and inaccurate pass or shot.

1. Introductory part of the coaching session
1.1 Juggling the ball ....*refer to page 39*
1.2 Individual corrective technical–tactical coaching
2. Main part of the coaching session
2.1 Helpful tactical games ....*refer to page 40*
2.2 Deceptive dribbling and feinting techniques ....*refer to page 44*
2.3 Technical–tactical program element

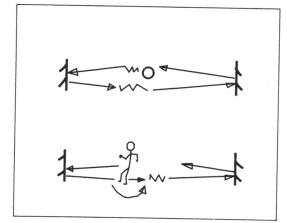
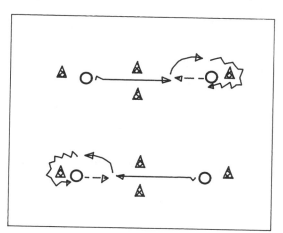

2.4 Technical–tactical shooting element

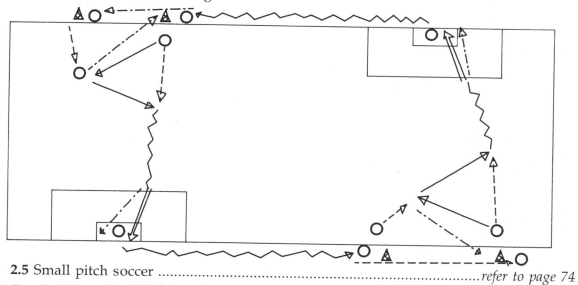

2.5 Small pitch soccer ....*refer to page 74*
3. Concluding part of the coaching session
3.1 Summary of the coaching session

Kicking the ball with the inside of the foot

The part used with this technique is the large flat area on the inside of the foot. The advantage with this pass is that it is easy to learn and the large surface area guarantees control and accuracy in passing.

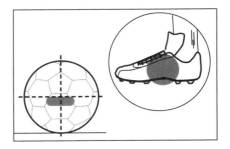

Accuracy and not power is what the inside of the foot pass is all about. On the other hand, its greatest disadvantage is that it is a pass that is easy to predict. It signals in advance, to the opponent, the intended direction of the pass.

The inside of the foot pass is also known as the push pass, as the ball is pushed and not struck with a sharp blow.

The technique involves the toes of the supporting leg facing in the direction of the intended pass near the ball. The kicking foot is turned outward, locked at the ankle joint and at 90° to the supporting foot. The hands are raised and wide for balance while the eyes are fixed on the ball. The body is behind the ball with the inside of the foot being pushed to made contact just below the centre axis of the ball. After contact the inside of the foot follows through, with the player maintaining body balance.

COMMON FAULTS — CORRECTIONS

1. Eyes are not fixed on the ball at the moment of contact.
2. The ankle joint is not locked and hard but relaxed and soft at the moment of contact with the ball.
3. There is no controlled push on to the ball but a swing from the hip.
4. The body is too upright and over the ball.
5. The toes of the kicking foot are not pointing out and away from the ball.
6. The standing foot is too far back from the ball; the player gets under the horizontal axis and lifts the ball high.
7. The standing foot is too close to the ball, preventing the player from getting behind the ball and pushing his or her weight behind it.
8. The knee and ankle joints are too relaxed at the moment of contact. This could result in possible joint injury if pressurised.
9. The kicking foot moves across the supporting leg after contact, indicating poor balance.

1. Introductory part of the coaching session
1.2 Individual corrective technical–tactical coaching

2. Main part of the coaching session
2.3 Technical–tactical program element

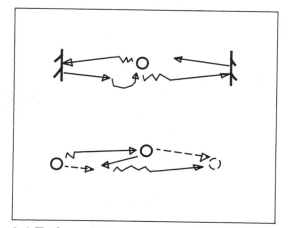 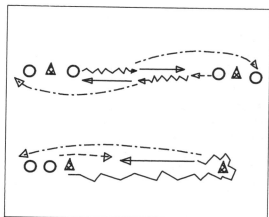

2.4 Technical–tactical shooting element

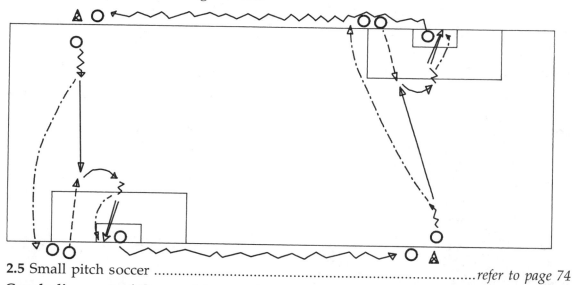

3. Concluding part of the coaching session
3.1 Summary of the coaching session

Receiving (amortisation) with the inside of the foot

The part used with this technique is the large flat area on the inside of the foot — the same surface area that is used when kicking with the inside of the foot.

The key to receiving (amortisation) with the inside of the foot is to treat the ball gently and have the receiving part relaxed to cushion the force of the oncoming ball.

The technique involves the surface area moving towards the oncoming ball and just before the moment of contact, the foot is withdrawn a little slower than the speed of the ball. This will have a 'deadening' effect on the ball, bringing it under control.

The hands are raised and the elbows are away from the side of the body for balance, with all weight on the supporting leg. The receiving leg is turned outward from the hip joint, flexed at the joints, relaxed and loose. The toes of the receiving foot are pointing at 90° to the supporting foot, with the sole horizontal to the ground.

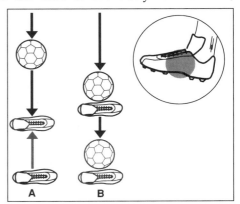

The toes should be pointing upwards to increase the area of control, with the ankle joint flexed at 90°.

The eyes are fixed on the ball to anticipate ball speed and direction.

Players of the highest quality will always have their heads up to look for possible solutions before the ball is about to be received. This habit is something the coach must insist on from an early age.

COMMON FAULTS — CORRECTIONS

1. The player's timing is too slow or too quick in moving the foot to or away from the ball.
2. The ankle joint is locked and hard when it should be relaxed and loose to absorb the ball force.
3. The hands and elbows are not raised and away from the body for balance.
4. There is no movement with the inside of the foot to meet the ball.
5. The eyes are not fixed on the ball.
6. The player does not get in flight with the ball but tends to stretch for it.
7. The receiving foot strikes the ground when contact is made with the ball. This is a direct result of poor body balance.

1. Introductory part of the coaching session
1.1 Juggling the ball ....*refer to page 39*
1.2 Individual corrective technical–tactical coaching

2. Main part of the coaching session
2.1 Helpful tactical games ....*refer to page 40*
2.2 Deceptive dribbling and feinting techniques ....*refer to page 44*
2.3 Technical–tactical program element

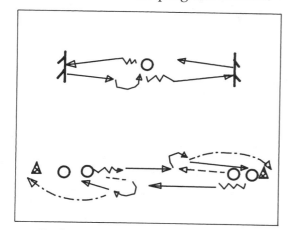
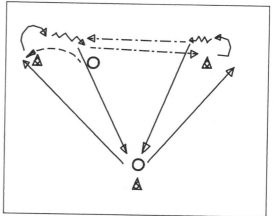

2.4 Technical–tactical shooting element

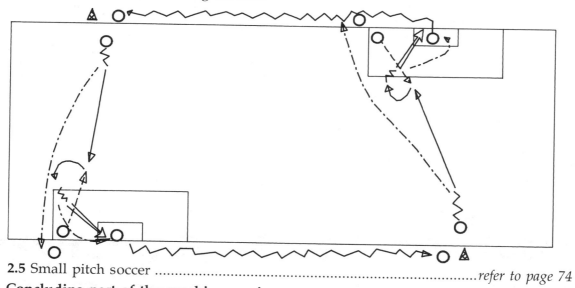

2.5 Small pitch soccer ....*refer to page 74*

3. Concluding part of the coaching session
3.1 Summary of the coaching session

Receiving (amortisation) with the full instep

When receiving (amortisation) with the full instep, the ankle joint should be loose and relaxed to absorb and cushion the speed of the ball.

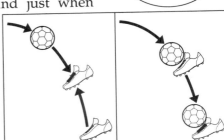

The area of the full instep corresponds exactly to the area where the boots are laced.

The technique is basically the same as with other parts of the body where we have the instep moving towards the ball and just when contact is about to be made, the surface area is withdrawn, a little slower than the ball speed, bringing the ball under control.

The player must get in flight of the ball and receive it by the instep through the vertical axis with the ankle joint relaxed and loose.

The hands and elbows are raised to the side of the body to assist in balance. If the receiving player is pressurised then the ball is to be controlled with the body between the ball and the defending player.

As with other techniques the eyes are fixed on the ball until contact is made, with solutions about what to do with the ball already in mind.

COMMON FAULTS — CORRECTIONS

1. The player is too late going to meet the ball with the instep.
2. The withdrawal is either too slow or too quick, resulting in both instances with the ball bouncing out of control.
3. The ankle joint is not relaxed and loose, but hard and locked.
4. The hands are tight and to the side of the body and not relaxed, raised and out to assist with balance.
5. The player does not anticipate the ball flight and instead of getting in flight stretches with the instep to one side to control the ball.
6. The eyes are not fixed on the ball in flight.
7. As soon as contact is made the receiving foot hits the ground, indicating poor body balance.
8. The standing foot is not flexed but straight, reducing effective body balance.

1. Introductory part of the coaching session
    1.1 Juggling the ball ....*refer to page 39*
    1.2 Individual corrective technical–tactical coaching

2. Main part of the coaching session
    2.1 Helpful tactical games ....*refer to page 40*
    2.2 Deceptive dribbling and feinting techniques ....*refer to page 44*
    2.3 Technical–tactical program element

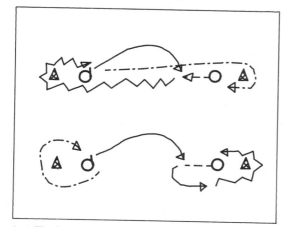 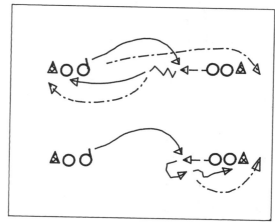

    2.4 Technical–tactical shooting element

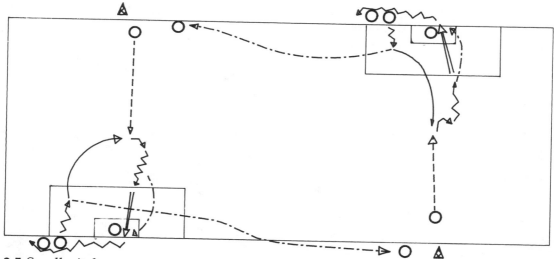

    2.5 Small pitch soccer ....*refer to page 74*

3. Concluding part of the coaching session
    3.1 Summary of the coaching session

Receiving (trapping) with the inside of the foot

The most frequently used 'trap' in the game is with the inside of the foot. The advantage with this technique is that with the large flat surface area, greater control over the ball can be exercised by the player.

The trapping inside of the foot is relaxed and loose, turned out at 90° to the supporting leg. The supporting leg is bent at the knee with the upper extremity leaning forward over the anticipated landing spot of the ball.

The ball is to be received behind the supporting leg, with the sole of the receiving foot raised off the ground, forming a 'wedge' to trap the ball.

The eyes are on the ball with the hands relaxed and raised to the side of the body to assist in body balance.

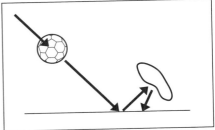

COMMON FAULTS — CORRECTIONS

1. The inside of the receiving foot is not behind the supporting leg forming the trap or wedge.
2. The supporting foot is too close to where the ball is going to make contact with the ground, allowing no space for the controlling foot to operate.
3. The ankle joint is not relaxed and loose.
4. The upper extremity is not leaning in the intended direction the player wants to go when getting the ball under control.
5. The player stands upright and simply steps on the ball.
6. The elbows and hands are not raised to assist in balance but are to the side.
7. The receiving inside of the foot moves to meet the ball and does not remain loose and relaxed to form the wedge trapping the ball.
8. The player is not leaning forward over the anticipated landing spot of the ball.

1. Introductory part of the coaching session
  1.1 Juggling the ball ....*refer to page 39*
  1.2 Individual corrective technical–tactical coaching
2. Main part of the coaching session
  2.1 Helpful tactical games ....*refer to page 40*
  2.2 Deceptive dribbling and feinting techniques ....*refer to page 44*
  2.3 Technical–tactical program element

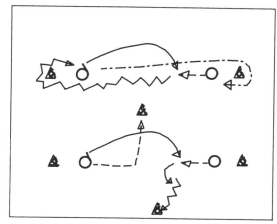 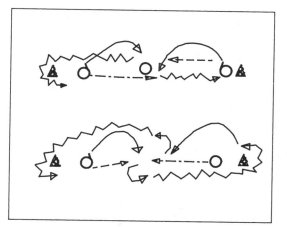

  2.4 Technical–tactical shooting element

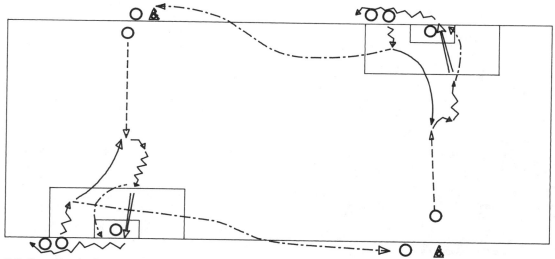

  2.5 Small pitch soccer ....*refer to page 74*
3. Concluding part of the coaching session
  3.1 Summary of the coaching session

UMBRO

Receiving (trapping) with the sole of the foot

With this technique the receiving foot is extended to control the ball in front of the supporting leg.

The supporting leg is bent, supporting the body weight, with the receiving leg relaxed and loose in the knee and ankle joints. The hands are away from the body for balance and the eyes are fixed on the ball.

The sole of the extended foot forms a wedge to trap the ball and at the moment of contact is rolled forward and down, thus bringing the ball close to the body and under control.

Beginners who are not leaning away tend to step hard down on the ball with the hands raised high in front of the body. What usually results is that the ball bounces under or in front of the receiving foot and up to hit the body or hands.

COMMON FAULTS — CORRECTIONS

1. There is no extension of the trapping foot.
2. The receiving foot is locked and hard when it should be relaxed and loose to cushion the impact of the ball.
3. No wedge is formed by the sole of the extended foot to trap the ball.
4. The player does not get in flight of the ball and cannot anticipate where the ball is going to land.
5. The hands are not raised to the side of the body for balance but high and in front to protect the face.
6. The eyes are not fixed on the ball while it is in flight.
7. The player steps down hard on the ball, losing balance and at times falling over.
8. The toes of the receiving foot are not facing the ball but are pointing away and beside the supporting leg. This results in the ball bouncing under or over the receiving foot.

1. Introductory part of the coaching session
   1.1 Juggling the ball ....*refer to page 39*
   1.2 Individual corrective technical–tactical coaching

2. Main part of the coaching session
   2.1 Helpful tactical games ....*refer to page 40*
   2.2 Deceptive dribbling and feinting techniques ....*refer to page 44*
   2.3 Technical–tactical program element

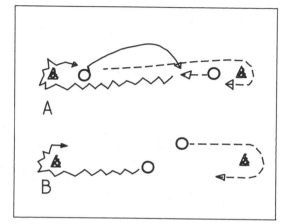

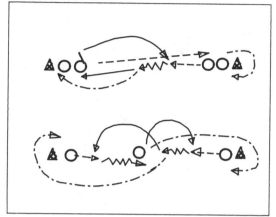

   2.4 Technical–tactical shooting element

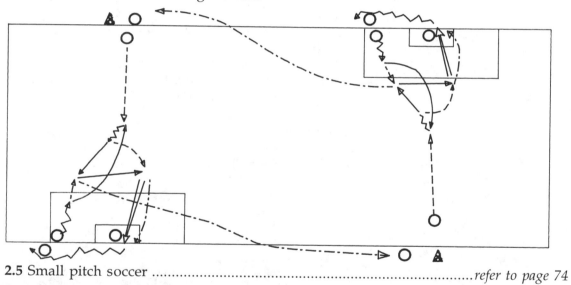

   2.5 Small pitch soccer ....*refer to page 74*

3. Concluding part of the coaching session
   3.1 Summary of the coaching session

The delay and basic block tackle

Tackling is simply taking the ball away from an attacking player. To be successful in any type of tackle the defending player has to be skilful, courageous and determined to win the ball.

With this element the muscle joints are opposite to when the player is receiving and must be locked and hard. This way the player will avoid any serious joint or muscle injury.

The delay and basic block tackle requires the defending player to pull back a distance of about 2 to 3 metres, setting the attacking player up before going in for the tackle.

Sometimes the defending player will have to outsmart the attacking player by making a 'dummy' movement, in order to tackle and force the attacking player into a position where she can then go in for the block tackle.

When tackling, the attacker's path is blocked with the defender's body and the ball is wedged with the locked inside of the foot. The body leans forward to counter the attacking player's forward motion, eyes are fixed on the ball and the hands are wide for balance.

Once the block has been made, on top of the horizontal ball line, the defending player rolls the ball forward over the attacking player's foot, winning possession.

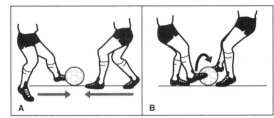

| COMMON FAULTS — CORRECTIONS |

1. At the moment of contact the joints are not locked and hard but loose and relaxed.
2. There is no rotation of the ball forward and out of the block after the tackle.
3. The eyes are not fixed on the ball.
4. The hands are to the side of the body and raised to assist in balance.
5. The player does not execute the block but more of a kick at the ball. This way the ball can go anywhere with a greater chance of the attacking player maintaining possession.
6. The block is performed under the horizontal axis of the ball, resulting in the ball rolling over the foot and out of the block.
7. The body is not leaning forward over the ball and locked in all joints but relaxed and loose. This can result in serious injury.
8. The defending player is not courageous and determined enough to win the ball.

1. Introductory part of the coaching session
    1.2 Individual corrective technical–tactical coaching

2. Main part of the coaching session
    2.3 Technical–tactical program element

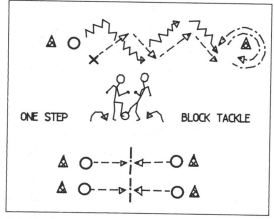
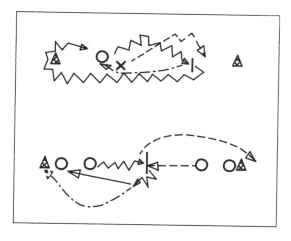

    2.4 Technical–tactical shooting element

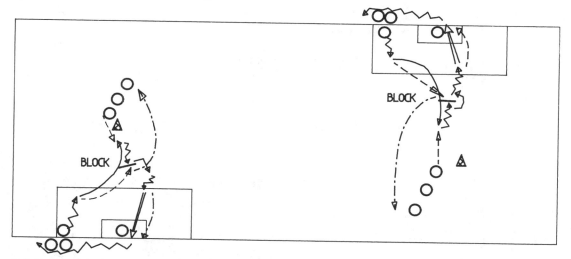

3. Concluding part of the coaching session
    3.1 Summary of the coaching session

Basic combinations — 1:1

The basic combination of 1:1 is where we create competitive situations for the individual player so that she can develop her individual technical–tactical ability.

The exercise starts without a ball, with the attacking player concentrating on the basic body movements to throw the defending player off-balance.

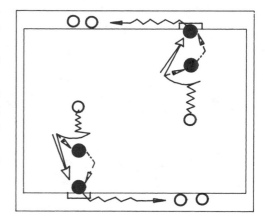

Progression is made with the introduction of a ball for the attacking player, with continued token defence.

When the coach is quite satisfied with the elements exercised, full match pressure is applied.

This is now the real match situation where the attacking player is required to use all his skill to beat the defender, while the defender has to outsmart the attacker to win possession.

When doing full pressure exercises always have a goal for the players to attack or defend.

COMMON FAULTS — CORRECTIONS

1. The player has too poor a dribbling and feinting repertoire with which to outsmart the defender.
2. The elbows and hands are not raised and away from the body to assist with body balance.
3. The head is continually fixed on the ball.
4. The defending player is always committing himself too early or too late to the ball and not trying to outsmart the attacking player.
5. The attacking player allows himself to be brought to a stationary position while dribbling. This is ideal for the defending player to select his moment to strike and tackle for the ball.
6. The defender reacts to a feint and slide tackles. A slide tackle should only be used as a last resort because if unsuccessful the defending player is left helpless on the ground.

1. Introductory part of the coaching session
1.1 Juggling the ball ....*refer to page 39*
1.2 Individual corrective technical–tactical coaching
2. Main part of the coaching session
2.1 Helpful tactical games ....*refer to page 40*
2.2 Deceptive dribbling and feinting techniques ....*refer to page 44*
2.3 Technical–tactical program element

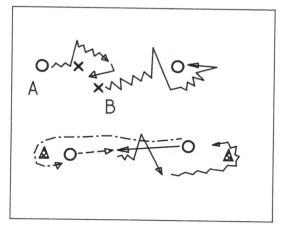
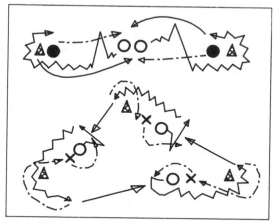

2.4 Technical–tactical shooting element

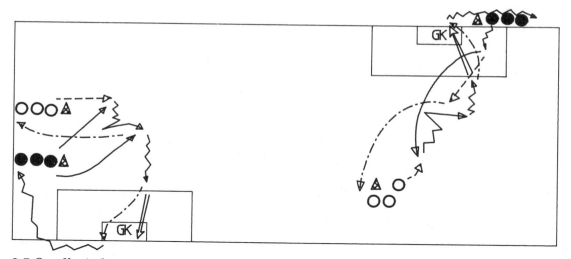

2.5 Small pitch soccer ....*refer to page 74*
3. Concluding part of the coaching session
3.1 Summary of the coaching session

2.5 SMALL PITCH SOCCER

Every coaching session, at this level, should end with a small-sided game on a small pitch. It is these small-sided situations that the young players enjoy most. They are in constant contact with the ball, enabling the technical–tactical and physical skills to be put into practice.

The aim when playing small-sided games is simply to attack the opponent's goal in the phase of attack and defend your goal in the phase of defence. The phase of attack is that moment your team gains possession, while the phase of defence is the moment the team has lost possession.

This is called soccer tactics — the art by which the player's technical and physical qualities are used to achieve the best possible result.

Tactics can be divided into 3 distinct categories:

1. *Individual tactics:* pressing the player, pressing the ball, creating space, dribbling, feinting, receiving, heading, passing, shooting, etc.
2. *Group tactics:* the mobility and interchange of players, the recovery behind the ball of the front attacking line, defending the goal, counter attacking, offside tactics, co-operation with the goalkeeper, playing wide or through the middle, etc.
3. *Team tactics:* keeping possession, slow build up, long direct penetrating passes, playing the high ball, keeping the ball low, switch of play, recovering behind the ball into a zone, pressing on all parts of the field, etc.

Team tactics used by the coach will also be determined by many factors that may include the way the opponents play, state of the playing surface, the team's position in the competition, phase of the game, the weather, etc.

The technical–tactical elements in the phase of attack are:

1. *Mobility:* the ability to move with or without the ball to create playing space.
2. *Penetration:* the ability to get past or behind defenders, with or without the ball.
3. *Width and depth:* the ability to create playing space across and along the field of play.
4. *Switch of play:* the ability to draw defenders out of position and exploit space on the opposite side.

The technical–tactical elements in the phase of defence are:

1. *Balance:* the ability to limit the creation of space, penetration and passing angles.
2. *Pressing the player without the ball:* the ability to reduce the time and playing space an attacking player will have when receiving the ball.
3. *Pressing the ball:* the ability to reduce the time and space the attacking player will have to receive, pass, dribble or shoot at goal.
4. *Zone and combined zone formations:* the ability to recover goal side of the ball, cover an area, and press any player entering that zone.

> **Note: It is necessary for coaches, coaching at all levels, to understand the technical–tactical elements in the phases of attack and defence. However, tactics must not be coached in level 2 at the expense of techniques.**

Order of coaching technical–tactical elements in attack and defence

The following technical–tactical elements in attack and defence are to be applied and reinforced at each level.

	TE–TA *elements in attack*				**TE–TA** *elements in defence*			
	Number 1	*Number 2*	*Number 3*	*Number 4*	*Number 1*	*Number 2*	*Number 3*	*Number 4*
Level 1 *(5 to 8 years)*	Unlimited touches with the ball Playing for fun				Unlimited touches with the ball Playing for fun			
Level 2 *(9 to 10 years)*	Mobility Maximum 3 touches Reinforce level 1				Balance Reinforce level 1			
Level 3 *(11 to 12 years)*	Mobility Maximum 2 touches Reinforce levels 1 and 2	Penetration			Balance Reinforce levels 1 and 2	Pressing the player without the ball		
Level 4 *(13 to 14 years)*	Mobility Maximum 1 touch Reinforce levels 1 to 3	Penetration Reinforce level 3	Width and depth		Balance Reinforce levels 1 to 3	Pressing the player without the ball Reinforce level 3	Pressing the ball	
Level 5 *(15 to 16 years)*	Mobility Maximum 1 touch Reinforce levels 1 to 4	Penetration Reinforce levels 3 and 4	Width and depth Reinforce level 4	Switch of play	Balance Reinforce levels 1 to 4	Pressing the player without the ball Reinforce levels 3 and 4	Pressing the ball Reinforce level 4	Zone and combined zone defence
Level 6 *(17+ years)*	Mobility Maximum 1 touch Reinforce levels 1 to 5	Penetration Reinforce levels 3 to 5	Width and depth Reinforce levels 4 and 5	Switch of play Reinforce level 5	Balance Reinforce levels 1 to 5	Pressing the player without the ball Reinforce levels 3 to 5	Pressing the ball Reinforce levels 4 and 5	Zone and combined zone defence Reinforce level 5

Technical–tactical elements in attack

MOBILITY — MAXIMUM 3 TOUCHES

Mobility is the ability to move with or without the ball to create playing space.

Before an attacking player can outsmart a well organised defence she must think in terms of creating space and time.

The role of the defending player is simply to deny space and time that the attacking player has with or without the ball. Today's better organised defenders will explain to a large degree why fewer goals are scored. The defending team will always wait confidently for the attacking team to make a mistake.

If an attacking player is being pressed without the ball, then he should use this to the team's advantage by making decoy diagonal runs and creating space for his team to use.

If a defending player is marking one attacking player for the whole game on the same part of the pitch, then certainly he is going to have an easy task.

One means of disturbing and disrupting the balance in defense is to have attacking players moving with or without the ball and continually changing positions. This type of movement, preferably diagonal, puts the defending player in 2 minds:

1. If she tracks down or presses the player she is marking then she will create space for another attacking player to work in.
2. If she stays and marks her zone area then the attacking player she was pressing is free to move into space and create a 2 attacking versus 1 defender situation.

When an attacking team achieves the above then they have shaken the confidence of the defence.

Without the continual movement of players, mobile fluid attacking play cannot be achieved.

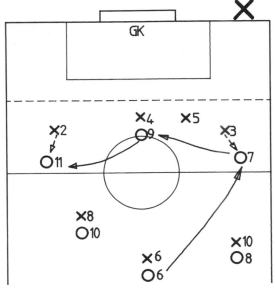

Team 0 lacks mobility and is constantly under pressure with very little working space

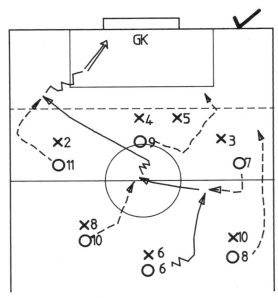

Team 0 is mobile and creating space to play or work in

Note: Introduce a maximum of 3 touches with the ball, in small-sided games, while reinforcing level 1.

Technical–tactical elements in defence

BALANCE

Balance is the ability to limit the creation of space, penetration and passing angles of the attacking team.

The aim of the attacking player, with or without the ball, is to draw the defenders out of position and create space and time. The defending team must be balanced against these threats.

The goalkeeper's main concern is to narrow angles. This same principle applies and must be taken into account by all defenders.

If one were to draw an arc 20 to 25 metres from the middle of the goal line, meeting 2 45° lines from the goalpost, then quite safely one could say that 90% or more goals are scored from this zone. If the defending team is able to recover behind the ball and maintain balance in front of this scoring zone then the creation of space, penetration and passing angles will be reduced to a bare minimum.

There is no such thing in today's modern game of just having defenders and attackers. When possession is gained all players attack and when possession is lost all players, regardless of their positions, are required to defend and pressurise to win back the ball.

When possession is lost all defending players must get goal side of the ball preventing any attacking superiority, player-wise, of the attacking team. From here the defenders adjust their positions to cut the passing angles and reduce the time and space that the attacking side may have on the ball.

In other words the team establishes balance in defence.

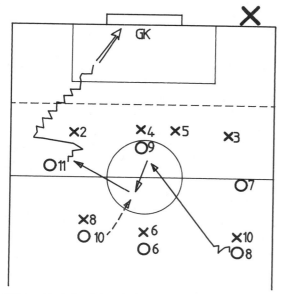

011 is able to beat the whole defence as it is square and out of balance

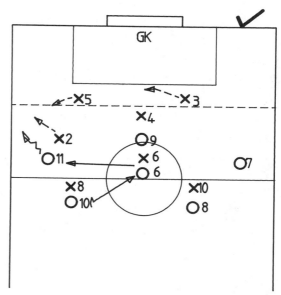

Support from X5 and X3 for X2 creates balance in defence and makes it difficult for 011 to penetrate

The laws of the game

1. *The field of play*
   Length — 44 to 59 yards
   Width — 21 to 46 yards
   The goal area — no marked goal area required at this level
   The penalty area — 20 × 8 yards
   The corner area — no marked corner area required at this level
   The goals — shall be 6 yards apart joined by a horizontal cross-bar 6 feet high
   The centre circle — shall have a radius of 6 yards

2. *The ball* — shall be a size 4 and of leather

3. *Number of players* — a match shall be played by 2 teams consisting of not more than 7 players each; in each team there is a goalkeeper

4. *Referees and linesmen* — a referee and linesmen shall officiate at each game

5. *Duration* — 30 minutes each way with 10 minutes for half-time

6. *The start of play* — before or after goals are scored, play is started by a player taking a place kick at the centre. All defending players must be in their half and outside the circle

7. *The ball out of play* — when it has wholly crossed the goal line or touch line, when in the air or on the ground

8. *Offside* — there are no offsides at this level

9. *Fouls and misconduct* — the player is penalised by awarding a free kick

10. *Free kicks* — all free kicks can result in a direct shot at goal. All opposing players shall be at least 6 yards from the ball

11. *Penalty kicks* — the penalty kick is taken 8 yards from the goal line

12. *Throw-in* — at the point where the ball crossed the line, the throw is taken with both hands behind the head and with both feet on the ground

13. *Goal kick* — at the side where the ball crossed the line, the ball is placed in the goal area and kicked into play

14. *Corner kick* — if the ball passes over the goal line, excluding the goals, and is last played by the defending team, then a player from the attacking team takes a free kick from the corner of the field

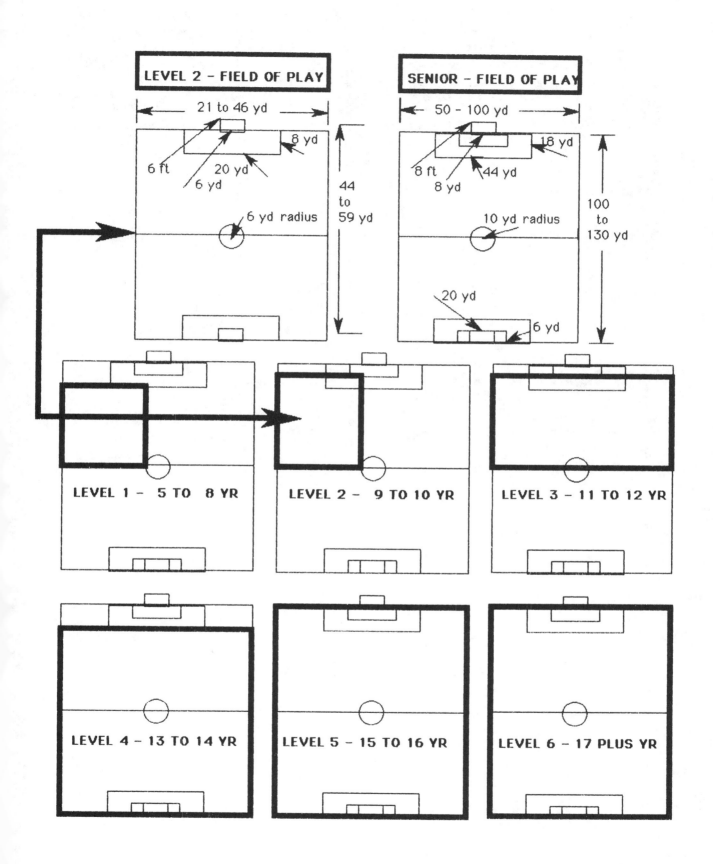

LEVEL 2 – FIELD OF PLAY

21 to 46 yd

8 yd

6 ft
20 yd
6 yd

44 to 59 yd

6 yd radius

SENIOR – FIELD OF PLAY

50 – 100 yd

18 yd

8 ft
44 yd
8 yd

100 to 130 yd

10 yd radius

20 yd

6 yd

LEVEL 1 – 5 TO 8 YR

LEVEL 2 – 9 TO 10 YR

LEVEL 3 – 11 TO 12 YR

LEVEL 4 – 13 TO 14 YR

LEVEL 5 – 15 TO 16 YR

LEVEL 6 – 17 PLUS YR

Superstar Alfredo di Stefano crouched in the centre with the famous Real Madrid side, 5 times winner of the European Champion Club Cup from 1955 to 1960

technical–tactical elements

Agility in the air and on the ground

Trampoline

The basic bounce: *can be used as a warm-up activity. The body and arms should be straight with head erect. At the top of the bounce, the legs are straight with toes pointing down. On the downward bounce flex the legs, hitting the mat with flat feet shou width*

The seat drop: *from the basic bounce position raise the legs to a horizontal position, moving arms forward and upwards. From here drop back on to the mat into the seat position and bounce back t vertical*

The tuck jump: *at the top of the bounce clasp the shins, bringing knees to the chest. Tuck in the elbows with eyes fixed on the cer end of the trampoline. The heels are against the seat while the to are pointing downward*

The closed pike jump: from the basic bounce bring the legs straight with toes pointing to a horizontal position. Bend the body forward at the hips with the hands straight with the legs

The half pirouette: on the bounce, raise 1 arm above the head while bending the other at 90° across the chest. Twist the body 180° around its vertical axis

The split pike jump: the split pike is similar to the closed pike jump except that both legs and arms are stretched apart during the bounce

The pirouette: this is similar to the half pirouette but twist a full 360° instead of 180°

FLOOR

The forward roll: *crouch on the toes with hands on the mat shoulder width apart. Place the chin to the chest, lift the hips and kick off the mat and overbalance. Roll over to the crouch position*

The backward roll: *squat on the mat with elbows bent and palms facing up. Curl the body and rock back, lowering the seat to the mat. Roll back and swing the feet over the head, rolling into a squat*

The mule kick: *place the hands on the mat shoulder width apart. All the weight is taken by the hands with a kick of 1 leg followed by the other high in the air*

The crouch balance: *place the hands on the mat shoulder width apart, palms down. Kick both legs high in the air, bent together while balancing on the hands in the crouch position*

The twist crouch: *the player stands with 1 foot forward, bends and places hands flat on the mat. Travelling sideways, the legs are bent and together, twisting at the hips*

BALANCE BEAM

Walking forward   *Walking backwards*

Walking through hoops   *Bouncing a ball*

Balancing objects   *Picking up objects*

Catching a ball

Walking over objects

Hopping

MINI-TRAMPOLINE/VAULTING BOX

The basic bounce: *on hitting the trampoline mat swing the arms down and bend the legs with the feet flat. To get the upward bounce, push hard on the heels with the forward and upward swing of the hands*

The tuck jump: *the same technique as with the basic bounce but bring the knees to the chest, clasping the shins. Land softly on the mat*

The closed pike jump: *following the bounce bring the legs straight and to a horizontal position. Bend the body at the hips with the hands pointing down the shins*

The split pike jump: *the technique with this element is the same as with the closed pike jump, only the legs and arms are stretched apart*

The side vault: *from the mini-trampoline bounce place the hands on either side of the box. Twist the body to 1 side with a soft landing side-on to the box*

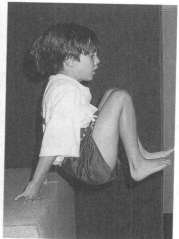

The bent leg squat vault: *following the bounce the stretched out arms touch the box while the legs are bent and close to the chest. The upper extremity is leaning forward. The legs straighten for a soft landing*

Phase 2: 7 to 8 years

TRAMPOLINE — Reinforce basic elements: 5 to 6 years

Swivel hips: *from a basic bounce, go into a seat drop. At the top of the bounce do a half twist and drop into another seat drop*

FLOOR — Reinforce basic elements: 5 to 6 years

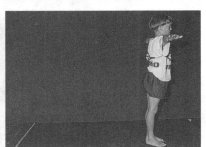

The dive roll: *dive forward, stretching the body to land on the hands. Tuck the chin to the chest. Roll over the shoulders and on to the back*

BALANCE BEAM — Reinforce basic elements: 5 to 6 years

Inclined bench balances   *See-saw*   *Passing over arms*

Mini-trampoline/vaulting box

Straddle vault: *following the bounce, lean forward and straighten the legs, keeping them apart with toes pointed. Extend the hands quickly so that they make contact with the apparatus and the body can straddle over it. Land on 2 feet, hands wide*

Forward dive roll: *leap forward with the body and arms stretched. The hands make contact first with the mat, softening the fall, the chin tucked into the chest and knees likewise. Staying curled, roll to your feet*

Forward somersault: *from the forward bounce, clasp the shins by the hands with the chin tucked into the chest. With the quick rotation spin into the somersault, opening out before coming to the vertical axis*

Trampoline

Floor

Balance beam

Mini-trampoline/vaulting box

Superstar Ferenc Puskas (on the left) leads the Hungarian side which beat England 6–3 at Wembley in 1953

LEVEL 3

technical–tactical development program

Core learning areas in the soccer development program

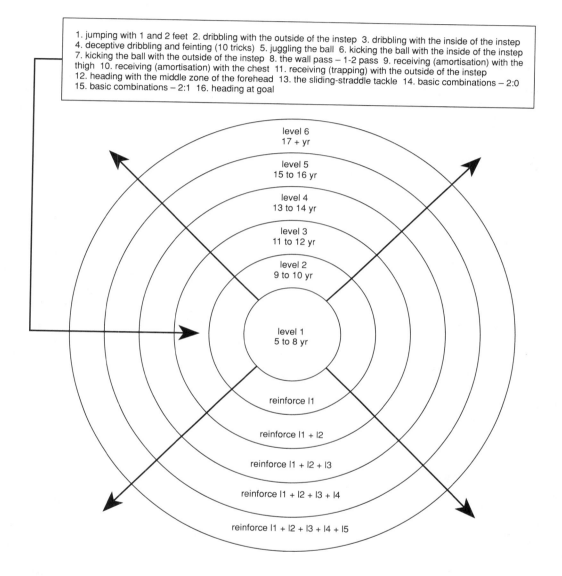

1. jumping with 1 and 2 feet 2. dribbling with the outside of the instep 3. dribbling with the inside of the instep
4. deceptive dribbling and feinting (10 tricks) 5. juggling the ball 6. kicking the ball with the inside of the instep
7. kicking the ball with the outside of the instep 8. the wall pass – 1-2 pass 9. receiving (amortisation) with the
thigh 10. receiving (amortisation) with the chest 11. receiving (trapping) with the outside of the instep
12. heading with the middle zone of the forehead 13. the sliding-straddle tackle 14. basic combinations – 2:0
15. basic combinations – 2:1 16. heading at goal

level 6
17 + yr

level 5
15 to 16 yr

level 4
13 to 14 yr

level 3
11 to 12 yr

level 2
9 to 10 yr

level 1
5 to 8 yr

reinforce l1

reinforce l1 + l2

reinforce l1 + l2 + l3

reinforce l1 + l2 + l3 + l4

reinforce l1 + l2 + l3 + l4 + l5

Technical–tactical program

Element	Level 1 (5–8 yr)	Level 2 (9–10 yr)	Level 3 (11–12 yr)	Level 4 (13–14 yr)	Level 5 (15–16 yr)	Level 6 (17+ yr)
Agility in the air and on the ground	1	Reinforce	Reinforce	Reinforce	Reinforce	Reinforce
Basic running and sprinting technique		1	Reinforce	Reinforce	Reinforce	Reinforce
The start technique (forward side)		2	Reinforce	Reinforce	Reinforce	Reinforce
Jumping with 1 and 2 feet			1	Reinforce	Reinforce	Reinforce
Changing direction and speed				1	Reinforce	Reinforce
Dribbling with the full instep		3	Reinforce	Reinforce	Reinforce	Reinforce
Dribbling with the sole of the foot		4	Reinforce	Reinforce	Reinforce	Reinforce
Dribbling with the outside of the instep			2	Reinforce	Reinforce	Reinforce
Dribbling with the inside of the instep			3	Reinforce	Reinforce	Reinforce
Deceptive dribbling and feinting (15 tricks)		5	Reinforce	Reinforce	Reinforce	Reinforce
Deceptive dribbling and feinting (10 tricks)			4	Reinforce	Reinforce	Reinforce
Deceptive dribbling and feinting (5 tricks)				2	Reinforce	Reinforce
Juggling the ball (individual)		6	Reinforce	Reinforce	Reinforce	Reinforce
Juggling the ball (partner)			5	Reinforce	Reinforce	Reinforce
Juggling the ball (group)				3	Reinforce	Reinforce
Kicking the ball with the full instep		7	Reinforce	Reinforce	Reinforce	Reinforce
Kicking the ball with the inside of the foot		8	Reinforce	Reinforce	Reinforce	Reinforce
Kicking the ball with the inside of the instep			6	Reinforce	Reinforce	Reinforce
Kicking the ball with the outside of the instep			7	Reinforce	Reinforce	Reinforce
The wall pass — 1–2 pass			8	Reinforce	Reinforce	Reinforce
Chipping the ball				4	Reinforce	Reinforce
Full volley kick (front side)				5	Reinforce	Reinforce
Half volley kick (front side)				6	Reinforce	Reinforce
Overhead (scissors) volley kick					1	Reinforce
Kicking with the toe, heel and knee					2	Reinforce
Receiving (amortisation) — inside of the foot		9	Reinforce	Reinforce	Reinforce	Reinforce
Receiving (amortisation) with the full instep		10	Reinforce	Reinforce	Reinforce	Reinforce
Receiving (amortisation) with the thigh			9	Reinforce	Reinforce	Reinforce
Receiving (amortisation) with the chest			10	Reinforce	Reinforce	Reinforce
Receiving (amortisation) with the head				7	Reinforce	Reinforce
Receiving (trapping) — inside of the foot		11	Reinforce	Reinforce	Reinforce	Reinforce
Receiving (trapping) with the sole of the foot		12	Reinforce	Reinforce	Reinforce	Reinforce
Receiving (trapping) with the outside of the instep			11	Reinforce	Reinforce	Reinforce
Receiving (trapping) with the stomach/chest				8	Reinforce	Reinforce
Heading with the middle zone of the forehead			12	Reinforce	Reinforce	Reinforce
Heading with the side zone of the forehead				9	Reinforce	Reinforce
The diving header					3	Reinforce
The delay and basic block tackle		13	Reinforce	Reinforce	Reinforce	Reinforce
The sliding–straddle tackle			13	Reinforce	Reinforce	Reinforce
The shoulder charge				10	Reinforce	Reinforce
Intercepting the pass					4	Reinforce
Basic combinations — 1:1		14	Reinforce	Reinforce	Reinforce	Reinforce
Basic combinations — 2:0			14	Reinforce	Reinforce	Reinforce
Basic combinations — 2:1			15	Reinforce	Reinforce	Reinforce
Basic combinations — 2:2				11	Reinforce	Reinforce
Basic combinations — 3:0					5	Reinforce
Basic combinations — 3:2					6	Reinforce
Helpful tactical games		15	Reinforce	Reinforce	Reinforce	Reinforce
Kicking at goal		16	Reinforce	Reinforce	Reinforce	Reinforce
Heading at goal			16	Reinforce	Reinforce	Reinforce
Team technical–tactical playing patterns — attack					7	Reinforce
Team technical–tactical playing patterns — defence					8	Reinforce
Set play — attacking situations					9	Reinforce
Set play — defending situations					10	Reinforce
Small pitch soccer — TE–TA elements	2	Reinforce	Reinforce	Reinforce	Reinforce	Reinforce
Full pitch soccer — TE–TA elements				12	Reinforce	Reinforce
	2	16	16	12	10	0

Total soccer development program elements = 56 elements

Technical–tactical elements to be coached

1. Jumping with 1 and 2 feet
2. Dribbling with the outside of the instep
3. Dribbling with the inside of the instep
4. Deceptive dribbling and feinting (10 tricks)
5. Juggling the ball
6. Kicking the ball with the inside of the instep
7. Kicking the ball with the outside of the instep
8. The wall pass — 1–2 pass
9. Receiving (amortisation) with the thigh
10. Receiving (amortisation) with the chest
11. Receiving (trapping) with the outside of the instep
12. Heading with the middle zone of the forehead
13. The sliding–straddle tackle
14. Basic combinations — 2:0
15. Basic combinations — 2:1
16. Heading at goal

Total elements = 16

Time allocation for the 80 minute coaching session

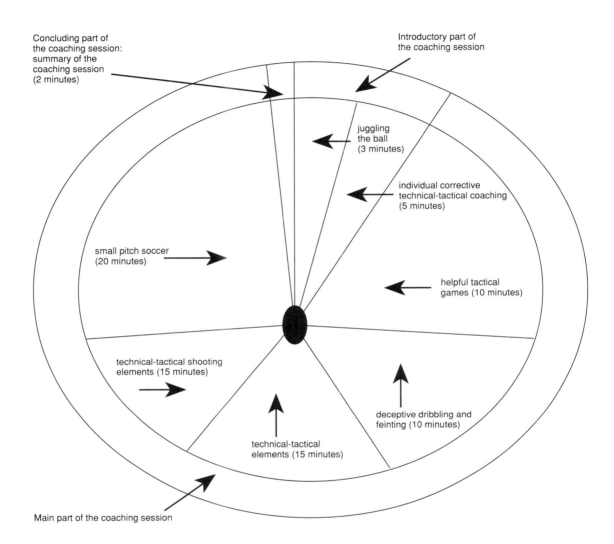

Concluding part of
the coaching session:
summary of the
coaching session
(2 minutes)

Introductory part of
the coaching session

juggling
the ball
(3 minutes)

individual corrective
technical-tactical coaching
(5 minutes)

small pitch soccer
(20 minutes)

helpful tactical
games (10 minutes)

technical-tactical shooting
elements (15 minutes)

deceptive dribbling and
feinting (10 minutes)

technical-tactical
elements (15 minutes)

Main part of the coaching session

Structure of the practical coaching session — 80 minutes

Total practical coaching time = 80 minutes

1. Introductory part of the coaching session

1.1 JUGGLING THE BALL

Juggling the ball is simply keeping the ball off the ground, playing it with all parts of the body except from the arms to the hands.

There is no better exercise for young players than juggling the ball to get universal feeling and confidence with the ball.

When juggling, it is necessary to be relaxed and have good body balance.

Juggling the ball is an important introductory part of each coaching session.

1. Juggling with the use of the outside of the foot

2. Juggling with the use of the chest

3. Juggling with the use of the head

2. Main part of the coaching session

2.1 HELPFUL TACTICAL GAMES

1. Parallel 4-goal soccer

One team attacks either 1 of the opponent's goals or defends its own. There are no offsides but corners are taken. The team can have goalkeepers or play without.

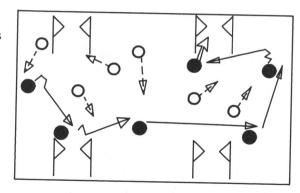

2. Soccer tennis

The ball is served from the bottom right corner behind the base line. The ball must pass over the net on the full and bounce in the opponent's court before being played. The ball can be played a maximum of 2 times in succession by the same player before passing or playing directly over the net. The net height is above the hips or below the shoulders.

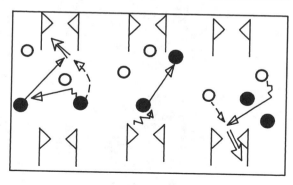

3. Mini-competition — 4:4, 3:3, 2:2

Four or 6 teams are selected to play in an organised mini-competition. There are no outs and a goal can only be scored from the front of the goal. Games are played equal time, with each team playing one another once. The team with the most number of points is declared winner.

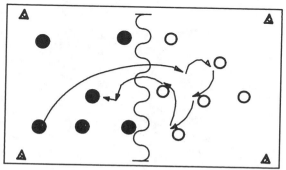

4. Medicine balls as goals

Two medicine balls are placed 20 metres apart. Two teams compete against each other in a game of small-sided soccer. There are no outs, with the goal being scored by hitting the medicine ball from any angle. There are no offsides.

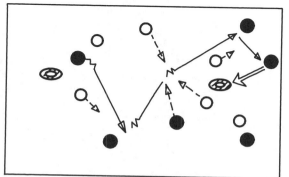

2.2 DECEPTIVE DRIBBLING AND FEINTING

In the previous level 15 deceptive dribbling and feinting elements of the game were exercised.

In level 3, 10 more deceptive dribbling and feinting elements are implemented. This brings the total number of dribbling and feinting elements to 25.

Dribbling is running with the ball under close control, using any part of the foot.

Feinting is the art of making deceptive body movements to delude the opponent.

So we could describe both dribbling and feinting as deception, where we use the body or ball or both to throw the defenders off balance to get past them.

In today's modern game every player must be able to master the art of dribbling and feinting.

No technique in the game of soccer causes greater pleasure than a good piece of dribbling and feinting.

As players progress through the soccer development program they will discover the dribbling and feinting techniques that suit them best.

Superstar Pele, the greatest goalscorer of all time. He scored over 1000 goals in his career

Methods of progress

The following exercises represent the methods of progress when coaching deceptive dribbling and feinting techniques.

1. *No pressure — 1 player*

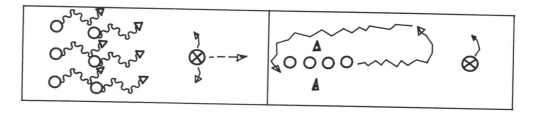

2. *Token pressure — 2 players*

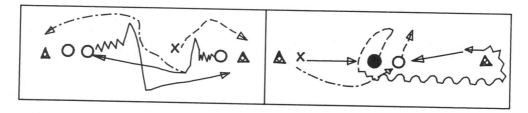

3. *Token pressure — 3 players*

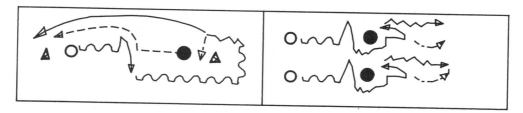

4. *Token pressure — 4 players*

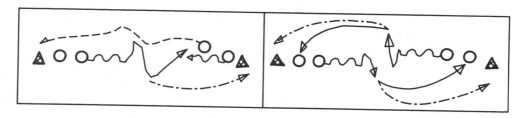

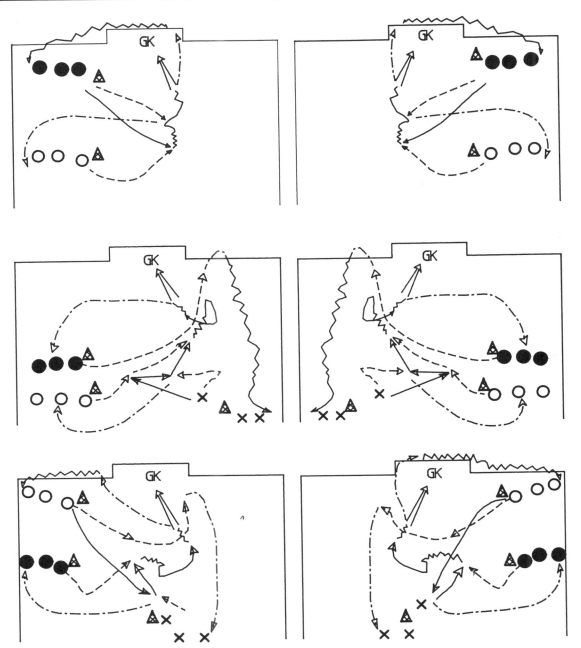

5. Full pressure — 1:1 combinations: combine the full pressure situations with goalscoring opportunities. This develops both the attacking and defending functions of players

Deceptive dribbling and feinting techniques

The following represent the 10 deceptive dribbling and feinting techniques to be executed in level 3.

1. Cutting the ball left and right

2. Flick the ball with the inside of the instep out of tackle

3. Dummy inside of foot pass and roll away

4. *Cross over dummy heel pass*

5. *Side trick pass*

6. *Run over heel pass*

7. Around the world

8. Run over heel stop

9. Flick, turn and receive

10. Twister

2.3 TECHNICAL–TACTICAL PROGRAM ELEMENTS

Jumping with 1 and 2 feet

A player will generally jump in the game simply to strike at the ball in order to win possession. In the majority of cases there will be an opponent who has similar intentions, so the decisive factor in such situations is the technique. A jump made with a run or a player moving is much more effective than a jump from a stationary position; however a player is in no position to decide the type of jump as this will be determined by the speed, flight of the ball and basic playing conditions.

As a result, exercises in jumping with 1 or 2 feet should be combined with a run or made without a run and made forward, backwards or to the side.

Players should be encouraged to use the 1 foot jump where there is sufficient time and space. This technique will give greater height in the jump. However, as the 2 foot jump is easier it is important to start learning this technique.

With the *2 foot jump* the extended step is made so that both feet are bent shoulder width apart with the hands away from the body, bent at the elbows. The leg muscles contract quickly so that there is complete extension of the ankle joint. The hands quickly move upwards, blocking at shoulder level with the back arching away from the imaginary ball. The landing must be soft and elastic with all joints bent and the player being able to move quickly in the selected direction.

The preparatory phase with the *jump 1 foot* is made up with the last 2 extended steps lowering the centre of gravity. This lowering and extension is necessary so that the force does not throw the body forward. The extended or stretched foot is bent to cushion the forward force and direct it vertically. To achieve this, the upper extremity of the body has to be leaning slightly backwards. The hands and free knee energetically move upwards following the sudden extension of the supporting ankle joint. The body, arching off the back foot, imitates the header at the highest point. The landing should be soft with the player quickly moving off in the intended direction. Even though with both techniques the player is required to imitate the header, this is of secondary importance.

With the jumping technique there are 4 phases: the preparatory phase, the take off phase, the flight phase and the landing phase. All 4 phases are of equal importance when executing the jump with 1 or 2 feet.

COMMON FAULTS — CORRECTIONS

1. The player is static and upright. **2.** There is no extended step. **3.** The player does not lean slightly backwards before the jump. **4.** The hands and free knee do not move energetically upwards. **5.** The player is not relaxed in the phase of flight. **6.** The head movement to strike the imaginary ball is not at the highest point. **7.** The back is not arched during the phase of flight. **8.** The landing is not soft and controlled.

1. Introductory part of the coaching session
1.1 Juggling the ball ....*refer to page 98*
1.2 Individual corrective technical–tactical coaching

2. Main part of the coaching session
2.1 Helpful tactical games ....*refer to page 99*
2.2 Deceptive dribbling and feinting techniques ....*refer to page 103*
2.3 Technical–tactical program element

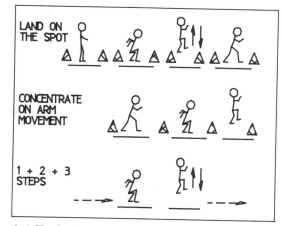 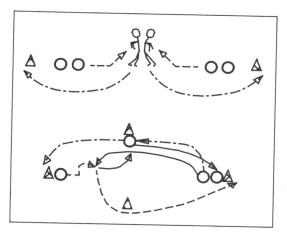

2.4 Technical–tactical shooting element

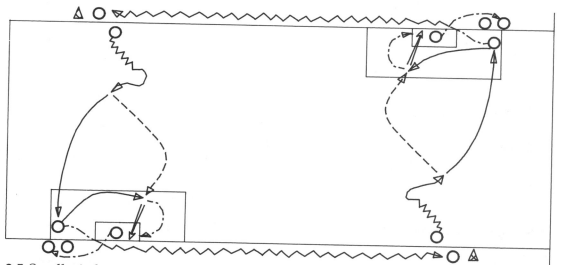

2.5 Small pitch soccer ....*refer to page 132*

3. Concluding part of the coaching session
3.1 Summary of the coaching session

Dribbling with the outside of the instep

Whenever the player has the ball at her feet to dribble, no matter what technique she is using, she always has the initiative. The defending player has to take particular care as she doesn't know which way the attacking player will move or what she is going to do.

Dribbling with the outside of the instep is where the dribbling foot is turned inward with the heels raised and toes pointing down. With the foot turned inward the controlling surface area is enlarged, enabling effective guiding control over the ball. The ball is pushed below its horizontal axis which results in a slight backspin of the ball. This is important as it prevents the ball from running too far in front and out of control. The ideal place to strike the ball is just below the axis. If the ball is struck too low then there is too much backspin with the possibility of the player kicking the ground. When striking the ball the ankle joint is to be loose and relaxed to enable the soft cushioned controlled kicks of the ball.

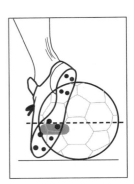

The eyes are on the ball at the moment of contact but the head is then raised to view the playing field. The body has a lean forward with the hands raised and elbows away from the body for balance.

This technique is commonly used when feinting a defender and then pushing and dribbling the ball with the outside of the instep past him. This technique can also quite successfully be used to keep the body between the ball and the opponent. This is known as shielding or screening the ball.

COMMON FAULTS — CORRECTIONS

1. The heel is not raised and the foot turned down and inwards.
2. The ankle joint is hard and locked with the ball being kicked along out of control.
3. The eyes are continually fixed on the ball, indicating lack of confidence and control.
4. The hands are to the side of the body and not away for balance.
5. The ball is not struck just below the horizontal axis but too low or on top. Both executions result in poor control.
6. There is no forward incline of the body but the player is upright.
7. At the moment of execution the legs are not bent, lowering the centre of gravity to assist balance with the ball.

1. Introductory part of the coaching session
1.1 Juggling the ball ....*refer to page 98*
1.2 Individual corrective technical–tactical coaching

2. Main part of the coaching session
2.1 Helpful tactical games ....*refer to page 99*
2.2 Deceptive dribbling and feinting techniques ....*refer to page 103*
2.3 Technical–tactical program element

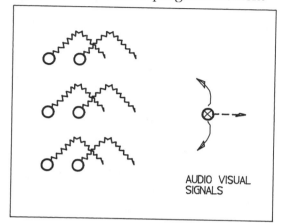

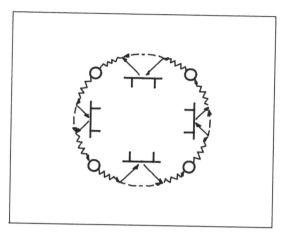

AUDIO VISUAL
SIGNALS

2.4 Technical–tactical shooting element

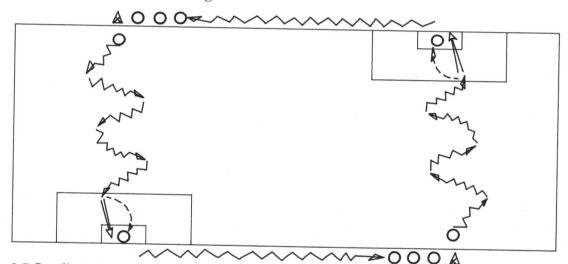

2.5 Small pitch soccer ....*refer to page 132*

3. Concluding part of the coaching session
3.1 Summary of the coaching session

Dribbling with the inside of the instep

With dribbling with the inside of the instep the opposite occurs to that of dribbling with the outside of the instep. With this technique we have the toe raised and foot turning outward, exposing the inside of the foot to the ball. The foot should be soft and relaxed when guiding or dribbling the ball. The ball is pushed forward with the inner surface which corresponds with the area from the toe to the ankle joint.

The ball is pushed under the horizontal axis which will create a slight backspin preventing the ball from running away out of control. Before the player makes contact with the ball the foot is turned outward.

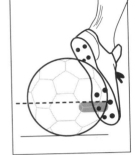

The body is leaning forward and the hands and elbows are raised and out to assist with balance. The eyes are on the ball and the field of play is viewed peripherally. When the ball is pushed and dribbled the eyes now are on the field of play while peripheral view is maintained over the ball. Whatever dribbling technique is used the player must avoid keeping his eyes always on the ball. With all forms of dribbling it should be noted that increased defending pressure on the attacking player must result in closer control over the ball.

COMMON FAULTS — CORRECTIONS

1. The ankle joint is hard and locked with the ball being kicked along out of control.
2. The toe is not raised and the foot is turned outwards.
3. The eyes are continually fixed on the ball, indicating lack of confidence and control.
4. The hands are to the side of the body and not away for balance.
5. The ball is not struck just below the horizontal axis but too low or on top. Both executions result in poor control.
6. There is no forward incline of the body but the player is upright.
7. At the moment of execution the legs are not bent, lowering the centre of gravity to assist balance with the ball.

1. Introductory part of the coaching session
    1.1 Juggling the ball ....*refer to page 98*
    1.2 Individual corrective technical–tactical coaching
2. Main part of the coaching session
    2.1 Helpful tactical games ....*refer to page 99*
    2.2 Deceptive dribbling and feinting techniques ....*refer to page 103*
    2.3 Technical–tactical program element

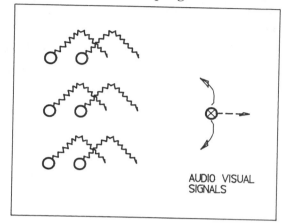
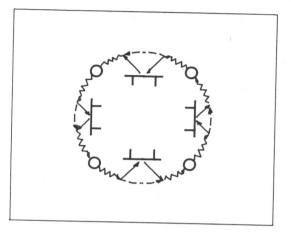

    2.4 Technical–tactical shooting element

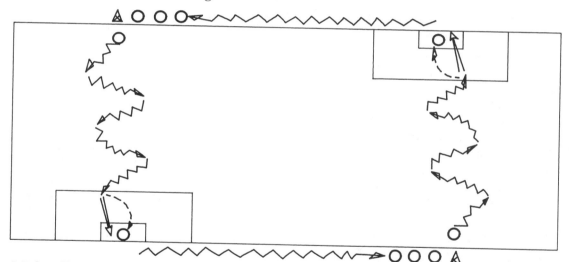

    2.5 Small pitch soccer ....*refer to page 132*
3. Concluding part of the coaching session
    3.1 Summary of the coaching session

Kicking the ball with the inside of the instep

The inner surface of the foot from the toe to the ankle joint corresponds to the inside of the instep.

There are times in the game when the path to goal or supporting players is blocked and only by 'bending' the pass, around opponents, is one able to find the target. This technique of kicking allows the player to swerve or, as it is better known, 'banana' the ball. The kick is made off centre to the vertical axis, giving the ball lateral spin. The more spin the ball has the greater the swerve. However, the greater the spin the less power of the kick. Therefore a balance between power and spin has to be established by the player.

The supporting leg is bent at the knee with the foot forming a 'V' with the kicking foot. The kicking foot is turned outward to allow the foot to make contact with the ball off centre. The ankle joint is locked and hard with the toes pointing upward. The elbows and hands are raised and to the side to assist with balance. The eyes are fixed on the ball with a peripheral view of the target.

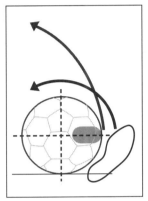

Some players have the capability to strike the ball to the side of the vertical axis and below the horizontal axis with the kicking foot moving upwards. This type of kick not only gives a side spin but also a top spin of the ball. Here the flight path of the ball will climb high and to the side and then quickly dip and swerve to the target. This type of kick or shot is extremley difficult for the goalkeepers to anticipate.

COMMON FAULTS — CORRECTIONS

1. The ankle joint is not hard and locked but loose.
2. The eyes are not fixed on the ball at the moment of contact.
3. There is no snap of the knee.
4. The ball is hit too far off centre from the vertical axis resulting in too much spin and no power.
5. The ball is struck too close to the vertical axis resulting in very little spin and swerve of the ball.
6. The player kicks through and not across the face of the ball.
7. The hands and elbows are not wide for balance.
8. The ball is struck too low below the horizontal axis giving it too much height.

1. Introductory part of the coaching session
    1.1 Juggling the ball ....*refer to page 98*
    1.2 Individual corrective technical–tactical coaching

2. Main part of the coaching session
    2.1 Helpful tactical games ....*refer to page 99*
    2.2 Deceptive dribbling and feinting techniques ....*refer to page 103*
    2.3 Technical–tactical program element

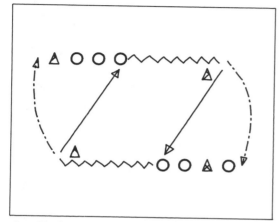 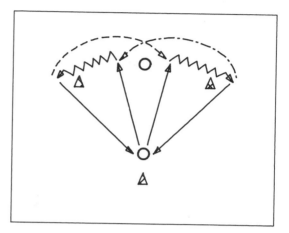

    2.4 Technical–tactical shooting element

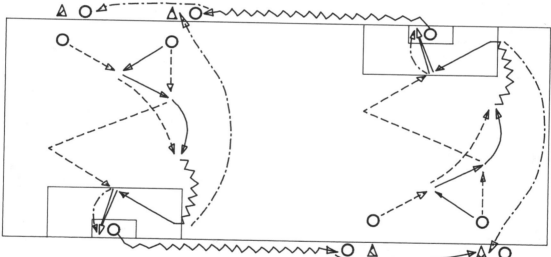

    2.5 Small pitch soccer ....*refer to page 132*

3. Concluding part of the coaching session
    3.1 Summary of the coaching session

Kicking the ball with the outside of the instep

The outside of the instep is the surface area that stretches from the small toe to the outside of the ankle joint.

There are times in the game when the supporting player or the path to goal is blocked. As with the inside of the foot technique, the kick with the outside of the foot can be successfully used to 'bend' or 'banana' the ball to its target.

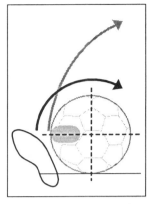

The use of this technique is quite popular with South American players but very unpopular with goalkeepers as they have to quickly adjust to the swerving ball in the air.

One great advantage with this technique compared with the inside of the instep is that greater power can be applied to the swerving ball without the player breaking his running stride. The kicking foot here is turned inward from the hip, toes are pointing down, the heel raised with the ankle joint locked and hard. The ball is kicked across the face of 1 side of the vertical axis. The greater the distance away from the vertical axis the more spin but the less power can be applied to the ball. The eyes are fixed on the ball at the moment of contact with the standing foot bent and away from the ball. The hands and elbows are raised and away from the body to assist with balance.

COMMON FAULTS — CORRECTIONS

1. The ankle joint is not locked and hard but soft and loose.
2. The toes are not pointing down and inward with heel raised.
3. The eyes are not fixed on the ball at the moment of contact.
4. The ball is struck too far off the vertical axis — too much spin and no power.
5. The ball is struck too close to the vertical axis — no spin or swerve of the ball.
6. Hands and elbows are not away from the body for balance.
7. The standing foot is too close to the ball preventing the kick across the ball face.
8. The kicking foot follows through to the target instead of away to the side.

1. Introductory part of the coaching session
  1.1 Juggling the ball ....*refer to page 98*
  1.2 Individual corrective technical–tactical coaching

2. Main part of the coaching session
  2.1 Helpful tactical games ....*refer to page 99*
  2.2 Deceptive dribbling and feinting techniques ....*refer to page 103*
  2.3 Technical–tactical program element

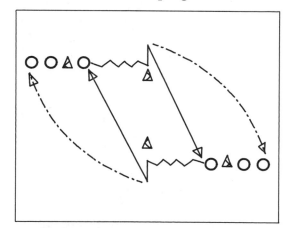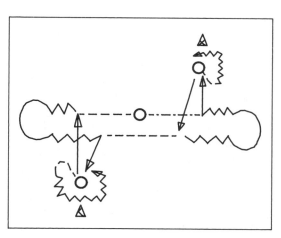

  2.4 Technical–tactical shooting element

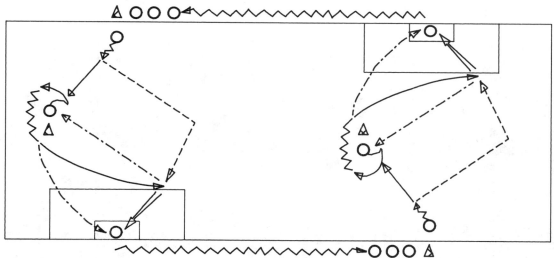

  2.5 Small pitch soccer ....*refer to page 132*

3. Concluding part of the coaching session
  3.1 Summary of the coaching session

The wall pass — 1–2 pass

This element is one of the most effective passes that can be used on any part of the playing field in order to release pressure in defence or to penetrate the opponent's defending quarter. It is also called the wall pass because the ball is 'bounced' off a supporting player back to the server. It is a quick exchange of passes between 2 attacking players.

This pass represents the basic co-operation between 2 players and also represents the basis for collective team play. The pass can be made with any part of the body but the inside of the foot or the outside of the instep is most commonly used. One great disadvantage with the inside of the foot is that the defending player is able to 'read' the attacking player's intentions and as a result intercept the pass. Also to use the inside of the foot the leg has to be turned at the hip which disrupts the player's running technique. This is less so with the outside of the instep as the attacking player is able to 'disguise' his movements and maintain his stride.

The movement is executed by the player with the ball slowing her movements to deceive the defender into thinking she is going to stop. At the moment the pass is made to her supporting player the attacking player moves into a sprint around the defender to receive the return 1–2 pass.

The role of the supporting player is particularly important because once the pass is made a mistake could result in a counter attack. The supporting player must disguise her intentions by deceiving the defender with a 'dummy' movement. At the moment of the pass the supporting player must be moving to the ball, to create space and time. At the same time she must have her body between the ball and the defender to make it much harder for the defending team to gain possession.

COMMON FAULTS — CORRECTIONS

1. The attacking player with the ball does not slow his movements before the pass. He looks in the direction of the intended pass. After executing the pass he does not go into a full sprint. The ball is delivered too slowly to the supporting player.

2. The supporting player does not disguise his run by starting to move in another direction. His eyes are fixed on the ball. There is no movement to the passed ball and his body is not between the ball and defender. The elbows and hands are not raised to assist with balance or more importantly to 'feel' for the defender's movement.

1. Introductory part of the coaching session
   1.1 Juggling the ball ....
   1.2 Individual corrective technical–tactical coaching *refer to page 98*

2. Main part of the coaching session
   2.1 Helpful tactical games ....*refer to page 99*
   2.2 Deceptive dribbling and feinting techniques ....*refer to page 103*
   2.3 Technical–tactical program element

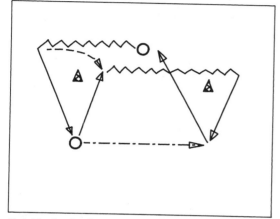
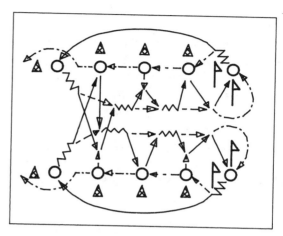

2.4 Technical–tactical shooting element

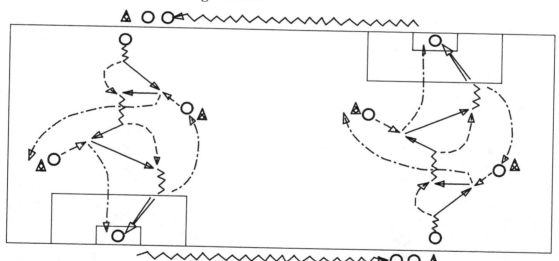

2.5 Small pitch soccer ....*refer to page 132*

3. Concluding part of the coaching session
   3.1 Summary of the coaching session

Receiving (amortisation) with the thigh

The secret of successful amortisation is to treat the ball gently and have the receiving part of the body relaxed and loose. The great advantage with receiving with the thigh is the thick layer of muscle (quadriceps) that covers the thigh bone (femur). This muscle alone at times is sufficient to cushion the ball and bring it under control.

The technique of receiving however requires the player to get in flight of the ball and anticipate the speed and place of contact.

All weight is on the supporting leg with eyes fixed on the ball. The elbows and hands are raised to the side of the body to assist in balance. As the ball approaches the receiving thigh goes to meet the ball and just before contact, contracts a little slower than the speed of the ball bringing it under control.

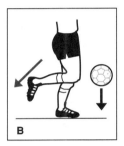

The receiving part of the thigh muscle must remain soft and relaxed at all times. The ideal amortisation is when the player moves the ball into position for the shot, dribble or pass while still being in complete control.

COMMON FAULTS — CORRECTIONS

1. The player does not get in flight with the ball but stretches for the ball.
2. The thigh is withdrawn too quickly missing the ball altogether.
3. The thigh is withdrawn too slowly resulting in the ball bouncing out of control.
4. The eyes are not fixed on the ball.
5. The receiving thigh muscle is not soft and relaxed to cushion or absorb the impact from the ball.
6. The hands and elbows are not raised to the side of the body for balance.
7. The supporting leg is not bent, lowering the centre of gravity and assisting in balance.

1. Introductory part of the coaching session
    1.1 Juggling the ball ....*refer to page 98*
    1.2 Individual corrective technical–tactical coaching

2. Main part of the coaching session
    2.1 Helpful tactical games ....*refer to page 99*
    2.2 Deceptive dribbling and feinting techniques ....*refer to page 103*
    2.3 Technical–tactical program element

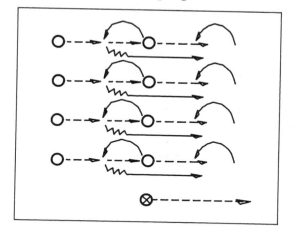
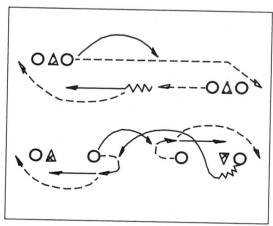

    2.4 Technical–tactical shooting element

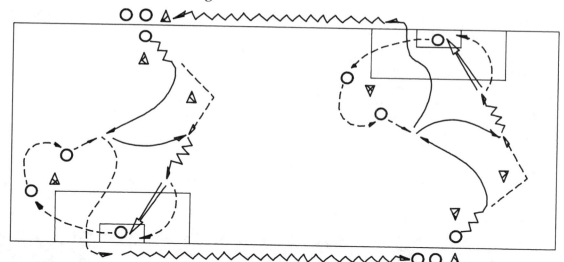

    2.5 Small pitch soccer ....*refer to page 132*

3. Concluding part of the coaching session
    3.1 Summary of the coaching session

Receiving (amortisation) with the chest

The ideal part of the chest to receive the ball is the central part of the breast bone (sternum); however many players prefer to use the soft side muscle.

There are two ways in which a player can receive with the chest. The quicker way is to have the ball bounce down; the slower way is to have the ball bounce up from the chest. With the quicker way the player must get in flight of the ball with elbows and hands raised for balance. At the moment of contact the hips have a backward movement with the hands moving forward to arch the chest down. The ball should quickly drop to the ground under control.

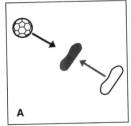

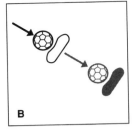

With the ball bouncing up from the chest the ball is usually arriving at a greater height. The technique here is the same as with all other techniques of amortisation. The part of the receiving chest moves to meet the ball and at the moment of contact withdraws a little slower than the ball, bringing it under control. The disadvantage here is that the ball will bounce up from the chest and at that moment it is temporarily out of control before it drops to the ground. If the receiving player is pressurised it is neccessary for him to get his body between the ball and the defender and 'screen' the ball.

Correct breathing technique will also assist in the control. As the ball arrives the player should inhale and at the moment of contact exhale.

In both examples of receiving (amortisation) with the chest, the eyes are fixed on the ball, hands raised to the side and the body relaxed.

COMMON FAULTS — CORRECTIONS

1. The eyes are not fixed on the ball.
2. The muscles are too tight and the body is not relaxed to cushion the force.
3. The player does not get in flight of the ball.
4. The hands are not raised and to the side of the body for balance.
5. The player does not withdraw the chest at the moment of contact.
6. Withdrawal of the chest is either too early or too late. In both instances the ball is not controlled.
7. The player does not exhale at the moment of contact.

1. Introductory part of the coaching session
   1.1 Juggling the ball ....*refer to page 98*
   1.2 Individual corrective technical–tactical coaching

2. Main part of the coaching session
   2.1 Helpful tactical games ....*refer to page 99*
   2.2 Deceptive dribbling and feinting techniques ....*refer to page 103*
   2.3 Technical–tactical program element

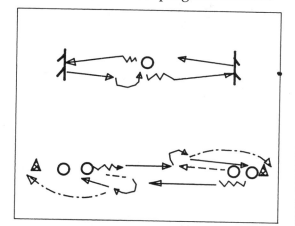
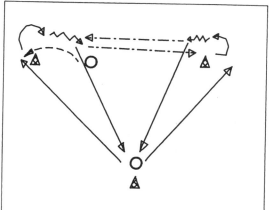

   2.4 Technical–tactical shooting element

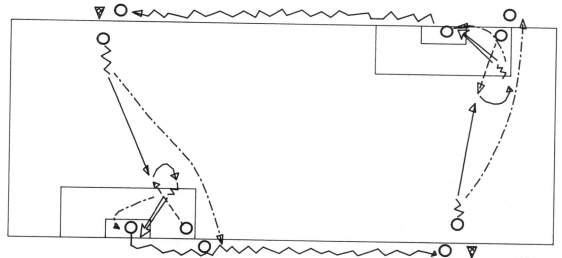

   2.5 Small pitch soccer ....*refer to page 132*

3. Concluding part of the coaching session
   3.1 Summary of the coaching session

Receiving (trapping) with the outside of the instep

The area from the small toe to the ankle is the part used when trapping with the outside of the instep. When a player cannot get in flight of the ball, then different techniques have to be used to control the ball. If in a particular situation the ball is arriving at the standing foot, then 1 technique the player can use is to trap the ball with the outside of the instep. This technique of control is the result of turning the foot inwards and not outwards.

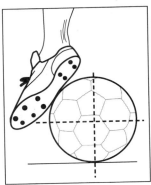

In this situation the receiving foot moves across the standing foot and 'traps' the ball. The receiving foot is relaxed and loose forming a 'wedge' for the ball to get caught in. The upper extremity of the body is leaning back and usually to the side of the receiving foot. The eyes are fixed on the ball with elbows and hands raised for balance.

With all receiving techniques the muscles and joints should be relaxed and loose.

COMMON FAULTS — CORRECTIONS

1. The muscles are too tight; the receiving ankle joint not loose and relaxed.
2. Eyes are not fixed on the ball.
3. There is no body lean to the side with hands raised and wide for balance.
4. The receiving foot is not turned inwards forming a wedge but the sole of the foot is flat to the ground.
5. All of the body weight is not balanced on the supporting leg.
6. Contact with the ball is not made above the horizontal axis of the ball.
7. The toes of the receiving foot are not pointing down and inward with the heel raised.
8. The ball is not received across and in front of the supporting leg.

1. Introductory part of the coaching session
    1.1 Juggling the ball ....*refer to page 98*
    1.2 Individual corrective technical–tactical coaching
2. Main part of the coaching session
    2.1 Helpful tactical games ....*refer to page 99*
    2.2 Deceptive dribbling and feinting techniques ....*refer to page 103*
    2.3 Technical–tactical program element

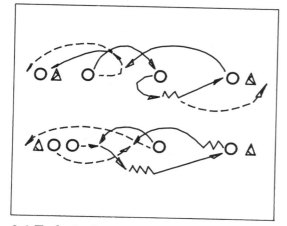 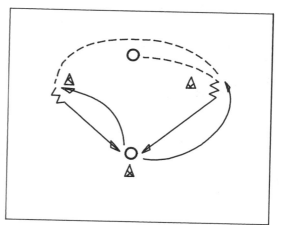

    2.4 Technical–tactical shooting element

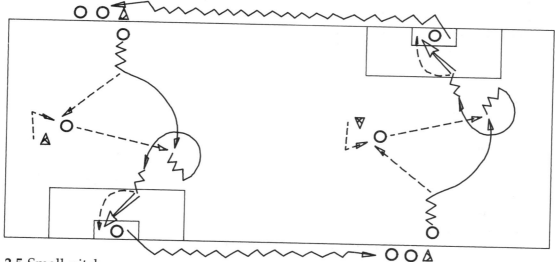

    2.5 Small pitch soccer ....*refer to page 132*
3. Concluding part of the coaching session
    3.1 Summary of the coaching session

Heading with the middle zone of the forehead

The greatest problem with teaching this element is the fear associated with an object hitting the head. If the ball is struck too low (nose or face) or too high (top of the head) then this fear will be justified by the pain. So the most important factor is to make certain that it is done correctly from the start and that the player is confident.

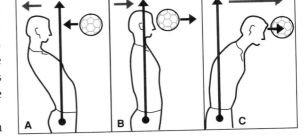

The middle zone of the forehead, where the ball is struck, is the part above the eyebrows in line with the nose. The ball can be headed from a standing position, a running position, with a jump or without a jump. It can be headed forward, to the side or even backwards over the head, in all situations using the middle zone of the forehead.

The technique requires the body to arch with the chin tucked in and neck muscles locked at the moment of contact. Eyes are on the ball at all times and the knees are bent. The elbows and hands are raised to support not only balance but also the forward thrust when the head attacks the ball. When the ball approaches the player must arch away from the ball involving as many joints as possible. The sudden contraction to the ball will harness all the available power into heading the ball.

If the player shows signs of fear when heading then let him practice by throwing the ball from his hand and heading to a partner then progress to the delivery from a partner. Start with stationary exercises and then progress to both players moving. This way the player will gradually develop confidence with heading the ball. If not then he will always have a poor technical habit that will be almost impossible to correct.

COMMON FAULTS — CORRECTIONS

1. The eyes are not fixed on the ball.
2. There is no arch of the body away from the arriving ball.
3. The head is lowered just before contact, allowing the ball to strike the top of the head. This is the result of the player being afraid of the ball hitting his face.
4. The legs are not bent resulting in the player just stretching to head the ball.
5. The elbows and hands are not raised and in front of the body to assist in the forward thrust and balance but held down to the side.
6. The neck muscles are not locked but relaxed.
7. The player waits, allowing the ball to hit the head instead of moving the head to meet and strike the ball.

1. Introductory part of the coaching session
    1.1 Juggling the ball ....*refer to page 98*
    1.2 Individual corrective technical–tactical coaching
2. Main part of the coaching session
    2.1 Helpful tactical games ....*refer to page 99*
    2.2 Deceptive dribbling and feinting techniques ....*refer to page 103*
    2.3 Technical–tactical program element

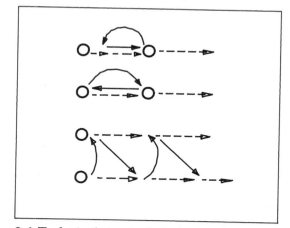 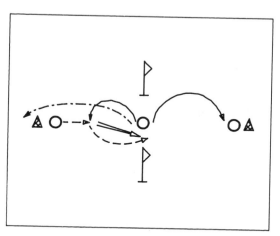

    2.4 Technical–tactical shooting element

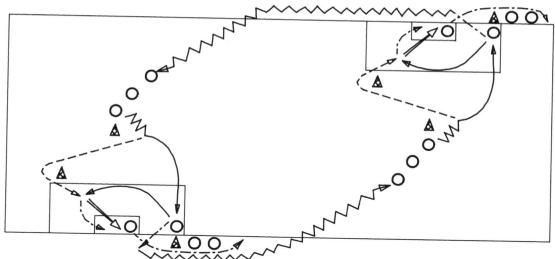

    2.5 Small pitch soccer ....*refer to page 132*
3. Concluding part of the coaching session
    3.1 Summary of the coaching session

The sliding–straddle tackle

The sliding tackle and straddle tackle are the two common tackles that leave the defending player stranded on the ground. The tackle needs perfect timing as the players and the ball are all moving. It is absolutely vital, as the defending player is on the ground and temporarily out of the game, that the technical execution is exact. If the attacking player gets out of the tackle she is able to continue penetration creating an attacking situation of 2 against 1 and completely upsetting the balance in defence. To be able to perform a successful tackle strength, courage and skill as well as technique all play an equally important role.

With *the sliding tackle* the defending and attacking players are side by side with the tackle performed slightly behind the attacking player. The supporting leg is bent allowing the body to fall to the side with the hand on the same side positioned to cushion the fall. When the ball is away from the attacking player precise timing and an explosive controlled jump to the ball are the essential elements of this type of tackle. The eyes are fixed at all times on the ball and not on the player's movements, while the joints are locked and hard.

With *the straddle tackle* the defending player takes up a position in front of the attacking player, keeping a distance of approximately 2 to 3 metres and moving with the ball. At the moment the attacking player loses control the defending player jumps to the ball, legs apart to block or kick the ball away and out of the attacking player's possession. The movement is explosive with joints locked and hands away from the body for balance and to cushion the fall.

COMMON FAULTS — CORRECTIONS

1. The tackling leg and body is too loose which could result in injury.
2. The player takes his eyes off the ball. This can result in an incorrect tackle giving away a free kick or penalty.
3. The hands are not away from the body to assist in balance and to cushion the fall.
4. Not choosing the right moment to tackle — too early or too late.
5. The defending player is not mobile and moving with the ball; easily beaten in a 1:1 situation.
6. The player is not certain, courageous and totally committed to the tackle.

1. Introductory part of the coaching session
1.1 Juggling the ball ....*refer to page 98*
1.2 Individual corrective technical–tactical coaching

2. Main part of the coaching session
2.1 Helpful tactical games ....*refer to page 99*
2.2 Deceptive dribbling and feinting techniques ....*refer to page 103*
2.3 Technical–tactical program element

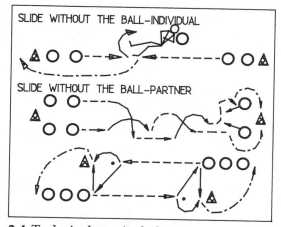
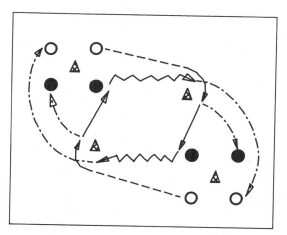

2.4 Technical–tactical shooting element

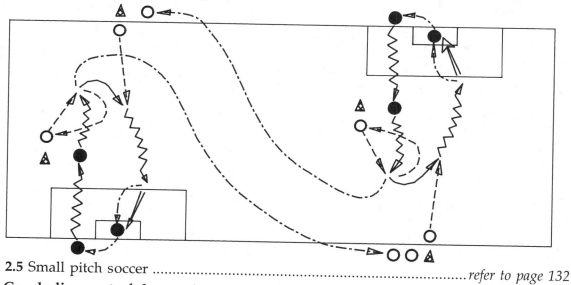

2.5 Small pitch soccer ....*refer to page 132*

3. Concluding part of the coaching session
3.1 Summary of the coaching session

Basic combinations – 2:0

These combinations represent the basic shape of the co-operation between 2 players and the basis for collective play.

When passing between each other the players are able to communicate. The better the communication with the ball the better the chances are of having a successful team.

The same type of pass and player movement will not be deceptive enough to outsmart defenders and in the majority of cases the pass will be intercepted and possession lost.

When making passes, even in the 2:0 situations, players must be encouraged to disguise their intentions and combine several combinations where there is the diagonal movement of the ball and the player. These diagonal movements are always confusing for defenders and make it difficult for them to balance against. Another important factor is the quality of the pass. A good player will be familiar with the qualities of his supporting player — his strengths and weaknesses — before delivering the pass.

Modern soccer demands the all round technical–tactical, physical and psychological quality of the player. Because of this priority in the game emphasis has to be given to the versatility of the player and the concept of play and not to the specialisation of the player in a specific function or position. As a result all the players must complete the attacking function of basic combinations of 2:0.

1. Introductory part of the coaching session

1.1 Juggling the ball ....*refer to page 98*

1.2 Individual corrective technical–tactical coaching

2. Main part of the coaching session

2.1 Helpful tactical games ....*refer to page 99*

2.2 Deceptive dribbling and feinting techniques ....*refer to page 103*

2.3 Technical–tactical program element

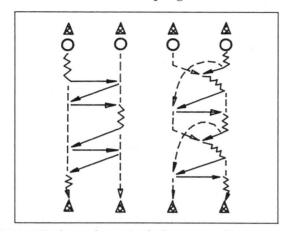 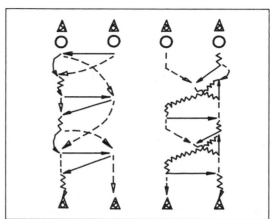

2.4 Technical–tactical shooting element

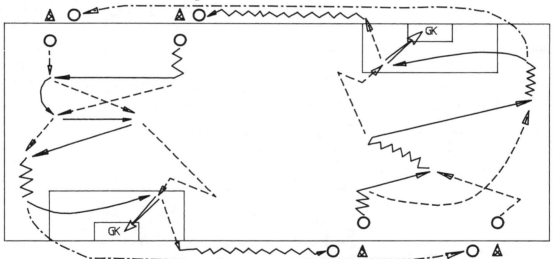

2.5 Small pitch soccer ....*refer to page 132*

3. Concluding part of the coaching session

3.1 Summary of the coaching session

Basic combinations – 2:1

These combinations are the same as the 2:0 combinations except that there is a defender. The elements again represent the basic shape of co-operation between 2 players trying to outsmart a defender.

The role of the defending player is simply to apply pressure on the attacking players while they are executing the element. This way we bring the element much closer to the conditions the attacking player will find in the game. The role of the defender starts with token pressure and when we are satisfied with the execution we then create the situation with full pressure. In this situation the player is defending as she would in the game and doing her best to prevent or break down the attack of the 2 players.

With passing between each other the players are able to communicate. The better the communication with the ball the better the chances of having a successful team. At the same time players must always be encouraged to disguise their intentions before releasing or receiving the ball.

Modern soccer demands the all round technical–tactical, physical and psychological quality of the player. Because of this priority in the game emphasis has to be given to the versatility of the player and the concept of play and not to specialisation of the player in a specific function or position. As a result all the players must complete the attacking and defending function of basic combinations of 2:1.

1. Introductory part of the coaching session
1.1 Juggling the ball ....*refer to page 98*
1.2 Individual corrective technical–tactical coaching

2. Main part of the coaching session
2.1 Helpful tactical games ....*refer to page 99*
2.2 Deceptive dribbling and feinting techniques ....*refer to page 103*
2.3 Technical–tactical program element

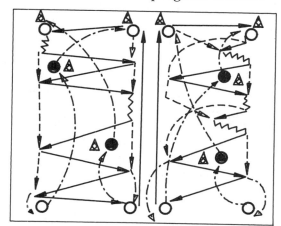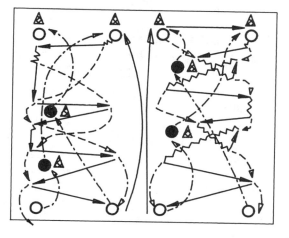

2.4 Technical–tactical shooting element

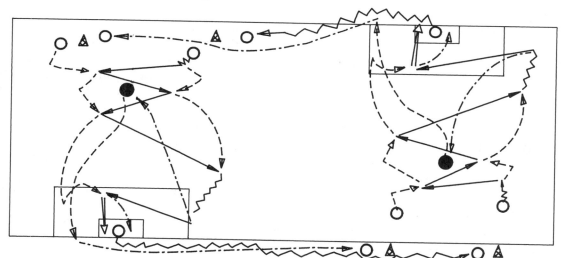

2.5 Small pitch soccer ....*refer to page 132*

3. Concluding part of the coaching session
3.1 Summary of the coaching session

2.5 SMALL PITCH SOCCER

Every coaching session, at this level, should end with a small-sided game on a small pitch. It is these small-sided situations that the young players enjoy most. They are in constant contact with the ball, enabling the technical–tactical and physical skills to be put into practice.

The aim when playing small-sided games is simply to attack the opponent's goal in the phase of attack and defend your goal in the phase of defence. The phase of attack is that moment your team gains possession, while the phase of defence is the moment the team has lost possession.

This is called soccer tactics — the art by which the player's technical and physical qualities are used to achieve the best possible result.

Tactics can be divided into 3 distinct categories:

1. *Individual tactics:* pressing the player, pressing the ball, creating space, dribbling, feinting, receiving, heading, passing, shooting, etc.
2. *Group tactics:* the mobility and interchange of players, the recovery behind the ball of the front attacking line, defending the goal, counter attacking, offside tactics, co-operation with the goalkeeper, playing wide or through the middle, etc.
3. *Team tactics:* keeping possession, slow build up, long direct penetrating passes, playing the high ball, keeping the ball low, switch of play, recovering behind the ball into a zone, pressing on all parts of the field, etc.

Team tactics used by the coach will also be determined by many factors that may include the way the opponent's play, state of the playing surface, the team's position in the competition, phase of the game, the weather, etc.

The technical–tactical elements in the phase of attack are:

1. *Mobility:* the ability to move with or without the ball to create playing space.
2. *Penetration:* the ability to get past or behind defenders, with or without the ball.
3. *Width and depth:* the ability to create playing space across and along the field of play.
4. *Switch of play:* the ability to draw defenders out of position and exploit space on the opposite side.

The technical–tactical elements in the phase of defence are:

1. *Balance:* the ability to limit the creation of space, penetration and passing angles.
2. *Pressing the player without the ball:* the ability to reduce the time and playing space an attacking player will have when receiving the ball.
3. *Pressing the ball:* the ability to reduce the time and space the attacking player will have to receive, pass, dribble or shoot at goal.
4. *Zone and combined zone formations:* the ability to recover goal side of the ball, cover an area, and press any player entering that zone.

It is necessary for coaches, coaching at all levels, to understand the technical–tactical elements in the phases of attack and defence. However, tactics must not be coached in level 3 at the expense of techniques.

Order of coaching technical–tactical elements in attack and defence

The following technical–tactical elements in attack and defence are to be applied and reinforced at each level.

	TE–TA *elements in attack*				**TE–TA** *elements in defence*			
	Number 1	*Number 2*	*Number 3*	*Number 4*	*Number 1*	*Number 2*	*Number 3*	*Number 4*
Level 1 (5 to 8 years)	Unlimited touches with the ball Playing for fun				Unlimited touches with the ball Playing for fun			
Level 2 (9 to 10 years)	Mobility Maximum 3 touches Reinforce level 1				Balance Reinforce level 1			
Level 3 (11 to 12 years)	Mobility Maximum 2 touches Reinforce levels 1 and 2	Penetration			Balance Reinforce levels 1 and 2	Pressing the player without the ball		
Level 4 (13 to 14 years)	Mobility Maximum 1 touch Reinforce levels 1 to 3	Penetration Reinforce level 3	Width and depth		Balance Reinforce levels 1 to 3	Pressing the player without the ball Reinforce level 3	Pressing the ball	
Level 5 (15 to 16 years)	Mobility Maximum 1 touch Reinforce levels 1 to 4	Penetration Reinforce levels 3 and 4	Width and depth Reinforce level 4	Switch of play	Balance Reinforce levels 1 to 4	Pressing the player without the ball Reinforce levels 3 and 4	Pressing the ball Reinforce level 4	Zone and combined zone defence
Level 6 (17+ years)	Mobility Maximum 1 touch Reinforce levels 1 to 5	Penetration Reinforce levels 3 to 5	Width and depth Reinforce levels 4 and 5	Switch of play Reinforce level 5	Balance Reinforce levels 1 to 5	Pressing the player without the ball Reinforce levels 3 to 5	Pressing the ball Reinforce levels 4 and 5	Zone and combined zone defence Reinforce level 5

Technical–tactical elements in attack

PENETRATION — MAXIMUM 2 TOUCHES

Penetration is the ability to get past or behind defenders, with or without the ball. It is not just restricted from play in the opponent's half but also from any part of the pitch. If the defenders are standing square at half way then there is no reason why a long penetrative pass could not be played from deep inside one's half, behind the defenders for a supporting player to attack.

Penetration is only possible with a mobile attack where the attacking players are continually moving to create space and time for themselves or their team mates. It is important that the player making the penetrative runs knows where to run to give the best possible support or decoy to the player with the ball.

Skilful players in a 1:1 situation can cause enormous damage to the opposing team by taking on defenders and getting behind them using their dribbling–feinting techniques. This penetrative play can completely destroy the balance in defence as the player with the ball, when beating the defender, is able to create a dangerous 2:1 situation. Players in the attacking quarter should always be encouraged to take on and dribble defending players if they cannot shoot at goal or make an effective pass to a supporting player.

The diagonal movement of the player and the diagonal movement of the ball are the most effective means of penetrating and piercing the balance in defence.

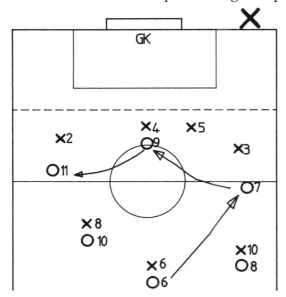

Team 0 is lacking mobility and penetration in attack

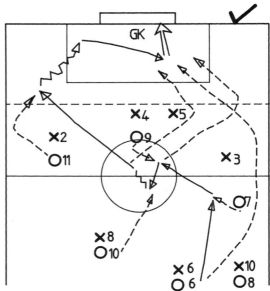

Team 0 is mobile and making diagonal penetrating runs, upsetting the balance in defence

---

Note: Introduce a maximum of 2 touches with the ball, in the small-sided games, while reinforcing levels 2 and 1.

Technical–tactical elements in defence

PRESSING THE PLAYER WITHOUT THE BALL

Pressing the player without the ball is the ability to reduce the time and playing space an attacking player will have when receiving the ball. This is also known as person to person marking.

Pressing a player is to mark and follow the attacking player with the intention of reducing his contribution to the game to a minimum. When pressing the player without the ball the defending player should:

- keep himself between the opposing player and his own goal;
- keep an eye on the ball and the opponent without losing balance;
- and try to maintain a distance of no more than 1 step or 1 metre from the opponent.

Pressing can be applied to a whole team or just to individual players. This will be determined by the individual quality of players and the conditions of play. If the opposition has an extremely gifted and dangerous player then it is wise to have 1 or even 2 players tightly press him out of the full game. Providing the defending player is never beaten, in theory this type of defensive pattern is perfect.

A big disadvantage with this element is pressing a player who is constantly moving out of position. These runs by the attacking player will open up the defence and allow other attacking players to use the working space. As a result total concentration and application by all defending players in these situations is required.

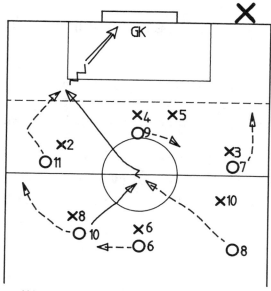

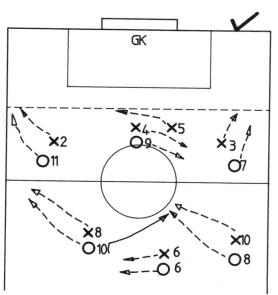

Team X is not pressing the 0 players and allows 08 to move into space and receive a pass from 010, then play a penetrating pass in behind the defenders for 011 to strike at goal

Here team X successfully applies pressing the player and reduces the time and space the attacking player has with or without the ball

The laws of the game

1. *The field of play*
   Length — 50 to 100 yards
   Width — 44 to 59 yards
   The goal area — 3×10 yards
   The penalty area — 22×9 yards
   The corner area — 0.5 yard
   The goals — shall be 6 yards apart joined by a horizontal cross-bar 6 feet high
   The centre circle — shall have a radius of 8 yards

2. *The ball* — shall be a size 4 and of leather

3. *Number of players* — a match shall be played by 2 teams consisting of not more than 9 players each; in each team there is a goalkeeper

4. *Referees and linesmen* — a referee and linesmen shall be appointed to officiate at each game

5. *Duration* — 35 minutes each way with 10 minutes for half-time

6. *The start of play* — before or after goals are scored, play is started by a player taking a place kick at the centre. All defending players must be in their half and outside the circle

7. *The ball out of play* — when it has wholly crossed the goal line or touch line, when in the air or on the ground

8. *Offside* — there are no offsides at this level

9. *Fouls and misconduct* — the player is penalised by awarding a free kick

10. *Free kicks* — all free kicks can result in a direct shot at goal. All opposing players shall be at least 8 yards from the ball

11. *Penalty kicks* — the penalty kick is taken 10 yards from the goal line

12. *Throw-in* — at the point where the ball crossed the line, the throw is taken with both hands behind the head and with both feet on the ground

13. *Goal kick* — at the side where the ball crossed the line, the ball is placed in the goal area and kicked into play

14. *Corner kick* — if the ball passes over the goal line, excluding the goals, and is last played by the defending team, then a player from the attacking team takes a free kick from the corner of the field

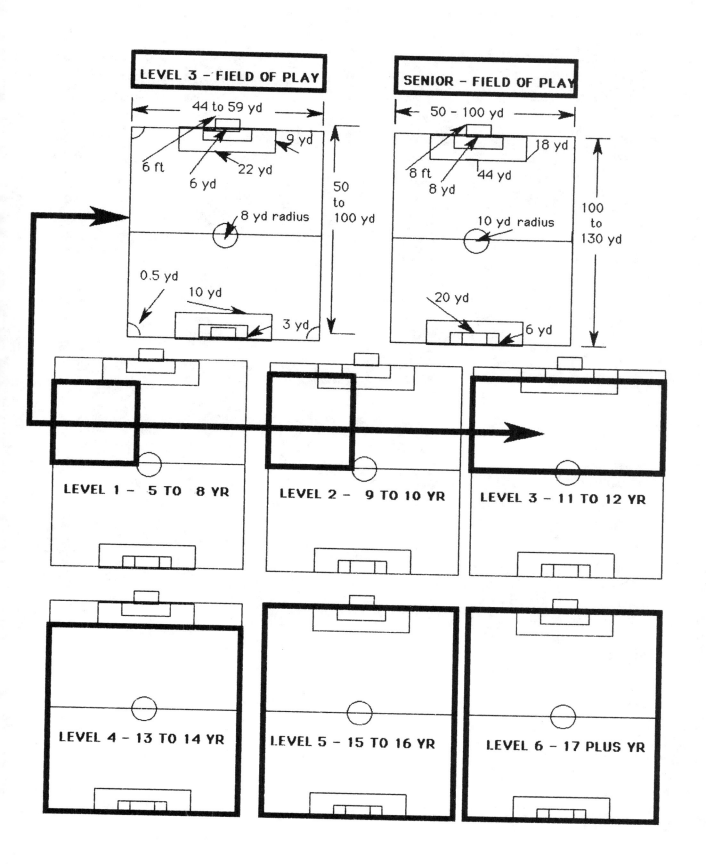

LEVEL 3 – FIELD OF PLAY

44 to 59 yd

9 yd

6 ft

22 yd

6 yd

50 to 100 yd

8 yd radius

0.5 yd

10 yd

3 yd

SENIOR – FIELD OF PLAY

50 – 100 yd

18 yd

8 ft

44 yd

8 yd

100 to 130 yd

10 yd radius

20 yd

6 yd

LEVEL 1 – 5 TO 8 YR

LEVEL 2 – 9 TO 10 YR

LEVEL 3 – 11 TO 12 YR

LEVEL 4 – 13 TO 14 YR

LEVEL 5 – 15 TO 16 YR

LEVEL 6 – 17 PLUS YR

UMBRO

Superstar Garrincha ('Little Bird') of the World Cup champion team Brazil dribbles past a defender

technical–tactical elements

Juggling the ball

Juggling the ball is simply keeping the ball off the ground, playing it with all parts of the body except from the arms to the hands.

There is no better exercise for young players than juggling the ball to get universal feeling and confidence with the ball.

When juggling, it is necessary to be relaxed and have good body balance.

Juggling the ball is an important introductory part of each coaching session.

1. Juggling with the use of the instep

2. Juggling with the use of the thigh

3. Juggling with the use of the inside of the foot

Helpful tactical games

1. Soccer handball

One team attacks and 1 team defends until a goal is scored or possession lost. Players interpass by throwing the ball with a maximum of 1 step with the ball. The attacking player with the ball must play a 1–2 pass and switch to another team player. Goals can only be scored by throwing the ball through the small goals. There are no outs or offside.

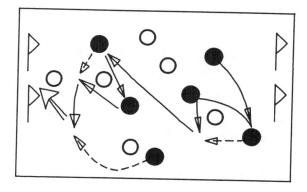

2. Piggy in the middle — 3:1

Three players, in a marked grid, keep possession of the ball away from the defending player in the middle. The defending player in the middle tries to intercept the ball being passed. If the ball is intercepted, the defending player changes places with the attacking player who lost possession.

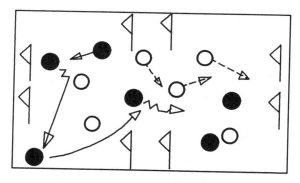

3. Soccer with 4 goals

Each team has 2 goals to attack and 2 goals to defend. There are no goalkeepers, no offside and no outs. Goals can only be scored from shooting from inside the grid.

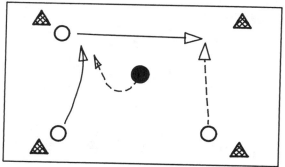

4. Hit your coloured marker

The playing area is covered with 2 different types of coloured markers, evenly distributed. The players must hit any 1 of their markers to score a goal. There are no outs and offside. Teams must defend their coloured marker.

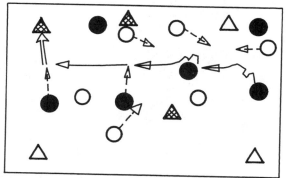

Deceptive dribbling and feinting techniques

The following represent the 15 deceptive dribbling and feinting techniques to be executed in level 2.

1. Cutting the ball back inside

2. Cutting the ball back under the bottom

3. Scissors 1 way and go the other way

4. *Dipping the shoulder 1 way and go the other*

5. *The shuffle*

6. *Inside and outside the instep*

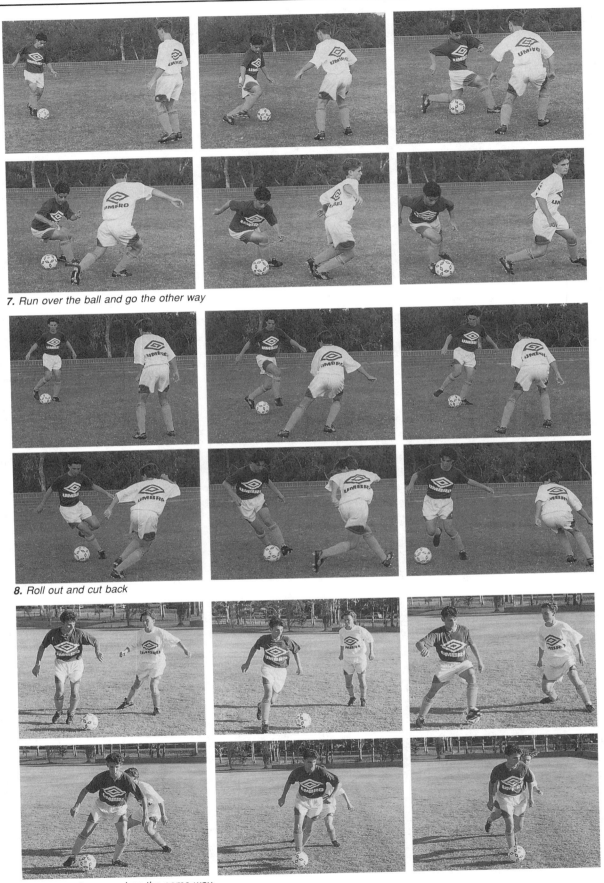

7. Run over the ball and go the other way

8. Roll out and cut back

9. Scissors 1 way and go the same way

10. *Dummy kick and roll back*

11. *Placing the ball between the legs*

12. *Dummy heel pass*

13. Cross over heel pass

14. Roll under the bottom and change direction

15. Overhead heel of the ball

Superstar Bobby Charlton, the hero of England's 1966 World Cup team, with an airborne shot in 1966 for Manchester United

Technical–tactical program elements

Basic running and sprinting technique

1. Introductory part of the coaching session
1.1 Juggling the ball ....*refer to page 140*
1.2 Individual corrective technical–tactical coaching

2. Main part of the coaching session
2.1 Helpful tactical games ....*refer to page 141*
2.2 Deceptive dribbling and feinting techniques ....*refer to page 142*
2.3 Technical–tactical program element

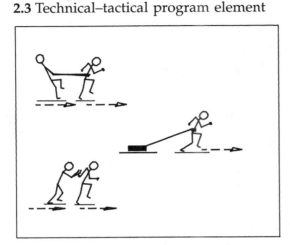
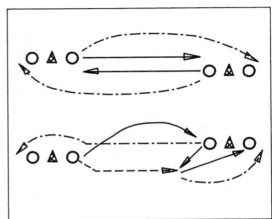

2.4 Technical–tactical shooting element

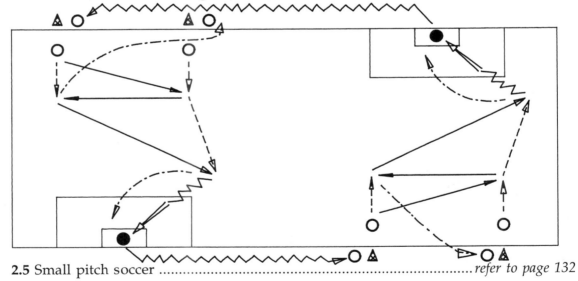

2.5 Small pitch soccer ....*refer to page 132*

3. Concluding part of the coaching session
3.1 Summary of the coaching session

UMBRO

The start technique (forward side)

1. Introductory part of the coaching session

1.2 Individual corrective technical–tactical coaching

2. Main part of the coaching session

2.3 Technical–tactical program element

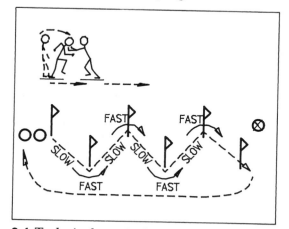 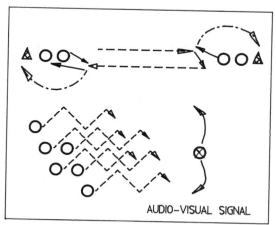

AUDIO–VISUAL SIGNAL

2.4 Technical–tactical shooting element

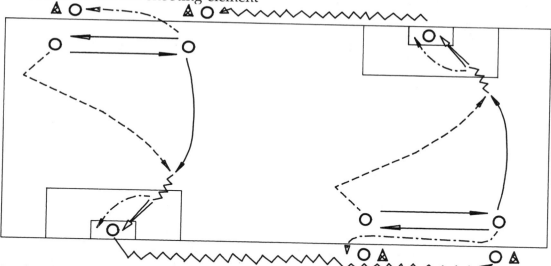

3. Concluding part of the coaching session

3.1 Summary of the coaching session

Dribbling with the full instep

1. Introductory part of the coaching session
1.2 Individual corrective technical–tactical coaching

2. Main part of the coaching session
2.3 Technical–tactical program element

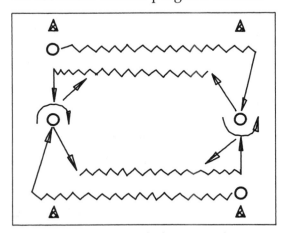 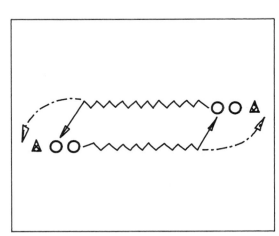

2.4 Technical–tactical shooting element

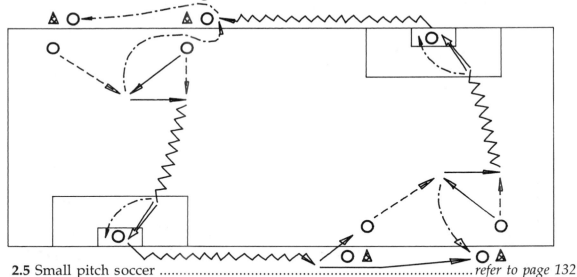

3. Concluding part of the coaching session
3.1 Summary of the coaching session

Dribbling with the sole of the foot

1. Introductory part of the coaching session
1.1 Juggling the ball ....*refer to page 140*
1.2 Individual corrective technical–tactical coaching

2. Main part of the coaching session
2.1 Helpful tactical games ....*refer to page 141*
2.2 Deceptive dribbling and feinting techniques ....*refer to page 142*
2.3 Technical–tactical program element

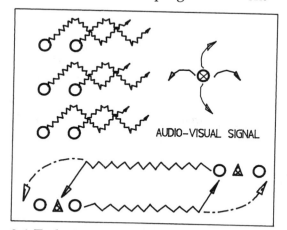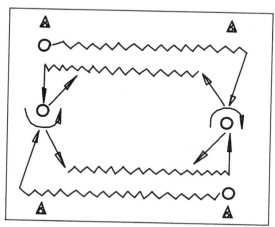

2.4 Technical–tactical shooting element

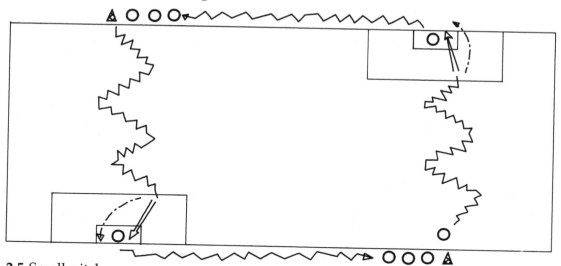

2.5 Small pitch soccer ....*refer to page 132*

3. Concluding part of the coaching session
3.1 Summary of the coaching session

Kicking the ball with the full instep

1. Introductory part of the coaching session
   1.1 Juggling the ball ....*refer to page 140*
   1.2 Individual corrective technical–tactical coaching

2. Main part of the coaching session
   2.1 Helpful tactical games ....*refer to page 141*
   2.2 Deceptive dribbling and feinting techniques ....*refer to page 142*
   2.3 Technical–tactical program element

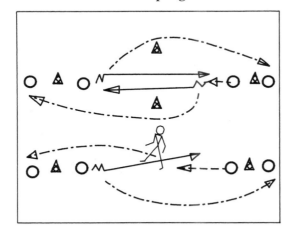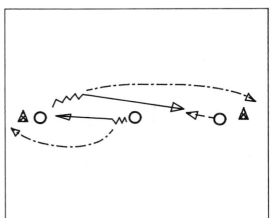

   2.4 Technical–tactical shooting element

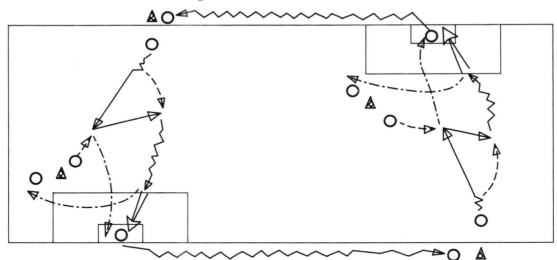

   2.5 Small pitch soccer ....*refer to page 132*

3. Concluding part of the coaching session
   3.1 Summary of the coaching session

Kicking the ball with the inside of the foot

1. Introductory part of the coaching session
   1.1 Juggling the ball ....*refer to page 140*
   1.2 Individual corrective technical–tactical coaching

2. Main part of the coaching session
   2.1 Helpful tactical games ....*refer to page 141*
   2.2 Deceptive dribbling and feinting techniques ....*refer to page 142*
   2.3 Technical–tactical program element

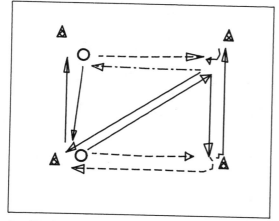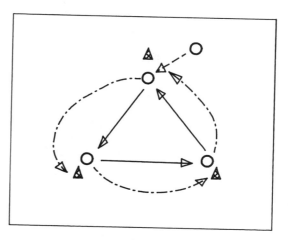

2.4 Technical–tactical shooting element

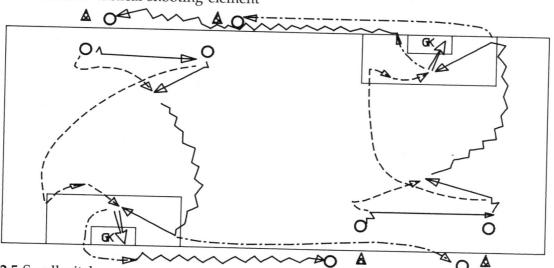

2.5 Small pitch soccer ....*refer to page 132*

3. Concluding part of the coaching session
   3.1 Summary of the coaching session

Receiving (amortisation) with the inside of the foot

1. Introductory part of the coaching session
   1.1 Juggling the ball ....*refer to page 140*
   1.2 Individual corrective technical–tactical coaching

2. Main part of the coaching session
   2.1 Helpful tactical games ....*refer to page 141*
   2.2 Deceptive dribbling and feinting techniques ....*refer to page 142*
   2.3 Technical–tactical program element

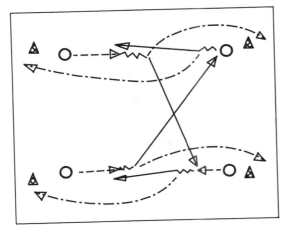 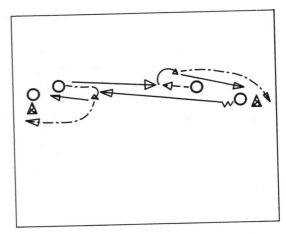

   2.4 Technical–tactical shooting element

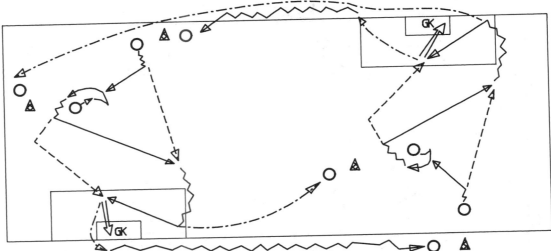

   2.5 Small pitch soccer ....*refer to page 132*

3. Concluding part of the coaching session
   3.1 Summary of the coaching session

Receiving (amortisation) with the full instep

1. Introductory part of the coaching session
   1.1 Juggling the ball
   1.2 Individual corrective technical–tactical coaching ....*refer to page 140*
2. Main part of the coaching session
   2.1 Helpful tactical games ....*refer to page 141*
   2.2 Deceptive dribbling and feinting techniques ....*refer to page 142*
   2.3 Technical–tactical program element

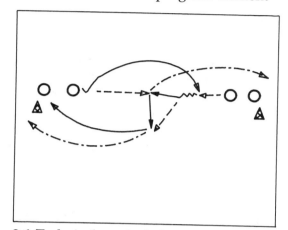 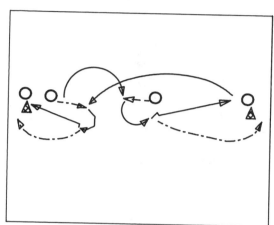

   2.4 Technical–tactical shooting element

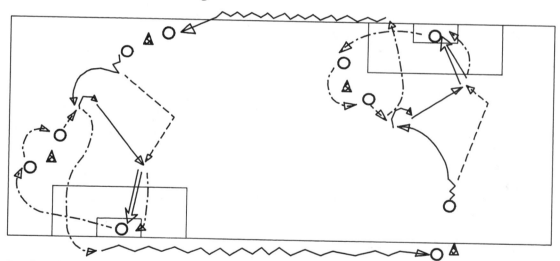

   2.5 Small pitch soccer ....*refer to page 132*
3. Concluding part of the coaching session
   3.1 Summary of the coaching session

Receiving (trapping) with the inside of the foot

1. Introductory part of the coaching session
1.1 Juggling the ball ....*refer to page 140*
1.2 Individual corrective technical–tactical coaching

2. Main part of the coaching session
2.1 Helpful tactical games ....*refer to page 141*
2.2 Deceptive dribbling and feinting techniques ....*refer to page 142*
2.3 Technical–tactical program element

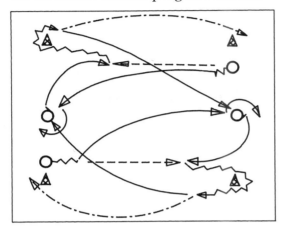 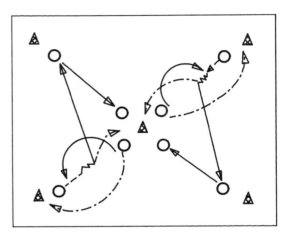

2.4 Technical–tactical shooting element

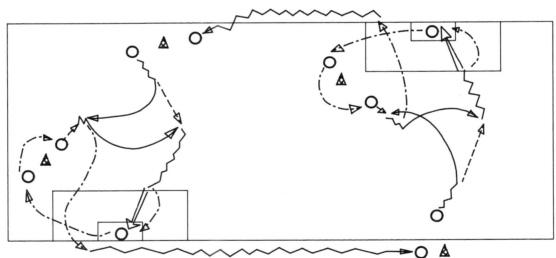

2.5 Small pitch soccer ....*refer to page 132*

3. Concluding part of the coaching session
3.1 Summary of the coaching session

Receiving (trapping) with the sole of the foot

1. Introductory part of the coaching session
1.1 Juggling the ball .... *refer to page 140*
1.2 Individual corrective technical–tactical coaching

2. Main part of the coaching session
2.1 Helpful tactical games .... *refer to page 141*
2.2 Deceptive dribbling and feinting techniques .... *refer to page 142*
2.3 Technical–tactical program element

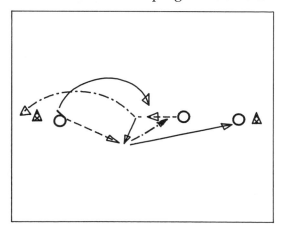 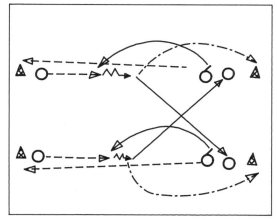

2.4 Technical–tactical shooting element

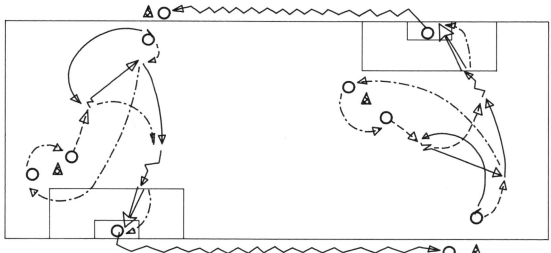

2.5 Small pitch soccer .... *refer to page 132*

3. Concluding part of the coaching session
3.1 Summary of the coaching session

The delay and basic block tackle

1. Introductory part of the coaching session
1.2 Individual corrective technical–tactical coaching

2. Main part of the coaching session
2.3 Technical–tactical program element

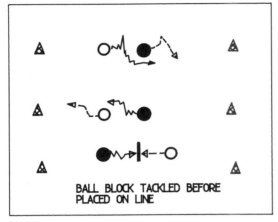

BALL BLOCK TACKLED BEFORE PLACED ON LINE

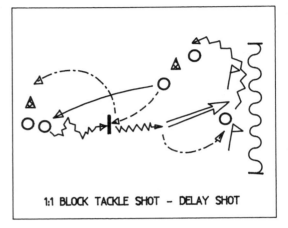

1:1 BLOCK TACKLE SHOT – DELAY SHOT

2.4 Technical–tactical shooting element

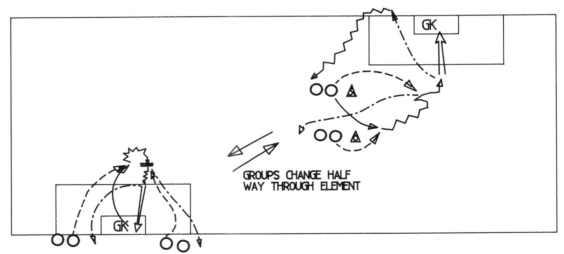

GROUPS CHANGE HALF WAY THROUGH ELEMENT

GK

GK

3. Concluding part of the coaching session
3.1 Summary of the coaching session

Basic combinations — 1:1

1. Introductory part of the coaching session
1.2 Individual corrective technical–tactical coaching

2. Main part of the coaching session
2.3 Technical–tactical program element

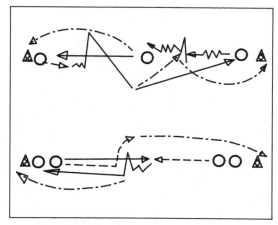 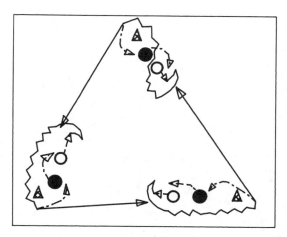

2.4 Technical–tactical shooting element

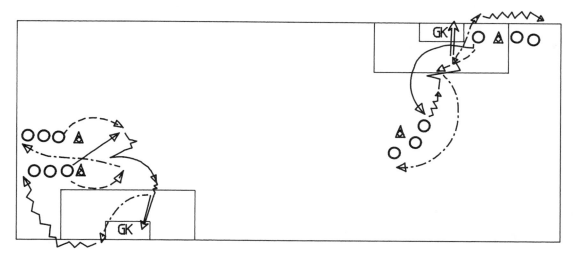

3. Concluding part of the coaching session
3.1 Summary of the coaching session

Superstar Dragan Dzajic, captain of the former Yugoslavian team in the 1970s, selected for the World 11, with the author

technical–tactical elements

Agility in the air and on the ground

Trampoline

The basic bounce: *can be used as a warm-up activity. The body and arms should be straight with head erect. At the top of the bounce, the legs are straight with toes pointing down. On the downward bounce flex the legs, hitting the mat with flat feet shou width*

The seat drop: *from the basic bounce position raise the legs to horizontal position, moving arms forward and upwards. From her drop back on to the mat into the seat position and bounce back vertical*

The tuck jump: *at the top of the bounce clasp the shins, bringin knees to the chest. Tuck in the elbows with eyes fixed on the ce end of the trampoline. The heels are against the seat while the t are pointing downward*

The closed pike jump: *from the basic bounce bring the legs straight with toes pointing to a horizontal position. Bend the body forward at the hips with the hands straight with the legs*

The half pirouette: *on the bounce, raise 1 arm above the head while bending the other at 90° across the chest. Twist the body 180° around its vertical axis*

The split pike jump: *the split pike is similar to the closed pike jump except that both legs and arms are stretched apart during the bounce*

The pirouette: *this is similar to the half pirouette but twist a full 360° instead of 180°*

FLOOR

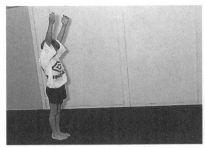

The forward roll: *crouch on the toes with hands on the mat shoulder width apart. Place the chin to the chest, lift the hips and kick off the mat and overbalance. Roll over to the crouch position*

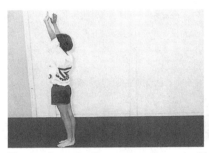

The backward roll: *squat on the mat with elbows bent and palms facing up. Curl the body and rock back, lowering the seat to the mat. Roll back and swing the feet over the head, rolling into a squat*

The mule kick: *place the hands on the mat shoulder width apart. All the weight is taken by the hands with a kick of 1 leg followed by the other high in the air*

The crouch balance: *place the hands on the mat shoulder width apart, palms down. Kick both legs high in the air, bent together while balancing on the hands in the crouch position*

UMBRO®

The twist crouch: *the player stands with 1 foot forward, bends and places hands flat on the mat. Travelling sideways, the legs are bent and together, twisting at the hips*

BALANCE BEAM

Walking forward   *Walking backwards*

    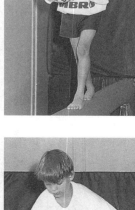

Walking through hoops   *Bouncing a ball*

Balancing objects   *Picking up objects*

UMBRO

Catching a ball

Walking over objects

Hopping

MINI-TRAMPOLINE/VAULTING BOX

The basic bounce: on hitting the trampoline mat swing the arms down and bend the legs with the feet flat. To get the upward bounce, push hard on the heels with the forward and upward swing of the hands

The tuck jump: the same technique as with the basic bounce but bring the knees to the chest, clasping the shins. Land softly on the mat

The closed pike jump: following the bounce bring the legs straight and to a horizontal position. Bend the body at the hips with the hands pointing down the shins

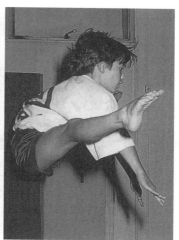

The split pike jump: *the technique with this element is the same as with the closed pike jump, only the legs and arms are stretched apart*

The side vault: *from the mini-trampoline bounce place the hands on either side of the box. Twist the body to 1 side with a soft landing side-on to the box*

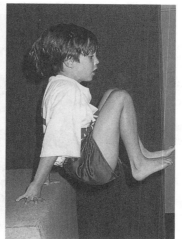

The bent leg squat vault: *following the bounce the stretched out arms touch the box while the legs are bent and close to the chest. The upper extremity is leaning forward. The legs straighten for a soft landing*

Phase 2: 7 to 8 years

TRAMPOLINE — Reinforce basic elements: 5 to 6 years

Swivel hips: *from a basic bounce, go into a seat drop. At the top of the bounce do a half twist and drop into another seat drop*

FLOOR — Reinforce basic elements: 5 to 6 years

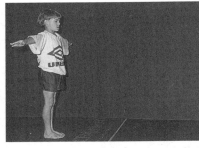  

The dive roll: *dive forward, stretching the body to land on the hands. Tuck the chin to the chest. Roll over the shoulders and on to the back*

BALANCE BEAM — Reinforce basic elements: 5 to 6 years

Inclined bench balances   See-saw   Passing over arms

Mini-trampoline/vaulting box

Straddle vault: *following the bounce, lean forward and straighten the legs, keeping them apart with toes pointed. Extend the hands quickly so that they make contact with the apparatus and the body can straddle over it. Land on 2 feet, hands wide*

Forward dive roll: *leap forward with the body and arms stretched. The hands make contact first with the mat, softening the fall, the chin tucked into the chest and knees likewise. Staying curled, roll to your feet*

Forward somersault: *from the forward bounce, clasp the shins by the hands, with the chin tucked into the chest. With the quick rotation spin into the somersault, opening out before coming to the vertical axis*

UMBRO

Superstar George Best engaged in a heading duel for Manchester United

Trampoline

Floor

Balance beam

Mini-trampoline/vaulting box

Superstar Eusebio in full flight for Benefica against AC Milan in 1963

technical–tactical development program

Core learning areas in the soccer development program

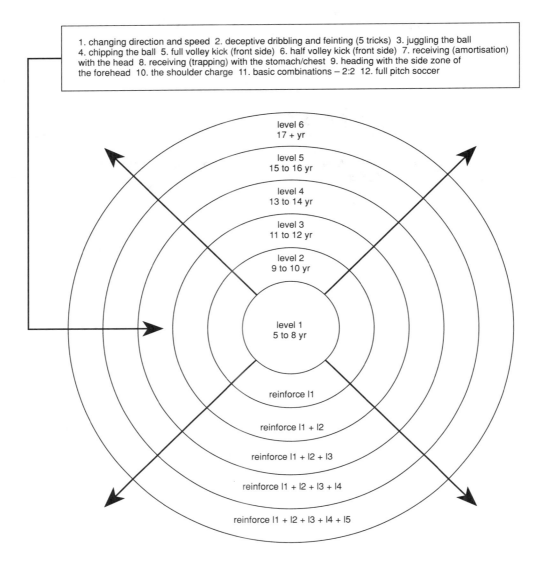

1. changing direction and speed 2. deceptive dribbling and feinting (5 tricks) 3. juggling the ball
4. chipping the ball 5. full volley kick (front side) 6. half volley kick (front side) 7. receiving (amortisation)
with the head 8. receiving (trapping) with the stomach/chest 9. heading with the side zone of
the forehead 10. the shoulder charge 11. basic combinations – 2:2 12. full pitch soccer

level 6
17 + yr

level 5
15 to 16 yr

level 4
13 to 14 yr

level 3
11 to 12 yr

level 2
9 to 10 yr

level 1
5 to 8 yr

reinforce l1

reinforce l1 + l2

reinforce l1 + l2 + l3

reinforce l1 + l2 + l3 + l4

reinforce l1 + l2 + l3 + l4 + l5

Technical–tactical program

Element	Level 1 (5–8 yr)	Level 2 (9–10 yr)	Level 3 (11–12 yr)	Level 4 (13–14 yr)	Level 5 (15–16 yr)	Level 6 (17+ yr)
Agility in the air and on the ground	1	Reinforce	Reinforce	Reinforce	Reinforce	Reinforce
Basic running and sprinting technique		1	Reinforce	Reinforce	Reinforce	Reinforce
The start technique (forward side)		2	Reinforce	Reinforce	Reinforce	Reinforce
Jumping with 1 and 2 feet			1	Reinforce	Reinforce	Reinforce
Changing direction and speed				1	Reinforce	Reinforce
Dribbling with the full instep		3	Reinforce	Reinforce	Reinforce	Reinforce
Dribbling with the sole of the foot		4	Reinforce	Reinforce	Reinforce	Reinforce
Dribbling with the outside of the instep			2	Reinforce	Reinforce	Reinforce
Dribbling with the inside of the instep			3	Reinforce	Reinforce	Reinforce
Deceptive dribbling and feinting (15 tricks)		5	Reinforce	Reinforce	Reinforce	Reinforce
Deceptive dribbling and feinting (10 tricks)			4	Reinforce	Reinforce	Reinforce
Deceptive dribbling and feinting (5 tricks)				2	Reinforce	Reinforce
Juggling the ball (individual)		6	Reinforce	Reinforce	Reinforce	Reinforce
Juggling the ball (partner)			5	Reinforce	Reinforce	Reinforce
Juggling the ball (group)				3	Reinforce	Reinforce
Kicking the ball with the full instep		7	Reinforce	Reinforce	Reinforce	Reinforce
Kicking the ball with the inside of the foot		8	Reinforce	Reinforce	Reinforce	Reinforce
Kicking the ball with the inside of the instep			6	Reinforce	Reinforce	Reinforce
Kicking the ball with the outside of the instep			7	Reinforce	Reinforce	Reinforce
The wall pass — 1–2 pass			8	Reinforce	Reinforce	Reinforce
Chipping the ball				4	Reinforce	Reinforce
Full volley kick (front side)				5	Reinforce	Reinforce
Half volley kick (front side)				6	Reinforce	Reinforce
Overhead (scissors) volley kick					1	Reinforce
Kicking with the toe, heel and knee					2	Reinforce
Receiving (amortisation) — inside of the foot		9	Reinforce	Reinforce	Reinforce	Reinforce
Receiving (amortisation) with the full instep		10	Reinforce	Reinforce	Reinforce	Reinforce
Receiving (amortisation) with the thigh			9	Reinforce	Reinforce	Reinforce
Receiving (amortisation) with the chest			10	Reinforce	Reinforce	Reinforce
Receiving (amortisation) with the head				7	Reinforce	Reinforce
Receiving (trapping) — inside of the foot		11	Reinforce	Reinforce	Reinforce	Reinforce
Receiving (trapping) with the sole of the foot		12	Reinforce	Reinforce	Reinforce	Reinforce
Receiving (trapping) with the outside of the instep			11	Reinforce	Reinforce	Reinforce
Receiving (trapping) with the stomach/chest				8	Reinforce	Reinforce
Heading with the middle zone of the forehead			12	Reinforce	Reinforce	Reinforce
Heading with the side zone of the forehead				9	Reinforce	Reinforce
The diving header					3	Reinforce
The delay and basic block tackle		13	Reinforce	Reinforce	Reinforce	Reinforce
The sliding–straddle tackle			13	Reinforce	Reinforce	Reinforce
The shoulder charge				10	Reinforce	Reinforce
Intercepting the pass					4	Reinforce
Basic combinations — 1:1		14	Reinforce	Reinforce	Reinforce	Reinforce
Basic combinations — 2:0			14	Reinforce	Reinforce	Reinforce
Basic combinations — 2:1			15	Reinforce	Reinforce	Reinforce
Basic combinations — 2:2				11	Reinforce	Reinforce
Basic combinations — 3:0					5	Reinforce
Basic combinations — 3:2					6	Reinforce
Helpful tactical games		15	Reinforce	Reinforce	Reinforce	Reinforce
Kicking at goal		16	Reinforce	Reinforce	Reinforce	Reinforce
Heading at goal			16	Reinforce	Reinforce	Reinforce
Team technical–tactical playing patterns — attack					7	Reinforce
Team technical–tactical playing patterns — defence					8	Reinforce
Set play — attacking situations					9	Reinforce
Set play — defending situations					10	Reinforce
Small pitch soccer — TE–TA elements	2	Reinforce	Reinforce	Reinforce	Reinforce	Reinforce
Full pitch soccer — TE–TA elements				12	Reinforce	Reinforce
	2	16	16	12	10	0

Total soccer development program elements = 56 elements

Technical–tactical elements to be coached

1. Changing direction and speed
2. Deceptive dribbling and feinting (5 tricks)
3. Juggling the ball
4. Chipping the ball
5. Full volley kick (front side)
6. Half volley kick (front side)
7. Receiving (amortisation) with the head
8. Receiving (trapping) with the stomach/chest
9. Heading with the side zone of the forehead
10. The shoulder charge
11. Basic combinations — 2:2
12. Small pitch and full pitch soccer

Total elements = 12

Time allocation for the 100 minute coaching session

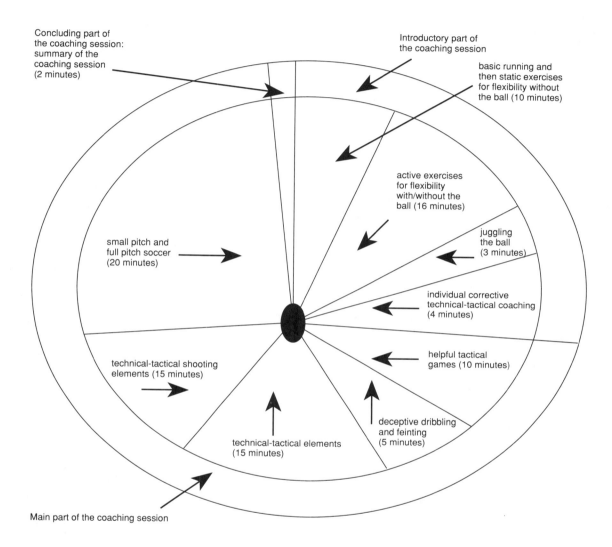

Concluding part of
the coaching session:
summary of the
coaching session
(2 minutes)

Introductory part of
the coaching session

basic running and
then static exercises
for flexibility without
the ball (10 minutes)

active exercises
for flexibility
with/without the
ball (16 minutes)

juggling
the ball
(3 minutes)

small pitch and
full pitch soccer
(20 minutes)

individual corrective
technical-tactical coaching
(4 minutes)

helpful tactical
games (10 minutes)

technical-tactical shooting
elements (15 minutes)

deceptive dribbling
and feinting
(5 minutes)

technical-tactical elements
(15 minutes)

Main part of the coaching session

Structure of the practical coaching session — 100 minutes

Total practical coaching time = 100 minutes

1. Introductory part of the coaching session

1.1 STATIC EXERCISES FOR FLEXIBILITY WITHOUT THE BALL

These exercises are designed to prepare the body in order to prevent injury and to enhance performance. A sustained stretch of 15 seconds or longer is preferable.

1. Thigh quadriceps: opposite hand holds the instep

2. Calf gastrocnemius: feet pointing forward. Back straight, lunge forward, heel down

3. Inner thigh (adductors): push knees towards the ground

4. Back of thigh (hamstrings): knee is straight

5. Back of thigh (outside hamstrings): foot turned out, taken across the body (lateral hamstring)

6. Back of thigh (inside hamstrings): foot turned in, placed away from the body (medial hamstring)

7. Outer thigh (iliotibial band): step behind and stretch with leg straight. Rotate away

8. Buttocks (gluteals): both buttocks on the ground, back straight. Press knee and turn

9. Stomach (abdominals): hips remain on the ground

10. Back (erector spinae): curl and hold into a ball

11. Side (latissimus dorsi): hand over hand, raise the hips and stretch

12. Neck muscles (trapezius sternomastoid): stretch forward, back and to the sides

1.2 ACTIVE EXERCISES FOR FLEXIBILITY WITH/WITHOUT THE BALL

Group exercises no. 1

As with the static exercises, these active exercises are also designed to prepare the body for the coaching session and to enhance performance.

1.

2.

3.

4.

5.

6.

Group exercises no. 2

As with the static exercises, these active exercises are also designed to prepare the body for the coaching session and to enhance performance.

1.

2.

3.

4.

5.

6.

Group exercises no. 3

As with the static exercises, these active exercises are also designed to prepare the body for the coaching session and to enhance performance.

1.

2.

3.

4.

5.

6.

1.3 JUGGLING THE BALL

Juggling the ball is simply keeping the ball off the ground, playing it with all parts of the body except from the arms to the hands.

There is no better exercise for young players than juggling the ball to get universal feeling and confidence with the ball.

When juggling, it is necessary to be relaxed and have good body balance.

Juggling the ball is an important introductory part of each coaching session.

All elements of juggling from the previous levels must be reinforced as progression is made from individual, partner and group juggling.

1. Juggling with the use of the shoulder

2. Juggling and catching the ball on the back of the neck

3. Juggling with the use of the heel

2. Main part of the coaching session

2.1 HELPFUL TACTICAL GAMES

1. Head volleyball

The area on which the game is played is the size of a volleyball court with a net 2.5 metres high. The game is started with a serve, throwing the ball and heading over the net from behind the base line. Points can only be won while the team has service. The ball can be headed a maximum of 4 times before passing over the net. The ball is dead if it hits the ground or is played with any other part of the body.

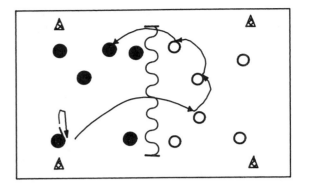

2. Play in your zone

Each player must play in his zone. Goals can only be scored from zone 1 and zone 3. In zone 1 and zone 3 each attacking team has an extra player advantage. In zone 2, 1 player gives an attacking advantage for both teams. The ball can be passed between the zones to supporting players but a goal can only be scored from the end zones.

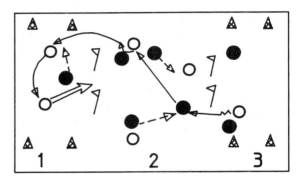

3. All up in attack

Teams play 2 or 1 touch in a small-sided game across the soccer field. All members of the attacking side must move up and support play in the opponent's half. Only if all attacking players are in the opponent's half, and a goal is scored, does it count. The team with the most number of goals wins.

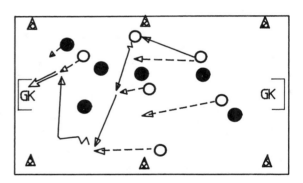

4. Soccer with 1 goal

The team in possession attacks and the team without possession defends. The goalkeeper plays for both teams with a goal being scored from any part of the pitch. The basic rule is that when a team gains possession of the ball it must be dribbled or passed over the 30 metre line before an attack can be mounted at goal. The normal rules of soccer apply. The team with the most number of goals wins.

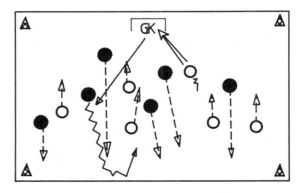

2.2 Deceptive dribbling and feinting

In the previous level 10 deceptive dribbling and feinting elements of the game were exercised.

In level 4, 5 more deceptive dribbling and feinting elements are implemented. This brings the total number of dribbling and feinting elements to 30.

Dribbling is running with the ball under close control, using any part of the foot.

Feinting is the art of making deceptive body movements to delude the opponent.

So we could describe both dribbling and feinting as deception, where we use the body or ball or both to throw the defenders off balance to get past them.

In today's game every player must be able to master the art of dribbling and feinting.

No technique in the game of soccer causes greater pleasure than a good piece of dribbling and feinting.

As players progress through the soccer development program they will discover the dribbling and feinting techniques that suit them best.

Superstar Pele with the author, while touring Australia in 1990

Methods of progress

1. *No pressure — 1 player*

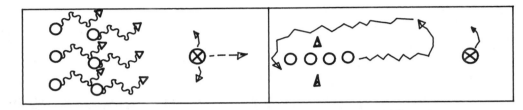

2. *Token pressure — 2 players*

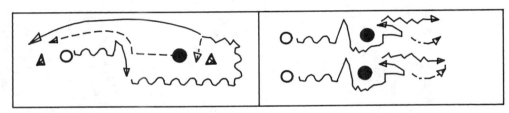

3. *Token pressure — 3 players*

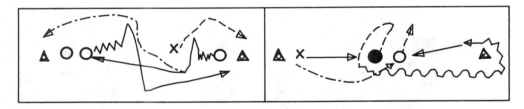

4. *Token pressure — 4 players*

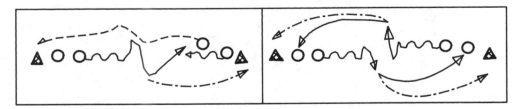

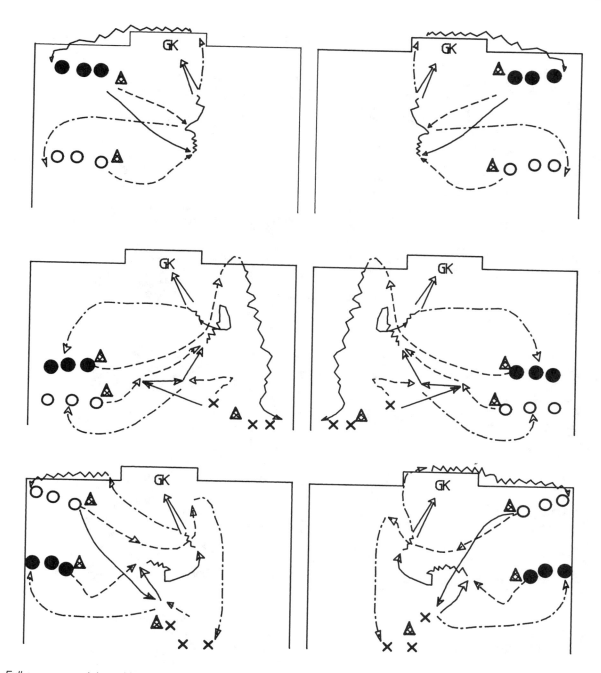

5. *Full pressure — 1:1 combinations*

Deceptive dribbling and feinting techniques

The following represent the 5 deceptive dribbling and feinting techniques to be executed in level 4.

1. *Double run over the ball*

2. *Roll out, in and away*

3. *Roll to the side and roll back*

4. *Flick the ball with the outside of the instep out of a tackle*

5. *Run over 1–2 pass*

2.3 TECHNICAL–TACTICAL PROGRAM ELEMENTS

Changing direction and speed

The ability, for a player, to effectively change direction and speed is playing an increasing role in today's game. Only this way will the player, if pressured, be able to create space and time for herself or for her supporting players to use.

Changing direction and speed will depend upon the initial speed of the player and the angle at which the player is going to move. This change of direction and speed can be forward, backwards or to the side.

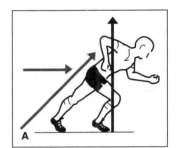

The technique requires the player to first stop and then quickly move off into another direction. Just before stopping the player leans away from the direction of movement, extending the last steps. The number of steps will be determined by the speed of the player. The last step, in front of the vertical axis, is the most important and must be longest. The leg is bent at the knee, ankle and hip joints, lowering the centre of gravity and absorbing the previous movement, thus bringing the body to a stop. The hands assist with balance by facing the direction and being 90° at the elbow joint.

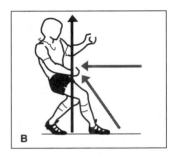

When stopping, the supporting leg should be bent and positioned with the upper extremity to enable the sudden and deceptive change of direction.

When the body movements have been successfully blocked then the start technique is used for the change of direction.

COMMON FAULTS — CORRECTIONS

1. The last steps are not extended in front of the vertical axis.
2. The player is vertical and does not lean away from the direction of movement. As a result it will take him extra steps to stop.
3. The stretched leg is not bent in the ankle, knee or hip joints to absorb and block the movement.
4. The hands are not bent at the elbows away from the body for balance but are straight and to the side.
5. When stopping the body is not relaxed and loose.

1. Introductory part of the coaching session

1.1 Basic running and then static exercises for flexibility
without the ball ....*refer to page 179*

1.2 Active exercises for flexibility with/without the ball ....*refer to page 180*

1.3 Juggling the ball ....*refer to page 183*

1.4 Individual corrective technical–tactical coaching

2. Main part of the coaching session

2.1 Helpful tactical games ....*refer to page 184*

2.2 Deceptive dribbling and feinting techniques ....*refer to page 188*

2.3 Technical–tactical program element

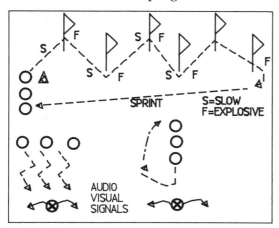
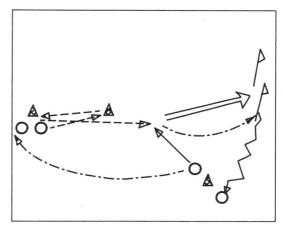

2.4 Technical–tactical shooting element

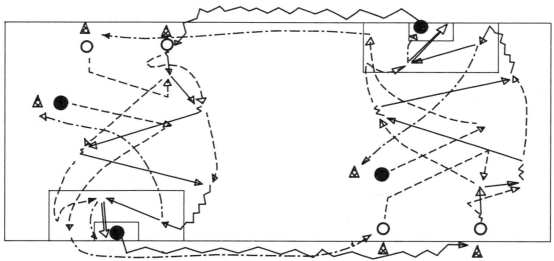

2.5 Small pitch or full pitch soccer ....*refer to page 208*

3. Concluding part of the coaching session

3.1 Summary of the coaching session

Chipping the ball

Often in the game the direct short pass to a supporting player becomes blocked. If this occurs then the chip pass is an excellent solution. This technique can be used to score goals by 'chipping' the goalkeeper when he is off his goal line. When struck, the ball will move in a short but high trajectory as a result of either an angled or straight approach.

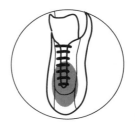

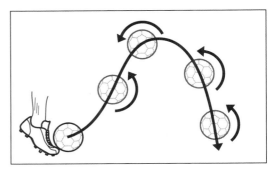

To make the ball rise quickly with the backspin, it must be struck well below the horizontal axis. The supporting foot is placed slightly back and to the side of the ball, with toes pointing in the direction of the intended kick. The hands and elbows are raised to the side for balance while the eyes are fixed on the ball.

The technique of the kicking foot involves a slight swing from the hip with a quick sharp snap of the knee with no follow through. The toes first make contact with the ball followed by the lower part of the full instep with the sole of the foot keeping horizontal to the ground.

If the ball is struck correctly it will have a backspin and rise quickly from the ground.

COMMON FAULTS — CORRECTIONS

1. There is a long swing from the hip instead of the short hip swing.
2. There is no sudden sharp snap of the knee.
3. Eyes are not fixed on the ball.
4. The supporting leg is too close to the ball, preventing the kicking foot from getting under the ball.
5. Hands and elbows are not raised to the side for balance.
6. The toes and sole of the foot do not keep horizontal to the ground after the ball is struck.
7. The player raises the toes and foot after the kick instead of blocking the follow through.
8. The ball is kicked too low with the toes hitting into the ground.
9. The ball is not hit through and under the vertical axis, thus not giving it full backspin but a combined back and side spin.

1. Introductory part of the coaching session

1.1 Basic running and then static exercises for flexibility
without the ball .... *refer to page 179*

1.2 Active exercises for flexibility with/without the ball .... *refer to page 180*

1.3 Juggling the ball .... *refer to page 183*

1.4 Individual corrective technical–tactical coaching

2. Main part of the coaching session

2.1 Helpful tactical games .... *refer to page 184*

2.2 Deceptive dribbling and feinting techniques .... *refer to page 188*

2.3 Technical–tactical program element

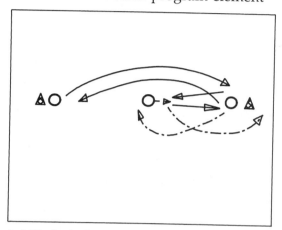 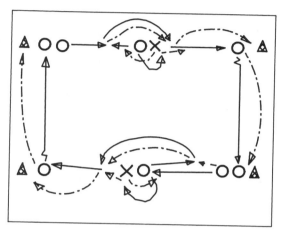

2.4 Technical–tactical shooting element

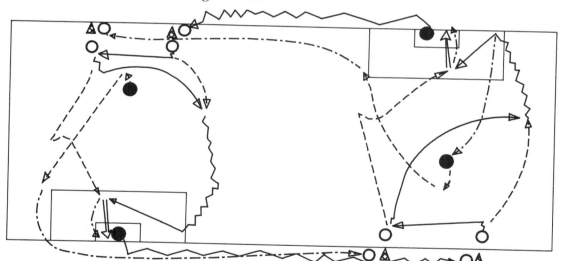

2.5 Small pitch or full pitch soccer .... *refer to page 208*

3. Concluding part of the coaching session

3.1 Summary of the coaching session

Full volley kick (front side)

The full volley kick is made with any part of the foot while the ball is in the air. If the ball is struck correctly the kicking foot will be able to transfer the force from the oncoming ball and create a powerful and efficient kick. If used for kicking at goal this type of kick is effective in that it catches everyone off balance. Not only is the volley an efficient technique but also very attractive as some players prefer to be airborne during its execution.

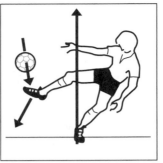 

Depending on whether the ball is to be kicked at goal or cleared, the point of ball contact is essential. If the ball is to be cleared then it is to be kicked under the horizontal axis; if kicked low it is to be kicked through or above the axis.

The technique with the *side volley*, also referred to as the 'hook volley', has the supporting leg placed well away from the ball with the upper extremity leaning to the ball. The hands are away from the body for balance and to cushion the body if the player falls to the side after execution. The eyes are fixed on the ball with the toes pointing away, the ankle joint locked and hard. As the ball approaches the arms and upper extremity turn away. Just before contact the hands, followed by the shoulders, trunk, hips and striking leg, move to attack the ball. This counter movement before kicking enables maximum elasticity and power to be transferred on to the ball.

For the ball to be kicked low the ball is to be struck with the extended instep on top of the horizontal axis while for the ball to be kicked high it must be kicked below the horizontal axis. With the *front volley* the ball is not to the side but in front of the player and in the air. With this technique a tremendous advantage can be gained by striking the ball as it is dropping with the full instep from below the horizontal axis, moving upwards to create a topspin drive. These topspin kicks are a goalkeeper's nightmare, as the ball seems to be going too high and out, then suddenly it will dip down into goal. The supporting leg is close to the ball with toes pointing in the direction of the intended kick. The kicking leg is raised by flexing the hip joint, enabling the instep to strike the airborne ball. Even though the swing starts at the hip it must always end with the sudden snap of the knee joint kicking through the vertical axis. The ankle joint is hard and locked with the arms and elbows raised to the side for balance. Following the kick the foot follows through into the normal running position.

COMMON FAULTS — CORRECTIONS

1. The ankle joint is not locked and hard but loose. Eyes are not fixed on the ball.
2. With the side volley there is no counter body movement. There is no follow through.
3. The hands are close to the side resulting in poor balance. There is no snap of the knee.

1. Introductory part of the coaching session

2. Main part of the coaching session

2.3 Technical–tactical program element

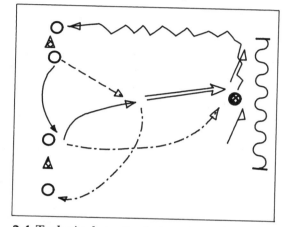 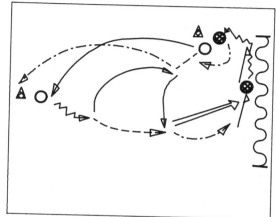

2.4 Technical–tactical shooting element

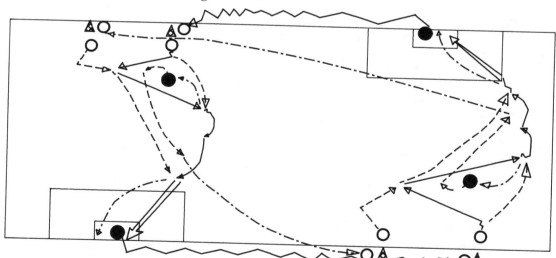

3. Concluding part of the coaching session

3.1 Summary of the coaching session

Half volley kick (front side)

There are times in the game when the player is unable to get to the ball and kick it before it hits the ground. However, at the moment the ball hits the ground the half volley kick can be used.

This technique of kicking is also referred to as the 'drop kick' which is kicking the ball the moment it drops and touches the ground. If the player wishes to keep the ball low the ball must be kicked early through or above the horizontal axis. If the player is late with contact then the ball will be kicked below the horizontal axis resulting in a high ball. The most difficult problem with this type of kick is to time the kick to coincide with the bounce of the ball.

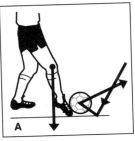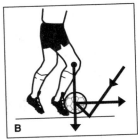

The *side half volley*, also referred to as the 'hook volley', requires the supporting leg to be placed well away from the oncoming ball with the upper extremity leaning to the ball. As the ball arrives there is a counter movement away from the ball by twisting the upper extremity, led by the hands and shoulders. Just before contact the hands, shoulders and upper extremity twist and lean explosively into the ball, transferring all the power on to the half volley kick. The hands are bent and away from the body to assist in balance and also to cushion the body if a fall results. The eyes are fixed on the ball, the ankle joint locked and hard with the toes pointing away from the ball. As with all kicking techniques the movement starts in the hip joint but must finish with the sudden snap of the knee. To keep the ball low the timing has to be perfect, with the kick executed above the horizontal axis.

With the *front half volley* many players prefer to strike with the instep across the face of the bouncing ball. Here the struck ball gets another dimension by swerving or bending to the target. The supporting foot is near and to the side of the ball with the ankle of the kicking foot extended hard and locked. The eyes are fixed on the ball with the hands and elbows raised to the side of the body for balance. The swing of the kicking foot starts in the hip, ending with the sudden snap of the knee. If the ball is to go low, the kick must take place above the horizontal axis with the knee joint in a vertical line with the centre vertical axis of the ball.

COMMON FAULTS — CORRECTIONS

1. Late timing of the bounce, the ball kicked low below the horizontal axis and going high.
2. The player not moving to get in line with the ball flight. Eyes are not fixed on the ball.
3. The ankle joint is not locked and hard but loose.
4. Hands and elbows are not away from the body for balance.
5. There is no follow through after the foot has struck the ball.
6. The kicking movement is only from the hip with no sudden snap of the knee.

1. Introductory part of the coaching session

1.4 Individual corrective technical–tactical coaching

2. Main part of the coaching session

2.3 Technical–tactical program element

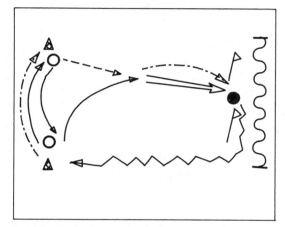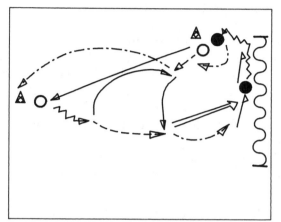

2.4 Technical–tactical shooting element

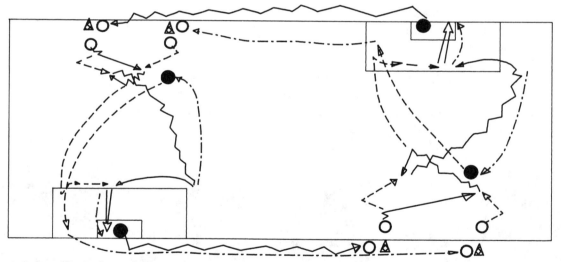

3. Concluding part of the coaching session

3.1 Summary of the coaching session

Receiving (amortisation) with the head

Receiving (amortisation) with the head is among the most difficult techniques to master. It is sometimes necessary to start with the analytic method before moving on to the situational method.

This technique is not commonly used in the game but a player may find himself in a situation where he needs to deaden the impact of the arriving ball with his head. The technique involves the surface area (forehead) moving to meet the ball and, just before contact is made, withdrawing it a little slower than the speed of the ball, bringing it under control.

At the moment just before contact is made, the body is extended towards the ball with the player balanced. At the moment of contact all joints are to be flexed, relaxed and loose so as to 'amortise' the ball and bring it under control. The ball should have a slight bounce off the forehead before dropping to the ground and being under control.

A   B

The first movement is for the player to get in flight with the ball with feet apart for balance and body moving to meet the ball. The elbows are bent and hands are raised to the side and in front of the body for balance with the eyes fixed on the ball. At the moment of contact the body is relaxed and withdrawing, but still in the path of the ball.

COMMON FAULTS — CORRECTIONS

1. The head is withdrawn too quickly and as a result the space used to cushion the ball will be used up at the moment of contact.
2. The head is withdrawn too late and as a result the ball will strike the head and bounce out of control.
3. The eyes close before contact. The head tilts downward allowing the ball to strike the top of the head. If this occurs apply the analytic method.
4. The body is not loose and relaxed and balanced on both feet.
5. The hands and elbows are not positioned to assist in the balanced movement.
6. There is no movement to meet the ball with the head.
7. The head does not withdraw away from the incoming ball.

1. Introductory part of the coaching session

2. Main part of the coaching session
   2.3 Technical–tactical program element

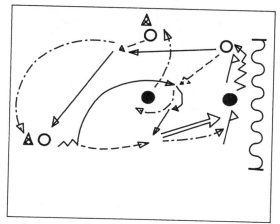 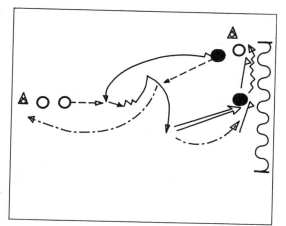

   2.4 Technical–tactical shooting element

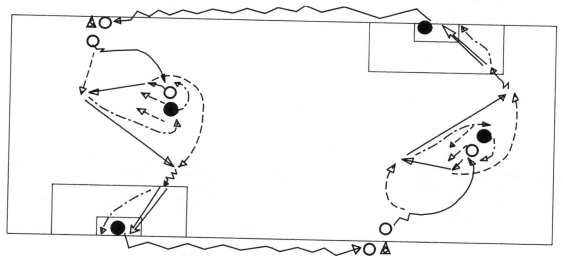

3. Concluding part of the coaching session
   3.1 Summary of the coaching session

Receiving (trapping) with the stomach/chest

The whole secret to receiving, whether it be trapping or amortisation, is that the player is relaxed and loose at the moment of contact with the ball. In today's game there is rarely time to bring the ball to a complete standstill as there is less time and space available for the player. As a result, with this and all other techniques of receiving, emphasis is to be placed on bringing the ball under control without stopping.

The moving player should get in flight of the ball, have eyes fixed on the ball, elbows and hands raised to the side and in front of the body. The legs are bent at the knees. At the moment the ball hits the ground the knee joints become fully extended with the body bending forward. This way the player creates a 'trap' for the ball, pushing it down to the ground under control for the player to play.

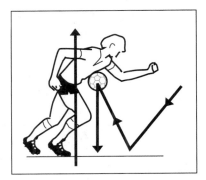

This type of control is usually made only with the high ball when the player cannot get to it on the full.

COMMON FAULTS — CORRECTIONS

1. Not moving to get in flight of the ball.
2. The hands are not away from the body for balance but too close to the side. The ball can hit the hand.
3. Poor anticipation of where the ball is going to land. If too close to the feet it hits the shins, if too far away from the body it bounces over the head.
4. The muscles are too tense and tight and not relaxed and loose.
5. There is no extension of the knee joints and the body is not bent over the ball the moment it hits the ground.
6. The upper extremity is vertical to the ground. There is no 'trap' and the ball bounces out of control.
7. At the moment the ball is about to bounce the eyes are taken off the ball and the head is turned away to the side.

1. Introductory part of the coaching session

2. Main part of the coaching session

2.3 Technical–tactical program element

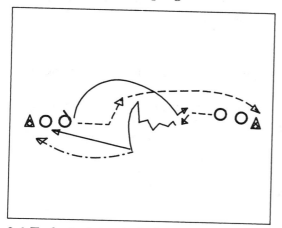
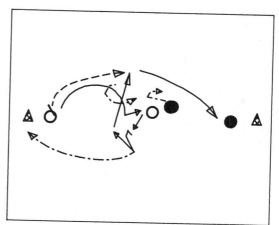

2.4 Technical–tactical shooting element

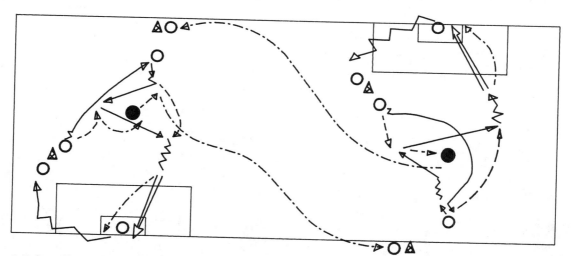

3. Concluding part of the coaching session

3.1 Summary of the coaching session

Heading with the side zone of the forehead

Over 40% of goals are scored and many more goals are defended with the use of the head. Modern soccer requires all players, no matter what role he or she is playing, to have the technical knowledge and ability to head the ball correctly.

In certain situations of the game the ball can be struck with the left or right side of the forehead. Using this technique the ball can be struck from a stationary position, a running position or a 1-footed or 2-footed jump. With this technique the player first takes up a side position in flight of the ball. This allows lateral movement along the vertical axis. This simply means that a greater amount of movement of the body mass can be achieved and applied on to the ball. The arching to the side gives greater elasticity in the movement than a player would have if facing the ball front.

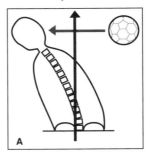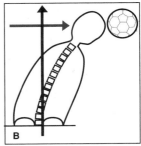

The body is arched away from the ball flight with the upper extremity quickly moving to meet the ball. As the ball is arriving the front leg is extended with the back leg bent, supporting the body weight. As the ball is about to be struck the back leg extends and thrusts the body on to a now bent supporting front leg with the upper extremity arching forward. The chin should be tucked in while waiting for the ball to arrive. Just before contact the head is extended to attack and strike the ball with the neck muscles locking the head in place. The hands and elbows are raised wide and in front of the body for balance while the eyes are fixed on the ball.

This arching of the body away and then forward to strike the ball provides the necessary balance for the swing on the ground and in the air.

COMMON FAULTS — CORRECTIONS

1. Players close their eyes and drop their heads, allowing the ball to strike the top of the head. If this occurs apply the analytic method.
2. There is no arch of the body away from the arriving ball.
3. The eyes are not fixed on the ball.
4. The hands and elbows are not to the side, raised and in front of the body.
5. The neck muscles are not locked and hard at the moment of contact.
6. At the moment of contact the head is not extended to meet the ball.
7. There is no arching of the body to strike and attack the ball.

1. Introductory part of the coaching session

1.1 Basic running and then static exercises for flexibility
  without the ball ....*refer to page 179*
1.2 Active exercises for flexibility with/without the ball ....*refer to page 180*
1.3 Juggling the ball ....*refer to page 183*
1.4 Individual corrective technical–tactical coaching

2. Main part of the coaching session

2.1 Helpful tactical games ....*refer to page 184*
2.2 Deceptive dribbling and feinting techniques ....*refer to page 188*
2.3 Technical–tactical program element

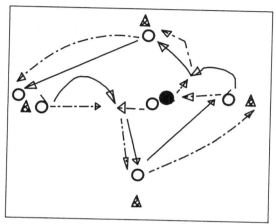 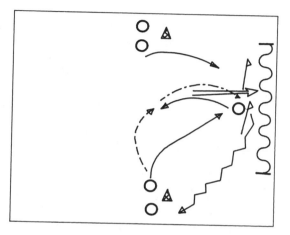

2.4 Technical–tactical shooting element

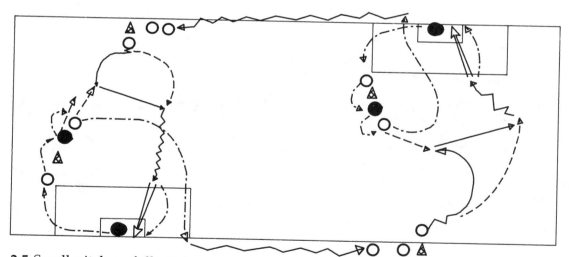

2.5 Small pitch or full pitch soccer ....*refer to page 208*

3. Concluding part of the coaching session

3.1 Summary of the coaching session

The shoulder charge

The laws of the game allow a player to charge the opponent with the shoulder while playing the ball. If the shoulder charge tackle has precise timing then the defending player will successfully win the ball in the tackle.

This type of tackle is of great importance in modern soccer as the amount of pressure on players with or without the ball is ever on the increase.

The technique involves the contacting shoulder and arm to be close as possible to the body with muscles locked and tight. The eyes are to be fixed on the ball and watching the outside foot of the opponent. When the outside foot has made contact with the ground then this is the perfect time to make the shoulder charge tackle. In this situation the attacking player has no area in which to counterbalance the tackle. As a result the player will find it very difficult to maintain balance and possession.

Just before the moment of contact the defending player should have his outside foot bent, lowering the centre of gravity and giving him better body balance. Then with extension he gives that power to support the tackle.

COMMON FAULTS — CORRECTIONS

1. Eyes are not fixed on the ball and the outside foot but on the player.
2. The leg playing the ball is loose and relaxed; there is chance of an injury.
3. Contacting hand is away from the body and not close with muscles locked tight.
4. The tackle is made too early or too late, resulting in missing the ball altogether or fouling.
5. The defending player is only playing the man and not the ball, again creating a foul.
6. The tackle is made with uncertainty and not with the player being courageous, totally committed and motivated in making the tackle and winning the ball.

1. Introductory part of the coaching session
    1.1 Basic running and then static exercises for flexibility
      without the ball ....*refer to page 179*
    1.2 Active exercises for flexibility with/without the ball ....*refer to page 180*
    1.3 Juggling the ball ....*refer to page 183*
    1.4 Individual corrective technical–tactical coaching

2. Main part of the coaching session
    2.1 Helpful tactical games ....*refer to page 184*
    2.2 Deceptive dribbling and feinting techniques ....*refer to page 188*
    2.3 Technical–tactical program element

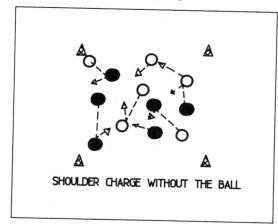

SHOULDER CHARGE WITHOUT THE BALL

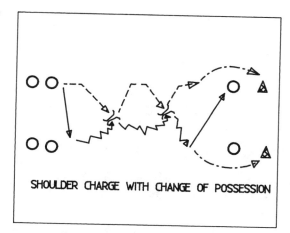

SHOULDER CHARGE WITH CHANGE OF POSSESSION

    2.4 Technical–tactical shooting element

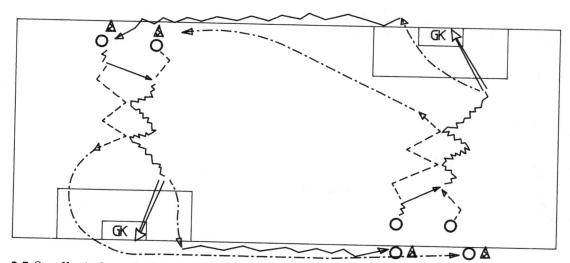

    2.5 Small pitch or full pitch soccer ....*refer to page 208*

3. Concluding part of the coaching session
    3.1 Summary of the coaching session

Basic combinations — 2:2

These basic combinations of 2:2 are now the result of progression from the 1:1, 2:0 and 2:1 exercises from previous levels.

These technical–tactical elements represent passing or communication between 2 attacking players against 2 defending players. The better the communication with the ball between the attacking players then the better the chances are of having a successful team. These combinations create specific situations that the player is going to experience in the game. The constant repetition of these specific technical–tactical elements will not only improve the player's technique but also to a high degree build on his or her tactical knowledge. In the game the player will find that these movements with or without the ball will eventually become automatic.

No matter what element is exercised the players must always be encouraged to be deceptive. They must disguise which way they are going to pass, dribble, receive, shoot and head the ball. They must always try to outwit the opponent.

The aim with these elements is simply through repetition to enable the player to solve similar situations that he or she will find in the game. The emphasis is always on the speed and sharpness with which all elements are to be executed. Casual and slow movements are not to be tolerated.

1. Introductory part of the coaching session

1.4 Individual corrective technical–tactical coaching

2. Main part of the coaching session

2.3 Technical–tactical program element

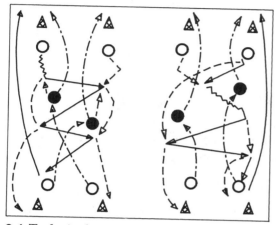 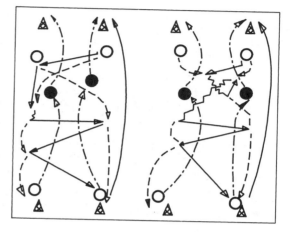

2.4 Technical–tactical shooting element

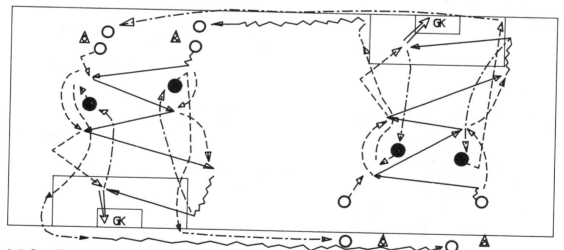

3. Concluding part of the coaching session

3.1 Summary of the coaching session

2.5 Small pitch and full pitch soccer

Every coaching session, at this level, should end with a small-sided game on a small pitch; however, there will be times when a coaching session will end with or consist of a full-sided game. But it is the small-sided situations that the young players enjoy most. They are in constant contact with the ball, enabling the technical–tactical and physical skills to be put into practice.

The aim when playing small-sided games is simply to attack the opponent's goal in the phase of attack and defend your goal in the phase of defence. The phase of attack is that moment your team gains possession, while the phase of defence is the moment the team has lost possession.

This is called soccer tactics — the art by which the player's technical and physical qualities are used to achieve the best possible result.

Tactics can be divided into 3 distinct categories:

1. *Individual tactics:* pressing the player, pressing the ball, creating space, dribbling, feinting, receiving, heading, passing, shooting, etc.
2. *Group tactics:* the mobility and interchange of players, the recovery behind the ball of the front attacking line, defending the goal, counter attacking, offside tactics, co-operation with the goalkeeper, playing wide or through the middle, etc.
3. *Team tactics:* keeping possession, slow build up, long direct penetrating passes, playing the high ball, keeping the ball low, switch of play, recovering behind the ball into a zone, pressing on all parts of the field, etc.

Team tactics used by the coach will also be determined by many factors that may include the way the opponents play, state of the playing surface, the team's position in the competition, phase of the game, the weather, etc.

The technical–tactical elements in the phase of attack are:

1. *Mobility:* the ability to move with or without the ball to create playing space.
2. *Penetration:* the ability to get past or behind defenders, with or without the ball.
3. *Width and depth:* the ability to create playing space across and along the field of play.
4. *Switch of play:* the ability to draw defenders out of position and exploit space on the opposite side.

The technical–tactical elements in the phase of defence are:

1. *Balance:* the ability to limit the creation of space, penetration and passing angles.
2. *Pressing the player without the ball:* the ability to reduce the time and playing space an attacking player will have when receiving the ball.
3. *Pressing the ball*: the ability to reduce the time and space the attacking player will have to receive, pass, dribble or shoot at goal.
4. *Zone and combined zone formations:* the ability to recover goal side of the ball, cover an area, and press any player entering that zone.

> **Note: It is necessary for coaches, coaching at all levels, to understand the technical–tactical elements in the phases of attack and defence. In level 4 greater emphasis is placed on tactical and physical development.**

Order of coaching technical–tactical elements in attack and defence

The following technical–tactical elements in attack and defence are to be applied and reinforced at each level.

TE–TA *elements in attack*				**TE–TA** *elements in defence*			
Number 1	*Number 2*	*Number 3*	*Number 4*	*Number 1*	*Number 2*	*Number 3*	*Number 4*
Level 1 (5 to 8 years) Unlimited touches with the ball Playing for fun				Unlimited touches with the ball Playing for fun			
Level 2 (9 to 10 years) Mobility Maximum 3 touches Reinforce level 1				Balance Reinforce level 1			
Level 3 (11 to 12 years) Mobility Maximum 2 touches Reinforce levels 1 and 2	Penetration			Balance Reinforce levels 1 and 2	Pressing the player without the ball		
Level 4 (13 to 14 years) Mobility Maximum 1 touch Reinforce levels 1 to 3	Penetration Reinforce level 3	Width and depth		Balance Reinforce levels 1 to 3	Pressing the player without the ball Reinforce level 3	Pressing the ball	
Level 5 (15 to 16 years) Mobility Maximum 1 touch Reinforce levels 1 to 4	Penetration Reinforce levels 3 and 4	Width and depth Reinforce level 4	Switch of play	Balance Reinforce levels 1 to 4	Pressing the player without the ball Reinforce levels 3 and 4	Pressing the ball Reinforce level 4	Zone and combined zone defence
Level 6 (17+ years) Mobility Maximum 1 touch Reinforce levels 1 to 5	Penetration Reinforce levels 3 to 5	Width and depth Reinforce levels 4 and 5	Switch of play Reinforce level 5	Balance Reinforce levels 1 to 5	Pressing the player without the ball Reinforce levels 3 to 5	Pressing the ball Reinforce levels 4 and 5	Zone and combined zone defence Reinforce level 5

Technical–tactical elements in attack

WIDTH AND DEPTH — MAXIMUM 1 TOUCH

Width and depth is the ability to create playing space across and along the field of play.

Creating width and depth simply serves to relieve and release pressure on the player with the ball. This is done by creating the diamond. The larger the diamond the greater the working space for the attacking team. This way the attacking team increases the chance of defenders making the mistake of being drawn out of position. If the attacking team has width and depth the player on the ball has numerous alternatives. In today's modern game the practice for teams without possession is to funnel back tight into a zone formation. This is to maintain balance and reduce the passing, dribbling and shooting angles. To counter this play every attempt must be made by the attacking team to draw the defending team out of position to get the ball deep or wide.

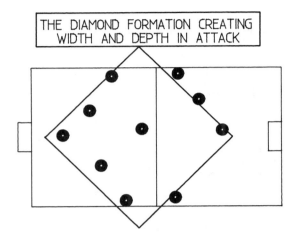

THE DIAMOND FORMATION CREATING WIDTH AND DEPTH IN ATTACK

Team 0 is showing very little width and depth in attack. As a result there is minimum attacking space in which to play

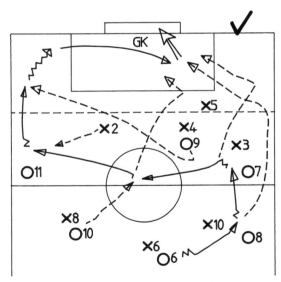

Team 0 has successfully drawn the defending team out of position and created width, depth and space in which to play

---

Note: Introduce into the small-sided/full-sided game a maximum of 1 touch, while reinforcing levels 3, 2 and 1.

Technical–tactical elements in defence

PRESSING THE BALL

Pressing the ball is the ability to reduce the time and space the attacking player has to make his pass, dribble or shoot at goal.

Ball pressing is applied by the nearest defending player to the ball. As soon as the ball is played to the supporting attacking player the defender quickly applies pressure to the ball.

The defending players do not mark person to person but mark a space or a zone and when the ball is played into their zone the pressing is applied.

When pressuring the pressure has to be applied with the purpose of preventing the attacking player from making a positive contribution to the game; in other words force him into nervous play and mistakes. With this type of pressing game the attacking team is not permitted to settle on the ball and establish a pattern in their build-up.

By applying the sudden pressure the peripheral view of the attacking player is reduced and as a result he is forced to keep his head down, focusing on the ball, concentrating on possession. This way he is unable to look for support to release the pressure.

If the attacking player manages to play the ball to a supporting player, then again the nearest defending player to the ball applies the pressure.

Pressing the ball can be applied on all parts of the pitch but it must be applied when the team is in balance. Applying pressure in the opponent's half is only recommended if the opposing team is not technically or physically equal or if the opposing team is leading and time is running out.

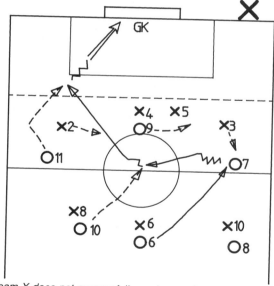

Team X does not successfully apply pressing of the ball and allows 07 to receive, dribble and pass to 010 who, with space and time, passes to 011 to strike at goal

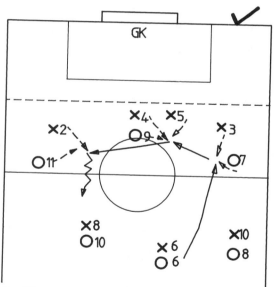

Here X3 pressures 07 into a pass to 09 who is pressured by both X5 and X4 and forced to make a bad pass to 011 that is intercepted by X2. From a defending position team X now move into the phase of attack

The laws of the game

1. *The field of play*
   Length — 100 to 130 yards
   Width — 50 to 100 yards
   The goal area — 6 × 20 yards
   The penalty area — 18×44 yards
   The corner area — 1 yard
   The goals — shall be 8 yards apart joined by a horizontal cross-bar 8 feet high
   The centre circle — shall have a radius of 10 yards

2. *The ball* — shall be a size 4 for players aged 13 years, size 5 for players aged 14 years, and of leather

3. *Number of players* — a match shall be played by 2 teams consisting of not more than 11 players each; each team includes a goalkeeper

4. *Referees and linesmen* — a referee and linesmen shall be appointed to officiate at each game

5. *Duration* — 40 minutes each way with 10 minutes for half-time

6. *The start of play* — before or after goals are scored, play is started by a player taking a place kick at the centre. All defending players must be in their half and outside the circle

7. *The ball out of play* — when it has wholly crossed the goal line or touch line, when in the air or on the ground

8. *Offside* — the offside law shall apply

9. *Fouls and misconduct* — the player is penalised by awarding a free kick

10. *Free kicks* — all free kicks can result in a direct or indirect shot at goal. All opposing players shall be at least 10 yards from the ball

11. *Penalty kicks* — the penalty kick is taken 12 yards from the goal line

12. *Throw-in* — at the point where the ball crossed the line, the throw is taken with both hands behind the head and with both feet on the ground

13. *Goal kick* — at the side where the ball crossed the line the ball is placed in the goal area and kicked into play

14. *Corner kick* — if the ball passes over the goal line, excluding the goals, and is last played by the defending team, then a player from the attacking team takes a free kick from the corner of the field

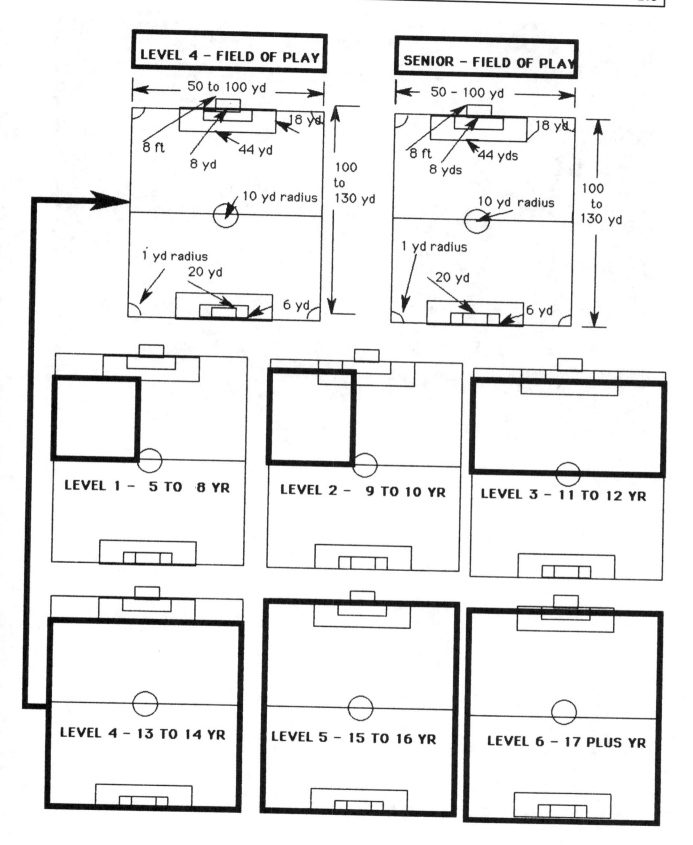

LEVEL 4 – FIELD OF PLAY

50 to 100 yd

18 yd

8 ft

44 yd

8 yd

100 to 130 yd

10 yd radius

1 yd radius

20 yd

6 yd

SENIOR – FIELD OF PLAY

50 – 100 yd

18 yd

8 ft

44 yds

8 yds

100 to 130 yd

10 yd radius

1 yd radius

20 yd

6 yd

LEVEL 1 – 5 TO 8 YR

LEVEL 2 – 9 TO 10 YR

LEVEL 3 – 11 TO 12 YR

LEVEL 4 – 13 TO 14 YR

LEVEL 5 – 15 TO 16 YR

LEVEL 6 – 17 PLUS YR

UMBRO

Superstar Franz Beckenbauer, then captain of Germany, holds high the 1974 World Cup trophy in Munich

technical–tactical elements

Juggling the ball

Juggling the ball is simply keeping the ball off the ground, playing it with all parts of the body except from the arms to the hands.

There is no better exercise for young players than juggling the ball to get universal feeling and confidence with the ball.

When juggling, it is necessary to be relaxed and have good body balance.

Juggling the ball is an important introductory part of each coaching session.

1. Juggling with the use of the outside of the foot

2. Juggling with the use of the chest

3. Juggling with the use of the head

Helpful tactical games

1. Parallel 4-goal soccer

One team attacks either 1 of the opponent's goals or defends its own. There are no offsides but corners are taken. The teams can have goalkeepers or play without.

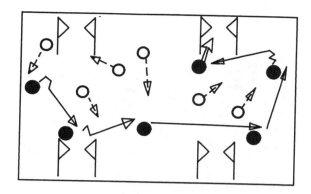

2. Soccer tennis

The ball is served from the bottom right corner behind the base line. The ball must pass over the net on the full and bounce in the opponent's court before being played. The ball can be played a maximum of 2 times in succession by the same player before passing or playing directly over the net. The net height is above the hips or below the shoulders.

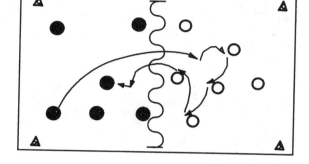

3. Mini-competition — 4:4, 3:3, 2:2

Four or 6 teams are selected to play in an organised mini-competition. There are no outs and a goal can only be scored from the front of the goal. Games are played equal time, with each team playing one another once. The team with the most number of points is declared winner.

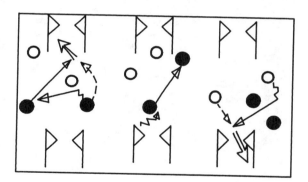

4. Medicine balls as goals

Two medicine balls are placed 20 metres apart. Two teams compete against each other in a game of small-sided soccer. There are no outs, with the goal being scored by hitting the medicine ball from any angle. There are no offsides.

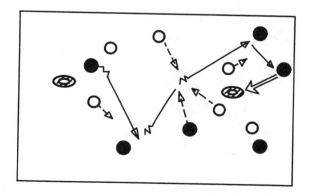

Deceptive dribbling and feinting techniques

The following represent the 10 deceptive dribbling and feinting techniques to be executed in level 3.

1. Cutting the ball left and right

2. Flick the ball with the inside of the instep out of tackle

3. Dummy inside of foot pass and roll away

4. *Cross over dummy heel pass*

5. *Side trick pass*

6. *Run over heel pass*

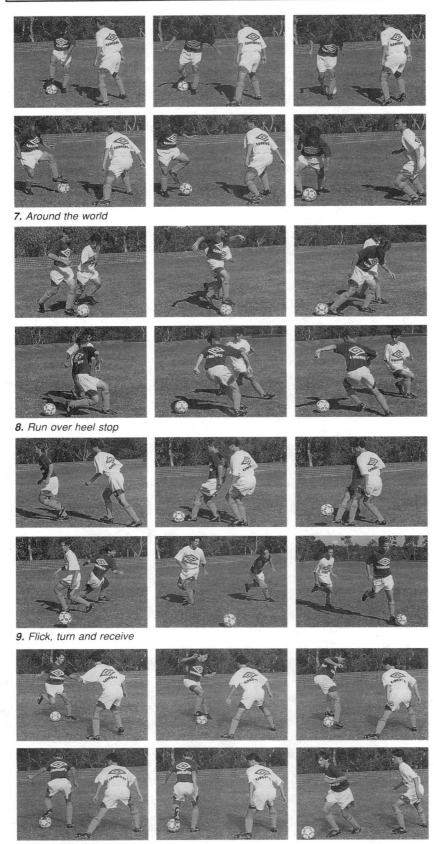

7. *Around the world*

8. *Run over heel stop*

9. *Flick, turn and receive*

10. *Twister*

Technical–tactical program elements

Jumping with 1 and 2 feet

1. Introductory part of the coaching session
    1.1 Basic running and then static exercises for flexibility
    without the ball ....*refer to page 179*
    1.2 Active exercises for flexibility with/without the ball ....*refer to page 180*
    1.3 Juggling the ball ....*refer to page 183*
    1.4 Individual corrective technical–tactical coaching

2. Main part of the coaching session
    2.1 Helpful tactical games ....*refer to page 184*
    2.2 Deceptive dribbling and feinting techniques ....*refer to page 188*
    2.3 Technical–tactical program element

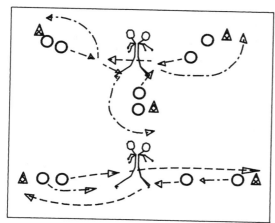 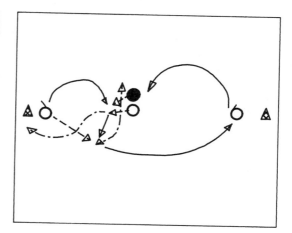

    2.4 Technical–tactical shooting element

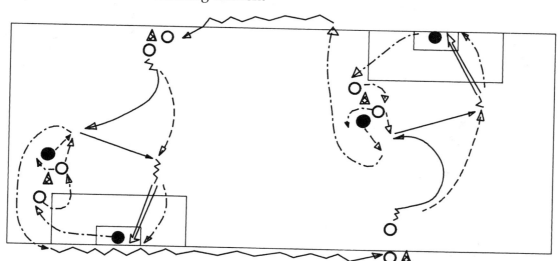

    2.5 Small pitch or full pitch soccer ....*refer to page 208*

3. Concluding part of the coaching session
    3.1 Summary of the coaching session

Dribbling with the outside of the instep

1. Introductory part of the coaching session

1.4 Individual corrective technical–tactical coaching

2. Main part of the coaching session

2.3 Technical–tactical program element

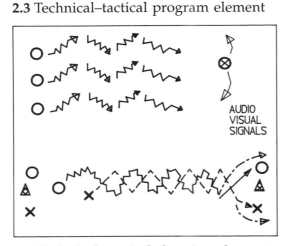 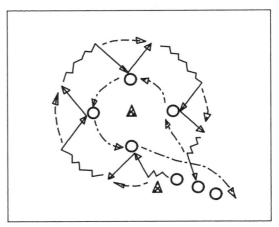

2.4 Technical–tactical shooting element

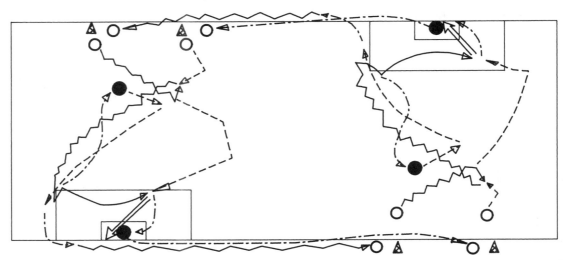

3. Concluding part of the coaching session

3.1 Summary of the coaching session

Dribbling with the inside of the instep

1. Introductory part of the coaching session
1.1 Basic running and then static exercises for flexibility
without the ball ....*refer to page 179*
1.2 Active exercises for flexibility with/without the ball ....*refer to page 180*
1.3 Juggling the ball ....*refer to page 183*
1.4 Individual corrective technical–tactical coaching

2. Main part of the coaching session
2.1 Helpful tactical games ....*refer to page 184*
2.2 Deceptive dribbling and feinting techniques ....*refer to page 188*
2.3 Technical–tactical program element

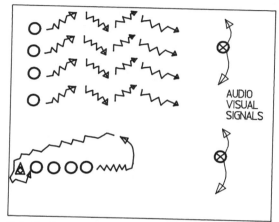
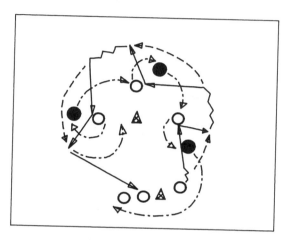

2.4 Technical–tactical shooting element

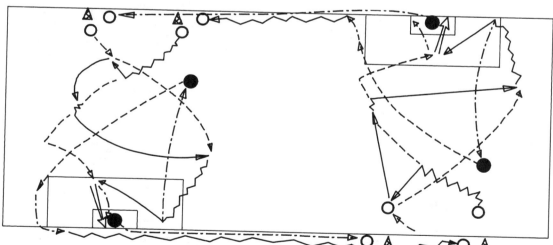

2.5 Small pitch or full pitch soccer ....*refer to page 208*

3. Concluding part of the coaching session
3.1 Summary of the coaching session

Kicking the ball with the inside of the instep

1. Introductory part of the coaching session

1.1 Basic running and then static exercises for flexibility
without the ball .... *refer to page 179*

1.2 Active exercises for flexibility with/without the ball .... *refer to page 180*

1.3 Juggling the ball .... *refer to page 183*

1.4 Individual corrective technical–tactical coaching

2. Main part of the coaching session

2.1 Helpful tactical games .... *refer to page 184*

2.2 Deceptive dribbling and feinting techniques .... *refer to page 188*

2.3 Technical–tactical program element

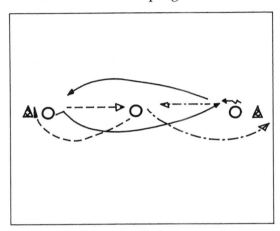 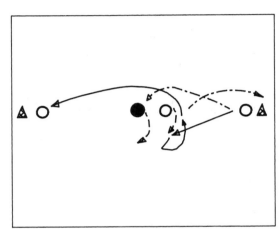

2.4 Technical–tactical shooting element

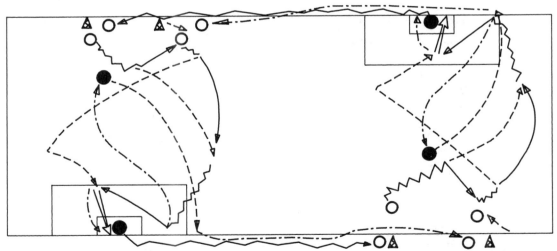

2.5 Small pitch or full pitch soccer .... *refer to page 208*

3. Concluding part of the coaching session

3.1 Summary of the coaching session

UMBRO

Kicking the ball with the outside of the instep

1. Introductory part of the coaching session
   1.1 Basic running and then static exercises for flexibility
     without the ball .... *refer to page 179*
   1.2 Active exercises for flexibility with/without the ball .... *refer to page 180*
   1.3 Juggling the ball .... *refer to page 183*
   1.4 Individual corrective technical–tactical coaching

2. Main part of the coaching session
   2.1 Helpful tactical games .... *refer to page 184*
   2.2 Deceptive dribbling and feinting techniques .... *refer to page 188*
   2.3 Technical–tactical program element

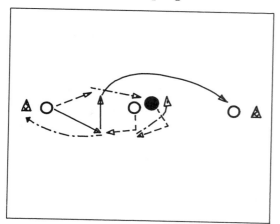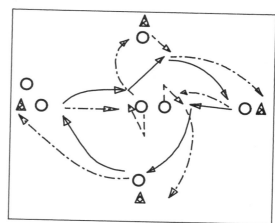

   2.4 Technical–tactical shooting element

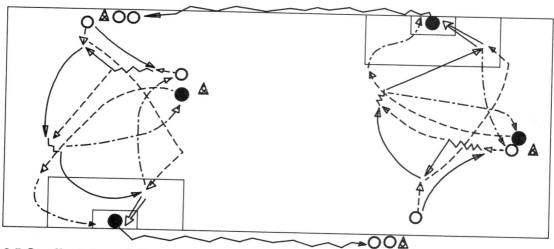

   2.5 Small pitch or full pitch soccer .... *refer to page 208*

3. Concluding part of the coaching session
   3.1 Summary of the coaching session

The wall pass — 1–2 pass

1. Introductory part of the coaching session
1.4 Individual corrective technical–tactical coaching

2. Main part of the coaching session
2.3 Technical–tactical program element

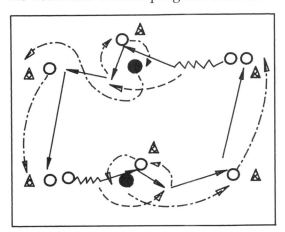 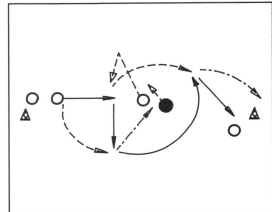

2.4 Technical–tactical shooting element

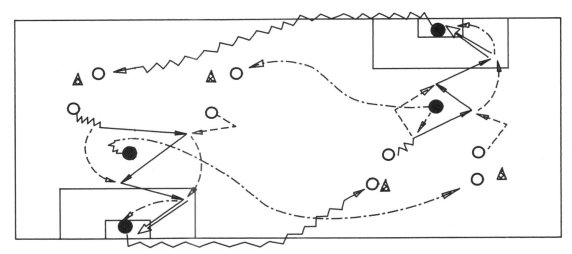

3. Concluding part of the coaching session
3.1 Summary of the coaching session

Receiving (amortisation) with the thigh

1. Introductory part of the coaching session

1.1 Basic running and then static exercises for flexibility
without the ball ....*refer to page 179*
1.2 Active exercises for flexibility with/without the ball ....*refer to page 180*
1.3 Juggling the ball ....*refer to page 183*
1.4 Individual corrective technical–tactical coaching

2. Main part of the coaching session

2.1 Helpful tactical games ....*refer to page 184*
2.2 Deceptive dribbling and feinting techniques ....*refer to page 188*
2.3 Technical–tactical program element

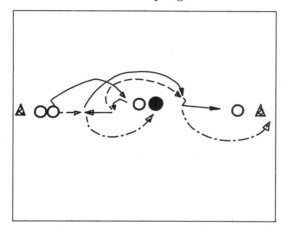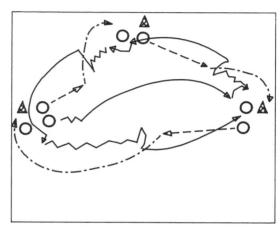

2.4 Technical–tactical shooting element

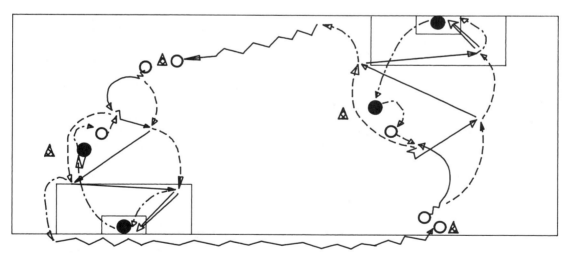

2.5 Small pitch or full pitch soccer ....*refer to page 208*

3. Concluding part of the coaching session

3.1 Summary of the coaching session

Receiving (amortisation) with the chest

1. Introductory part of the coaching session

1.1 Basic running and then static exercises for flexibility
without the ball .... *refer to page 179*

1.2 Active exercises for flexibility with/without the ball .... *refer to page 180*

1.3 Juggling the ball .... *refer to page 183*

1.4 Individual corrective technical–tactical coaching

2. Main part of the coaching session

2.1 Helpful tactical games .... *refer to page 184*

2.2 Deceptive dribbling and feinting techniques .... *refer to page 188*

2.3 Technical–tactical program element

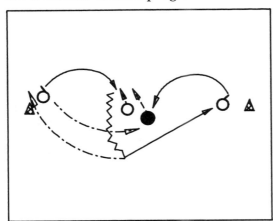 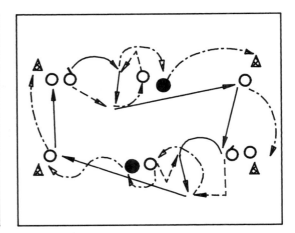

2.4 Technical–tactical shooting element

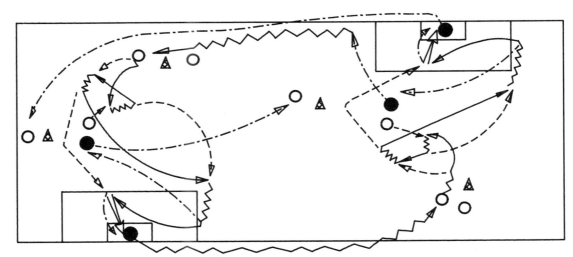

2.5 Small pitch or full pitch soccer .... *refer to page 208*

3. Concluding part of the coaching session

3.1 Summary of the coaching session

Receiving (trapping) with the outside of the instep

1. Introductory part of the coaching session
   1.1 Basic running and then static exercises for flexibility
      without the ball ....*refer to page 179*
   1.2 Active exercises for flexibility with/without the ball ....*refer to page 180*
   1.3 Juggling the ball ....*refer to page 183*
   1.4 Individual corrective technical–tactical coaching

2. Main part of the coaching session
   2.1 Helpful tactical games ....*refer to page 184*
   2.2 Deceptive dribbling and feinting techniques ....*refer to page 188*
   2.3 Technical–tactical program element

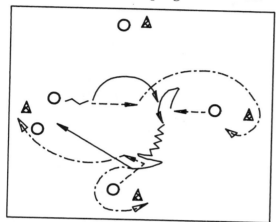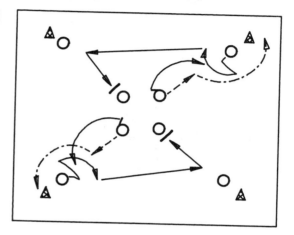

   2.4 Technical–tactical shooting element

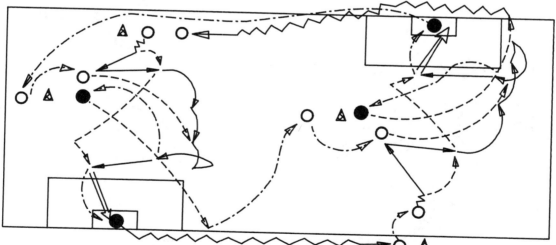

   2.5 Small pitch or full pitch soccer ....*refer to page 208*

3. Concluding part of the coaching session
   3.1 Summary of the coaching session

Heading with the middle zone of the forehead

1. Introductory part of the coaching session

1.4 Individual corrective technical–tactical coaching

2. Main part of the coaching session

2.3 Technical–tactical program element

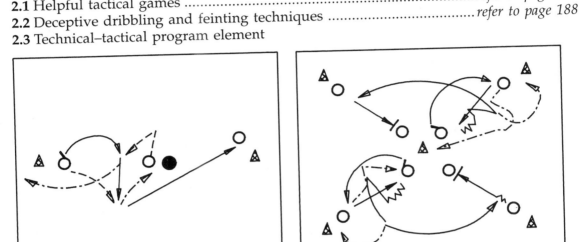

2.4 Technical–tactical shooting element

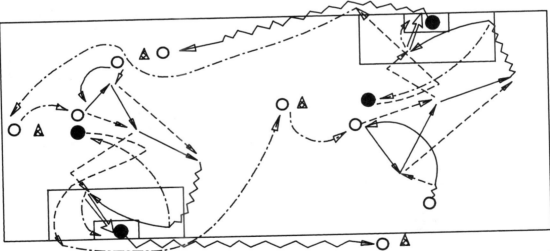

3. Concluding part of the coaching session

3.1 Summary of the coaching session

The sliding-straddle tackle

1. Introductory part of the coaching session
    1.1 Basic running and then static exercises for flexibility
        without the ball .... *refer to page 179*
    1.2 Active exercises for flexibility with/without the ball .... *refer to page 180*
    1.3 Juggling the ball .... *refer to page 183*
    1.4 Individual corrective technical–tactical coaching

2. Main part of the coaching session
    2.1 Helpful tactical games .... *refer to page 184*
    2.2 Deceptive dribbling and feinting techniques .... *refer to page 188*
    2.3 Technical–tactical program element

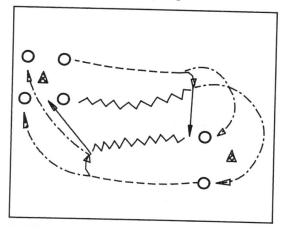 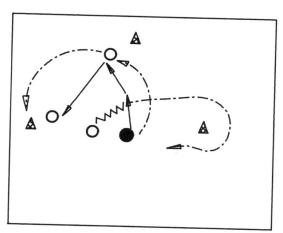

    2.4 Technical–tactical shooting element

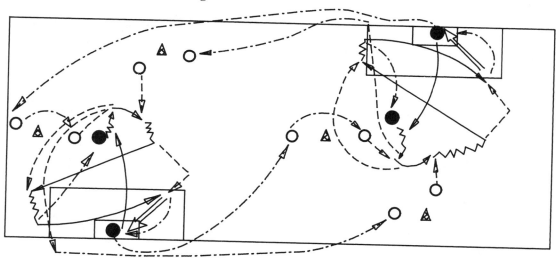

    2.5 Small pitch or full pitch soccer .... *refer to page 208*

3. Concluding part of the coaching session
    3.1 Summary of the coaching session

Basic combinations — 2:0

1. Introductory part of the coaching session

1.4 Individual corrective technical–tactical coaching

2. Main part of the coaching session

2.3 Technical–tactical program element

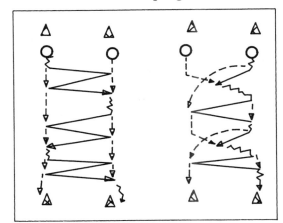 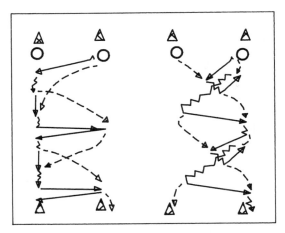

2.4 Technical–tactical shooting element

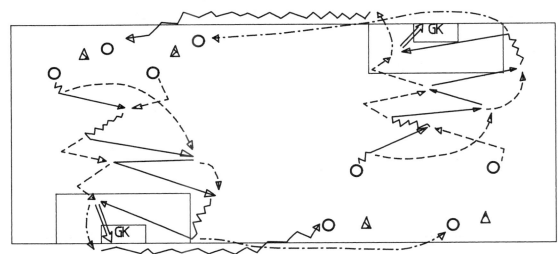

3. Concluding part of the coaching session

3.1 Summary of the coaching session

Basic combinations — 2:1

1. Introductory part of the coaching session

1.1 Basic running and then static exercises for flexibility without the ball ....*refer to page 179*

1.2 Active exercises for flexibility with/without the ball ....*refer to page 180*

1.3 Juggling the ball ....*refer to page 183*

1.4 Individual corrective technical–tactical coaching

2. Main part of the coaching session

2.1 Helpful tactical games ....*refer to page 184*

2.2 Deceptive dribbling and feinting techniques ....*refer to page 188*

2.3 Technical–tactical program element

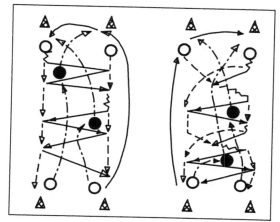 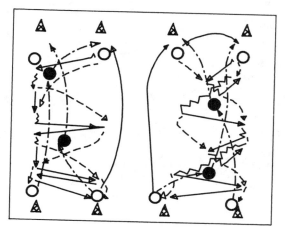

2.4 Technical–tactical shooting element

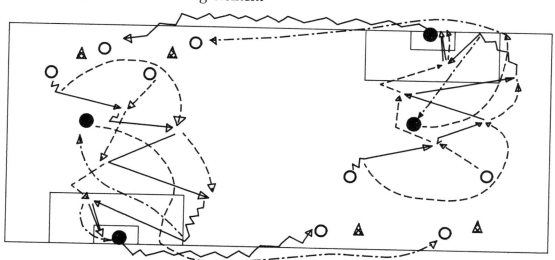

2.5 Small pitch or full pitch soccer ....*refer to page 208*

3. Concluding part of the coaching session

3.1 Summary of the coaching session

Superstar Johan Cruyff is fouled and awarded a penalty in the 1974 World Cup final against Germany

technical–tactical elements

Juggling the ball

Juggling the ball is simply keeping the ball off the ground, playing it with all parts of the body except from the arms to the hands.

There is no better exercise for young players than juggling the ball to get universal feeling and confidence with the ball.

When juggling, it is necessary to be relaxed and have good body balance.

Juggling the ball is an important introductory part of each coaching session.

1. Juggling with the use of the instep

2. Juggling with the use of the thigh

3. Juggling with the use of the inside of the foot

Helpful tactical games

1. Soccer handball

One team attacks and 1 team defends until a goal is scored or possession lost. Players interpass by throwing the ball with a maximum of 1 step with the ball. The attacking player with the ball must play a 1–2 pass and switch to another team player. Goals can only be scored by throwing the ball through the small goals. There are no outs or offside.

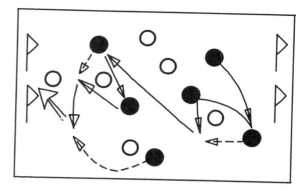

2. Piggy in the middle — 3:1

Three players, in a marked grid, keep possession of the ball away from the defending player in the middle. The defending player in the middle tries to intercept the ball being passed. If the ball is intercepted, the defending player changes places with the attacking player who lost possession.

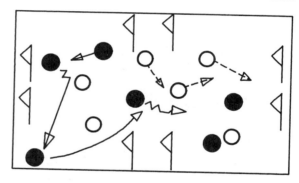

3. Soccer with 4 goals

Each team has 2 goals to attack and 2 goals to defend. There are no goalkeepers, no offside and no outs. Goals can only be scored from shooting from inside the grid.

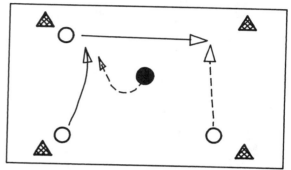

4. Hit your coloured marker

The playing area is covered with 2 different types of coloured markers, evenly distributed. The players must hit any 1 of their markers to score a goal. There are no outs and offside. Teams must defend their coloured marker.

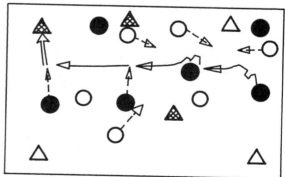

Deceptive dribbling and feinting techniques

The following represent the 15 deceptive dribbling and feinting techniques to be executed in level 2.

1. *Cutting the ball back inside*

2. *Cutting the ball back under the bottom*

3. *Scissors 1 way and go the other way*

4. *Dipping the shoulder 1 way and go the other*

5. *The shuffle*

6. *Inside and outside the instep*

7. Run over the ball and go the other way

8. Roll out and cut back

9. Scissors 1 way and go the same way

10. *Dummy kick and roll back*

11. *Placing the ball between the legs*

12. *Dummy heel pass*

13. *Cross over heel pass*

14. *Roll under the bottom and change direction*

15. *Overhead heel of the ball*

Technical–tactical program elements

Basic running and sprinting technique

1. Introductory part of the coaching session

1.1 Basic running and then static exercises for flexibility
without the ball ....*refer to page 179*

1.2 Active exercises for flexibility with/without the ball ....*refer to page 180*

1.3 Juggling the ball ....*refer to page 183*

1.4 Individual corrective technical–tactical coaching

2. Main part of the coaching session

2.1 Helpful tactical games ....*refer to page 184*

2.2 Deceptive dribbling and feinting techniques ....*refer to page 188*

2.3 Technical–tactical program element

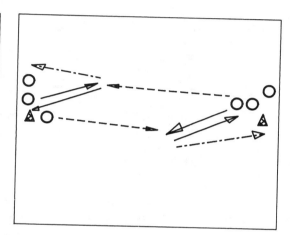

2.4 Technical–tactical shooting element

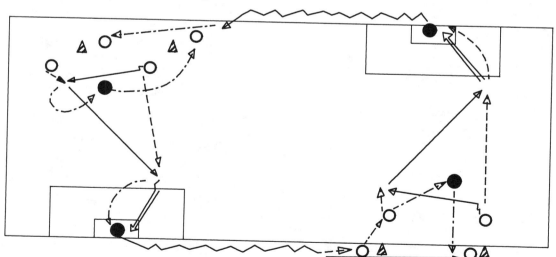

2.5 Small pitch or full pitch soccer ....*refer to page 208*

3. Concluding part of the coaching session

3.1 Summary of the coaching session

The start technique (forward side)

1. Introductory part of the coaching session
  1.1 Basic running and then static exercises for flexibility
   without the ball .... *refer to page 179*
  1.2 Active exercises for flexibility with/without the ball .... *refer to page 180*
  1.3 Juggling the ball .... *refer to page 183*
  1.4 Individual corrective technical–tactical coaching

2. Main part of the coaching session
  2.1 Helpful tactical games .... *refer to page 184*
  2.2 Deceptive dribbling and feinting techniques .... *refer to page 188*
  2.3 Technical–tactical program element

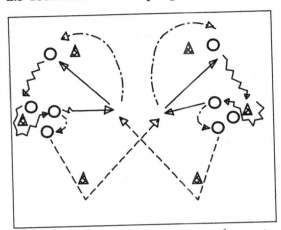 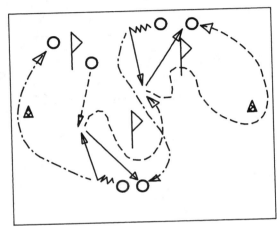

  2.4 Technical–tactical shooting element

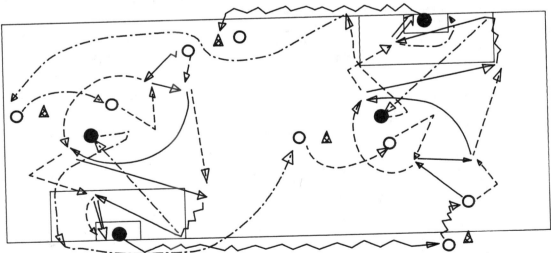

  2.5 Small pitch or full pitch soccer .... *refer to page 208*

3. Concluding part of the coaching session
  3.1 Summary of the coaching session

Dribbling with the full instep

1. Introductory part of the coaching session

1.4 Individual corrective technical–tactical coaching

2. Main part of the coaching session

2.3 Technical–tactical program element

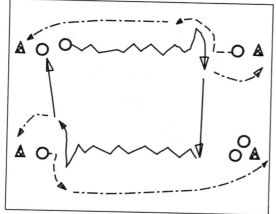
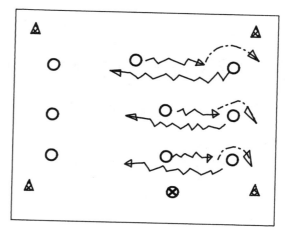

2.4 Technical–tactical shooting element

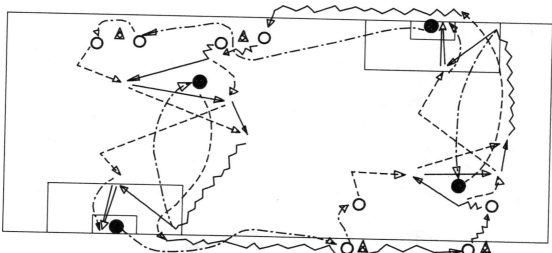

3. Concluding part of the coaching session

3.1 Summary of the coaching session

Dribbling with the sole of the foot

1. Introductory part of the coaching session

1.1 Basic running and then static exercises for flexibility
without the ball .... *refer to page 179*
1.2 Active exercises for flexibility with/without the ball .... *refer to page 180*
1.3 Juggling the ball .... *refer to page 183*
1.4 Individual corrective technical–tactical coaching

2. Main part of the coaching session

2.1 Helpful tactical games .... *refer to page 184*
2.2 Deceptive dribbling and feinting techniques .... *refer to page 188*
2.3 Technical–tactical program element

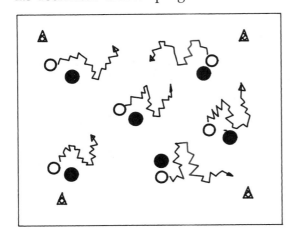 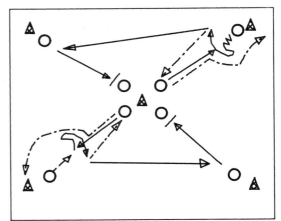

2.4 Technical–tactical shooting element

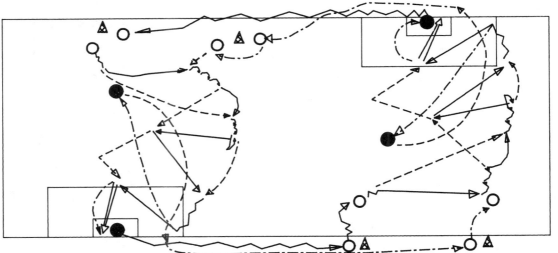

2.5 Small pitch or full pitch soccer .... *refer to page 208*

3. Concluding part of the coaching session

3.1 Summary of the coaching session

Kicking the ball with the full instep

1. Introductory part of the coaching session

1.1 Basic running and then static exercises for flexibility
without the ball ....*refer to page 179*

1.2 Active exercises for flexibility with/without the ball ....*refer to page 180*

1.3 Juggling the ball ....*refer to page 183*

1.4 Individual corrective technical–tactical coaching

2. Main part of the coaching session

2.1 Helpful tactical games ....*refer to page 184*

2.2 Deceptive dribbling and feinting techniques ....*refer to page 188*

2.3 Technical–tactical program element

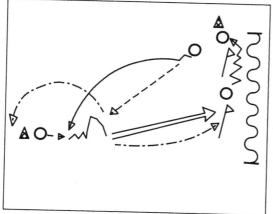
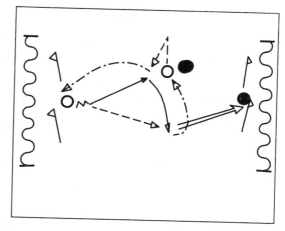

2.4 Technical–tactical shooting element

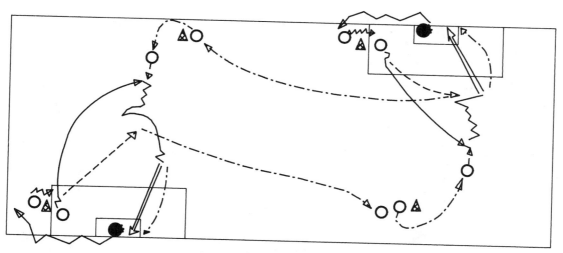

2.5 Small pitch or full pitch soccer ....*refer to page 208*

3. Concluding part of the coaching session

3.1 Summary of the coaching session

Kicking the ball with the inside of the foot

1. Introductory part of the coaching session

1.1 Basic running and then static exercises for flexibility
without the ball .... *refer to page 179*

1.2 Active exercises for flexibility with/without the ball .... *refer to page 180*

1.3 Juggling the ball .... *refer to page 183*

1.4 Individual corrective technical–tactical coaching

2. Main part of the coaching session

2.1 Helpful tactical games .... *refer to page 184*

2.2 Deceptive dribbling and feinting techniques .... *refer to page 188*

2.3 Technical–tactical program element

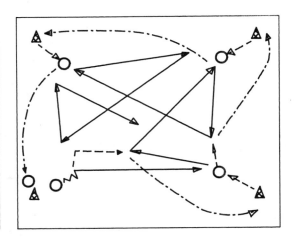

2.4 Technical–tactical shooting element

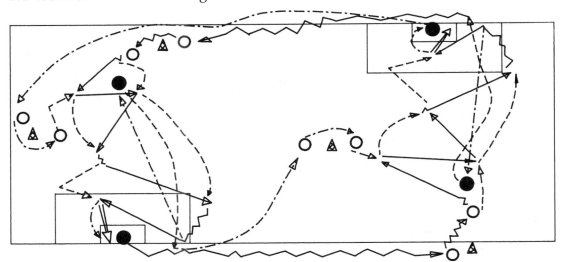

2.5 Small pitch or full pitch soccer .... *refer to page 208*

3. Concluding part of the coaching session

3.1 Summary of the coaching session

Receiving (amortisation) with the inside of the foot

1. Introductory part of the coaching session
    1.1 Basic running and then static exercises for flexibility
       without the ball ....*refer to page 179*
    1.2 Active exercises for flexibility with/without the ball ....*refer to page 180*
    1.3 Juggling the ball ....*refer to page 183*
    1.4 Individual corrective technical–tactical coaching

2. Main part of the coaching session
    2.1 Helpful tactical games ....*refer to page 184*
    2.2 Deceptive dribbling and feinting techniques ....*refer to page 188*
    2.3 Technical–tactical program element

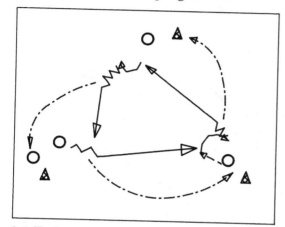
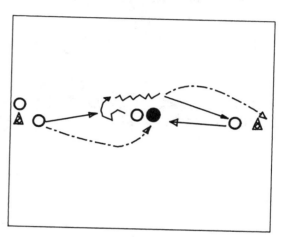

    2.4 Technical–tactical shooting element

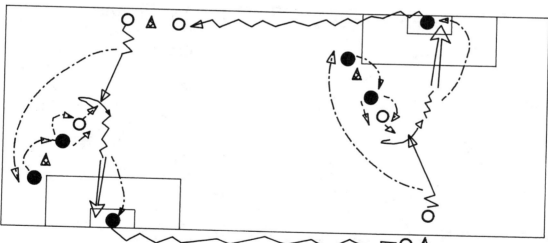

    2.5 Small pitch or full pitch soccer ....*refer to page 208*

3. Concluding part of the coaching session
    3.1 Summary of the coaching session

Receiving (amortisation) with the full instep

1. Introductory part of the coaching session

1.1 Basic running and then static exercises for flexibility
without the ball ....*refer to page 179*

1.2 Active exercises for flexibility with/without the ball ....*refer to page 180*

1.3 Juggling the ball ....*refer to page 183*

1.4 Individual corrective technical–tactical coaching

2. Main part of the coaching session

2.1 Helpful tactical games ....*refer to page 184*

2.2 Deceptive dribbling and feinting techniques ....*refer to page 188*

2.3 Technical–tactical program element

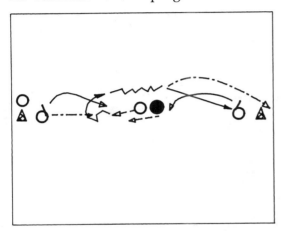 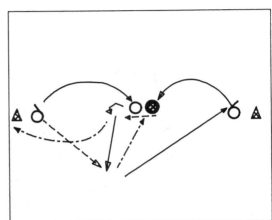

2.4 Technical–tactical shooting element

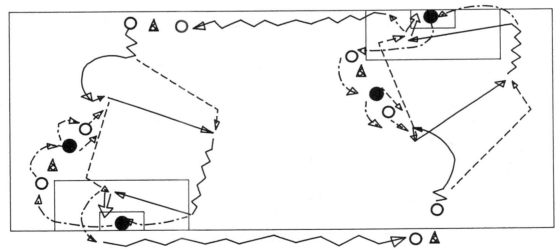

2.5 Small pitch or full pitch soccer ....*refer to page 208*

3. Concluding part of the coaching session

3.1 Summary of the coaching session

Receiving (trapping) with the inside of the foot

1. Introductory part of the coaching session

1.1 Basic running and then static exercises for flexibility
without the ball ....*refer to page 179*
1.2 Active exercises for flexibility with/without the ball ....*refer to page 180*
1.3 Juggling the ball ....*refer to page 183*
1.4 Individual corrective technical–tactical coaching

2. Main part of the coaching session

2.1 Helpful tactical games ....*refer to page 184*
2.2 Deceptive dribbling and feinting techniques ....*refer to page 188*
2.3 Technical–tactical program element

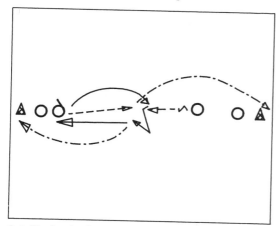
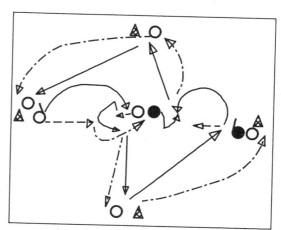

2.4 Technical–tactical shooting element

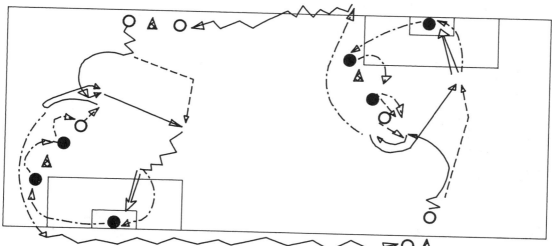

2.5 Small pitch or full pitch soccer ....*refer to page 208*

3. Concluding part of the coaching session

3.1 Summary of the coaching session

Receiving (trapping) with the sole of the foot

1. Introductory part of the coaching session
    1.1 Basic running and then static exercises for flexibility
without the ball .... *refer to page 179*
    1.2 Active exercises for flexibility with/without the ball .... *refer to page 180*
    1.3 Juggling the ball .... *refer to page 183*
    1.4 Individual corrective technical–tactical coaching

2. Main part of the coaching session
    2.1 Helpful tactical games .... *refer to page 184*
    2.2 Deceptive dribbling and feinting techniques .... *refer to page 188*
    2.3 Technical–tactical program element

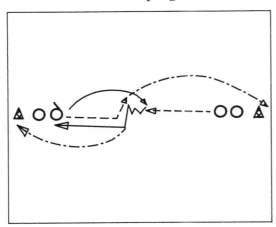 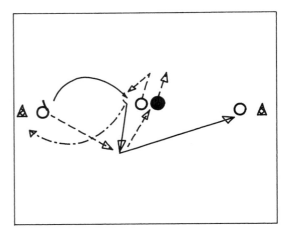

    2.4 Technical–tactical shooting element

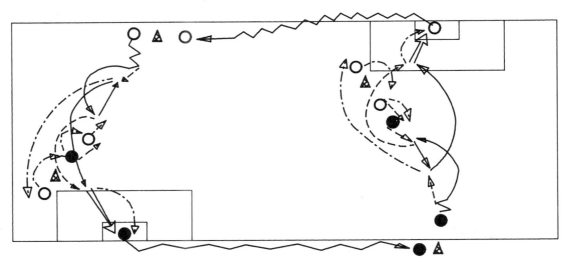

    2.5 Small pitch or full pitch soccer .... *refer to page 208*

3. Concluding part of the coaching session
    3.1 Summary of the coaching session

The delay and basic block tackle

1. Introductory part of the coaching session

1.4 Individual corrective technical–tactical coaching

2. Main part of the coaching session

2.3 Technical–tactical program element

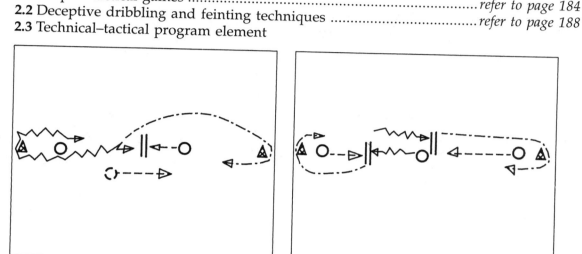
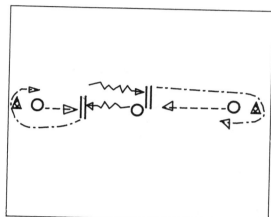

2.4 Technical–tactical shooting element

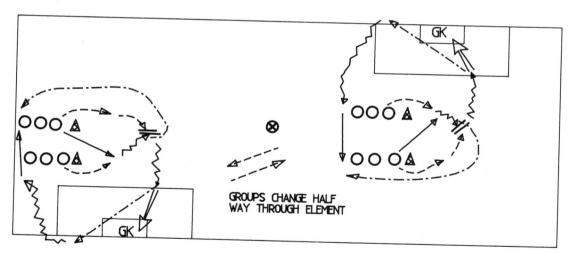

GROUPS CHANGE HALF
WAY THROUGH ELEMENT

3. Concluding part of the coaching session

3.1 Summary of the coaching session

Basic combinations — 1:1

1. Introductory part of the coaching session

1.1 Basic running and then static exercises for flexibility
without the ball .... *refer to page 179*

1.2 Active exercises for flexibility with/without the ball .... *refer to page 180*

1.3 Juggling the ball .... *refer to page 183*

1.4 Individual corrective technical–tactical coaching

2. Main part of the coaching session

2.1 Helpful tactical games .... *refer to page 184*

2.2 Deceptive dribbling and feinting techniques .... *refer to page 188*

2.3 Technical–tactical program element

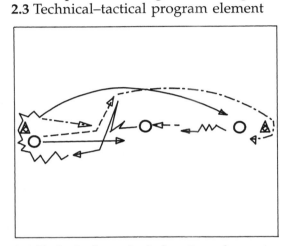 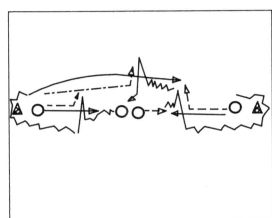

2.4 Technical–tactical shooting element

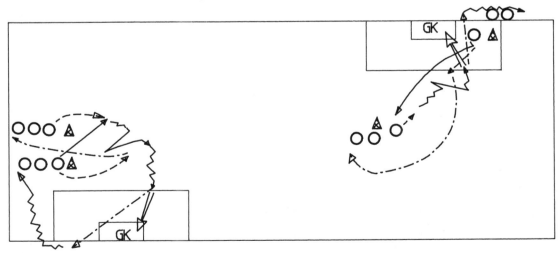

2.5 Small pitch or full pitch soccer .... *refer to page 208*

3. Concluding part of the coaching session

3.1 Summary of the coaching session

technical–tactical elements

Agility in the air and on the ground

Trampoline

The basic bounce: *can be used as a warm-up activity. The body and arms should be straight with head erect. At the top of the bounce, the legs are straight with toes pointing down. On the downward bounce flex the legs, hitting the mat with flat feet shou. width*

The seat drop: *from the basic bounce position raise the legs to a horizontal position, moving arms forward and upwards. From here drop back on to the mat into the seat position and bounce back t vertical*

The tuck jump: *at the top of the bounce clasp the shins, bringing knees to the chest. Tuck in the elbows with eyes fixed on the cer end of the trampoline. The heels are against the seat while the tc are pointing downward*

The closed pike jump: from the basic bounce bring the legs straight with toes pointing to a horizontal position. Bend the body forward at the hips with the hands straight with the legs

The half pirouette: on the bounce, raise 1 arm above the head while bending the other at 90° across the chest. Twist the body 180° around its vertical axis

The split pike jump: the split pike is similar to the closed pike jump except that both legs and arms are stretched apart during the bounce

The pirouette: this is similar to the half pirouette but twist a full 360° instead of 180°

UMBRO

FLOOR

The forward roll: *crouch on the toes with hands on the mat shoulder width apart. Place the chin to the chest, lift the hips and kick off the mat and overbalance. Roll over to the crouch position*

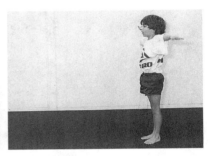

The backward roll: *squat on the mat with elbows bent and palms facing up. Curl the body and rock back, lowering the seat to the mat. Roll back and swing the feet over the head, rolling into a squat*

The mule kick: *place the hands on the mat shoulder width apart. All the weight is taken by the hands with a kick of 1 leg followed by the other high in the air*

The crouch balance: *place the hands on the mat shoulder width apart, palms down. Kick both legs high in the air, bent together while balancing on the hands in the crouch position*

The twist crouch: *the player stands with 1 foot forward, bends and places hands flat on the mat. Travelling sideways, the legs are bent and together, twisting at the hips*

BALANCE BEAM

Walking forward   *Walking backwards*

Walking through hoops   *Bouncing a ball*

Balancing objects   *Picking up objects*

Catching a ball

Walking over objects

Hopping

MINI-TRAMPOLINE/VAULTING BOX

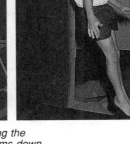

The basic bounce: *on hitting the trampoline mat swing the arms down and bend the legs with the feet flat. To get the upward bounce, push hard on the heels with the forward and upward swing of the hands*

The tuck jump: *the same technique as with the basic bounce but bring the knees to the chest, clasping the shins. Land softly on the mat*

The closed pike jump: *following the bounce bring the legs straight and to a horizontal position. Bend the body at the hips with the hands pointing down the shins*

The split pike jump: *the technique with this element is the same as with the closed pike jump, only the legs and arms are stretched apart*

The side vault: *from the mini-trampoline bounce place the hands on either side of the box. Twist the body to 1 side with a soft landing side-on to the box*

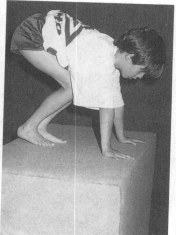
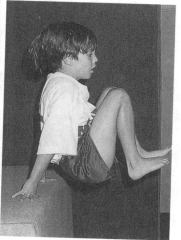

The bent leg squat vault: *following the bounce the stretched out arms touch the box while the legs are bent and close to the chest. The upper extremity is leaning forward. The legs straighten for a soft landing*

Phase 2: 7 to 8 years

TRAMPOLINE — Reinforce basic elements: 5 to 6 years

Swivel hips: *from a basic bounce, go into a seat drop. At the top of the bounce do a half twist and drop into another seat drop*

FLOOR — Reinforce basic elements: 5 to 6 years

The dive roll: *dive forward, stretching the body to land on the hands. Tuck the chin to the chest. Roll over the shoulders and on to the back*

BALANCE BEAM — Reinforce basic elements: 5 to 6 years

     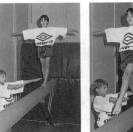 

Inclined bench balances   *See-saw*   *Passing over arms*

Mini-trampoline/vaulting box

Straddle vault: *following the bounce, lean forward and straighten the legs, keeping them apart with toes pointed. Extend the hands quickly so that they make contact with the apparatus and the body can straddle over it. Land on 2 feet, hands wide*

Forward dive roll: *leap forward with the body and arms stretched. The hands make contact first with the mat, softening the fall, the chin tucked into the chest and knees likewise. Staying curled, roll to your feet*

Forward somersault: *from the forward bounce, clasp the shins by the hands with the chin tucked into the chest. With the quick rotation spin into the somersault, opening out before coming to the vertical axis*

UMBRO

Superstar Karl-Heinz Rummenigge scores Germany's first goal in the 1986 World Cup final

technical–tactical development program

Core learning areas in the soccer development program

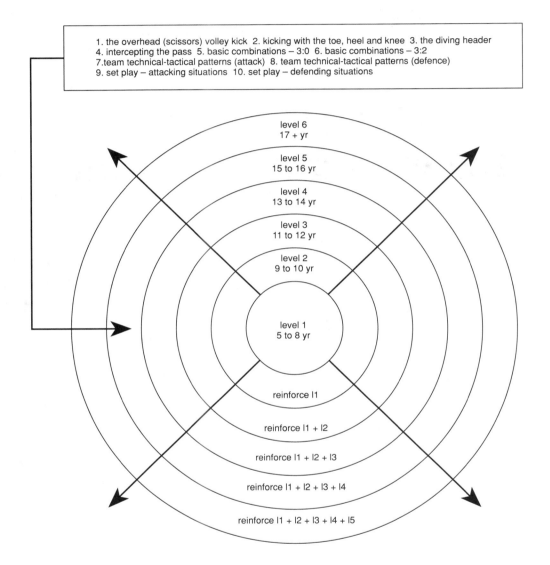

1. the overhead (scissors) volley kick 2. kicking with the toe, heel and knee 3. the diving header
4. intercepting the pass 5. basic combinations – 3:0 6. basic combinations – 3:2
7. team technical-tactical patterns (attack) 8. team technical-tactical patterns (defence)
9. set play – attacking situations 10. set play – defending situations

level 6
17 + yr

level 5
15 to 16 yr

level 4
13 to 14 yr

level 3
11 to 12 yr

level 2
9 to 10 yr

level 1
5 to 8 yr

reinforce l1

reinforce l1 + l2

reinforce l1 + l2 + l3

reinforce l1 + l2 + l3 + l4

reinforce l1 + l2 + l3 + l4 + l5

Technical–tactical program

Element	Level 1 (5–8 yr)	Level 2 (9–10 yr)	Level 3 (11–12 yr)	Level 4 (13–14 yr)	Level 5 (15–16 yr)	Level 6 (17+ yr)
Agility in the air and on the ground	1	Reinforce	Reinforce	Reinforce	Reinforce	Reinforce
Basic running and sprinting technique		1	Reinforce	Reinforce	Reinforce	Reinforce
The start technique (forward side)		2	Reinforce	Reinforce	Reinforce	Reinforce
Jumping with 1 and 2 feet			1	Reinforce	Reinforce	Reinforce
Changing direction and speed				1	Reinforce	Reinforce
Dribbling with the full instep		3	Reinforce	Reinforce	Reinforce	Reinforce
Dribbling with the sole of the foot		4	Reinforce	Reinforce	Reinforce	Reinforce
Dribbling with the outside of the instep			2	Reinforce	Reinforce	Reinforce
Dribbling with the inside of the instep			3	Reinforce	Reinforce	Reinforce
Deceptive dribbling and feinting (15 tricks)		5	Reinforce	Reinforce	Reinforce	Reinforce
Deceptive dribbling and feinting (10 tricks)			4	Reinforce	Reinforce	Reinforce
Deceptive dribbling and feinting (5 tricks)				2	Reinforce	Reinforce
Juggling the ball (individual)		6	Reinforce	Reinforce	Reinforce	Reinforce
Juggling the ball (partner)			5	Reinforce	Reinforce	Reinforce
Juggling the ball (group)				3	Reinforce	Reinforce
Kicking the ball with the full instep		7	Reinforce	Reinforce	Reinforce	Reinforce
Kicking the ball with the inside of the foot		8	Reinforce	Reinforce	Reinforce	Reinforce
Kicking the ball with the inside of the instep			6	Reinforce	Reinforce	Reinforce
Kicking the ball with the outside of the instep			7	Reinforce	Reinforce	Reinforce
The wall pass — 1–2 pass			8	Reinforce	Reinforce	Reinforce
Chipping the ball				4	Reinforce	Reinforce
Full volley kick (front side)				5	Reinforce	Reinforce
Half volley kick (front side)				6	Reinforce	Reinforce
Overhead (scissors) volley kick					1	Reinforce
Kicking with the toe, heel and knee					2	Reinforce
Receiving (amortisation) — inside of the foot		9	Reinforce	Reinforce	Reinforce	Reinforce
Receiving (amortisation) with the full instep		10	Reinforce	Reinforce	Reinforce	Reinforce
Receiving (amortisation) with the thigh			9	Reinforce	Reinforce	Reinforce
Receiving (amortisation) with the chest			10	Reinforce	Reinforce	Reinforce
Receiving (amortisation) with the head				7	Reinforce	Reinforce
Receiving (trapping) — inside of the foot		11	Reinforce	Reinforce	Reinforce	Reinforce
Receiving (trapping) with the sole of the foot		12	Reinforce	Reinforce	Reinforce	Reinforce
Receiving (trapping) with the outside of the instep			11	Reinforce	Reinforce	Reinforce
Receiving (trapping) with the stomach/chest				8	Reinforce	Reinforce
Heading with the middle zone of the forehead			12	Reinforce	Reinforce	Reinforce
Heading with the side zone of the forehead				9	Reinforce	Reinforce
The diving header					3	Reinforce
The delay and basic block tackle		13	Reinforce	Reinforce	Reinforce	Reinforce
The sliding–straddle tackle			13	Reinforce	Reinforce	Reinforce
The shoulder charge				10	Reinforce	Reinforce
Intercepting the pass					4	Reinforce
Basic combinations — 1:1		14	Reinforce	Reinforce	Reinforce	Reinforce
Basic combinations — 2:0			14	Reinforce	Reinforce	Reinforce
Basic combinations — 2:1			15	Reinforce	Reinforce	Reinforce
Basic combinations — 2:2				11	Reinforce	Reinforce
Basic combinations — 3:0					5	Reinforce
Basic combinations — 3:2					6	Reinforce
Helpful tactical games					7	Reinforce
Kicking at goal		15	Reinforce	Reinforce	Reinforce	Reinforce
Heading at goal		16	Reinforce	Reinforce	Reinforce	Reinforce
Team technical–tactical playing patterns — attack			16	Reinforce	Reinforce	Reinforce
Team technical–tactical playing patterns — defence					8	Reinforce
Set play — attacking situations					9	Reinforce
Set play — defending situations					10	Reinforce
Small pitch soccer — TE–TA elements	2	Reinforce	Reinforce	Reinforce	Reinforce	Reinforce
Full pitch soccer — TE–TA elements				12	Reinforce	Reinforce
	2	16	16	12	10	0

Total soccer development program elements = 56 elements

Technical–tactical elements to be coached

1. Overhead (scissors) volley kick
2. Kicking with the toe, heel and knee
3. The diving header
4. Intercepting the pass
5. Basic combinations — 3:0
6. Basic combinations — 3:2
7. Team technical–tactical playing patterns — attack
8. Team technical–tactical playing patterns — defence
9. Set play — attacking situations
10. Set play — defending situations

Total elements = 10

Time allocation for the 110 minute coaching session

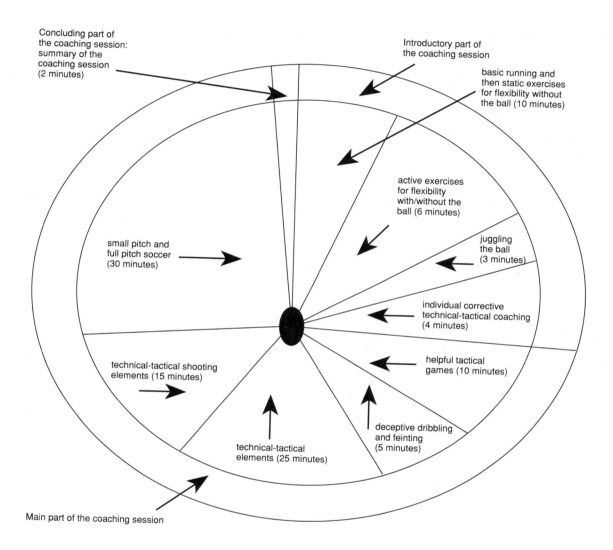

Concluding part of the coaching session: summary of the coaching session (2 minutes)

Introductory part of the coaching session

basic running and then static exercises for flexibility without the ball (10 minutes)

active exercises for flexibility with/without the ball (6 minutes)

juggling the ball (3 minutes)

small pitch and full pitch soccer (30 minutes)

individual corrective technical-tactical coaching (4 minutes)

helpful tactical games (10 minutes)

technical-tactical shooting elements (15 minutes)

deceptive dribbling and feinting (5 minutes)

technical-tactical elements (25 minutes)

Main part of the coaching session

Structure of the practical coaching session — 110 minutes

1. Introductory part of the coaching session

   1.4 Individual corrective technical–tactical coaching (4 minutes)

2. Main part of the coaching session

3. Concluding part of the coaching session

   3.1 Summary of the coaching session (2 minutes)

Total practical coaching time = 110 minutes

1. Introductory part of the coaching session

1.1 STATIC EXERCISES FOR FLEXIBILITY WITHOUT THE BALL

These exercises are designed to prepare the body in order to prevent injury and to enhance performance. A sustained stretch of 15 seconds or longer is preferable.

1. Thigh (quadriceps): opposite hand holds the instep

2. Calf (gastrocnemius): feet pointing forward. Back straight, lunge forward, heel down

3. Inner thigh (adductors): push knees towards the ground

4. Back of thigh (hamstrings): knee is straight

5. Back of thigh (outside hamstrings): foot turned out, taken across the body (lateral hamstring)

6. Back of thigh (inside hamstrings): foot turned in, placed away from the body (medial hamstring)

7. Outer thigh (iliotibial band): step behind and stretch with leg straight. Rotate away

8. Buttocks (gluteals): both buttocks on the ground, back straight. Press knee and turn

9. Stomach (abdominals): hips remain on the ground

10. Back (erector spinae): curl and hold into a ball

11. Side (latissimus dorsi): hand over hand, raise the hips and stretch

12. Neck (trapezius sternomastoid): stretch forward, back and to the sides

1.2 ACTIVE EXERCISES FOR FLEXIBILITY WITH/WITHOUT THE BALL

Group exercises no. 1

As with the static exercises, these active exercises are also designed to prepare the body for the coaching session and to enhance performance.

Group exercises no. 2

As with the static exercises, these active exercises are also designed to prepare the body for the coaching session and to enhance performance.

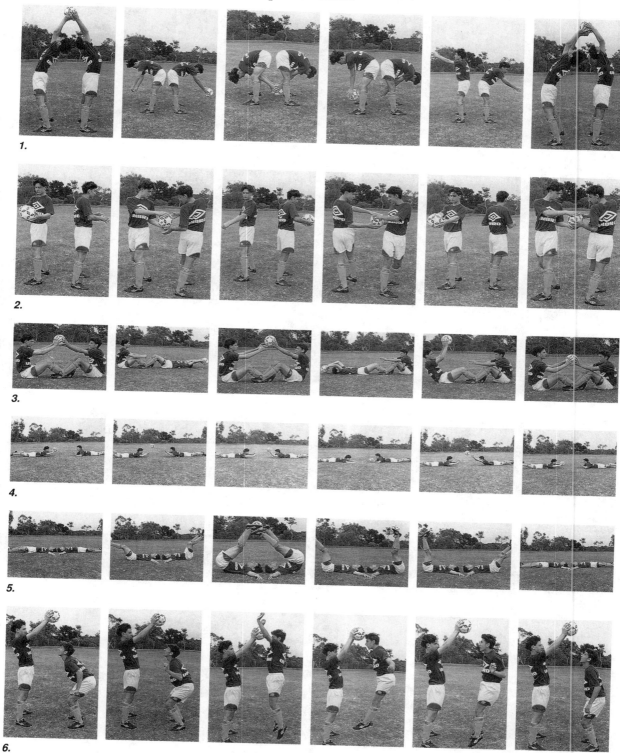

Group exercises no. 3

As with the static exercises, these active exercises are also designed to prepare the body for the coaching session and to enhance performance.

1.

2.

3.

4.

5.

6.

1.3 JUGGLING THE BALL

Juggling the ball is simply keeping the ball off the ground, playing it with all parts of the body except from the arms to the hands.

There is no better exercise for young players than juggling the ball to get universal feeling and confidence with the ball.

When juggling, it is necessary to be relaxed and have good body balance.

Juggling the ball is an important introductory part of each coaching session.

All elements of juggling from the previous levels must be reinforced as progression is made from individual, partner and group juggling.

1. Juggling individually

2. Juggling with a partner

3. Juggling with a group

2. Main part of the coaching session

2.1 HELPFUL TACTICAL GAMES

1. Switch of play and width game

Two teams play across the width of the field, each with goalkeepers. The attacking team must play and switch the ball from 1 side line to the other and then play the ball between a marker and the side line before a shot can be taken at goal. The ball can pass between any marker and the side line by either a pass or dribble. A goal can only count if the attacking team did not lose possession after the ball passed the outer markers.

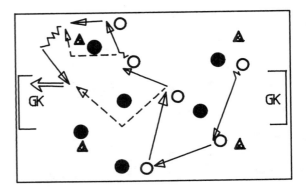

2. Horseback soccer

Two equal teams play small-sided soccer without goalkeepers. The jockey is carried on the back of the 'horse' and must not interfere in the game by obstructing others. The rider changes with the horse when the horse gets tired. There are no offsides and throw-ins are taken with a pass.

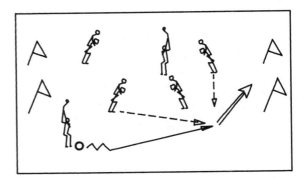

3. One touch — head to score

Two equal teams play across the field of play with or without goalkeepers. The attacking players are allowed a maximum of just 1 touch of the ball. A goal can only be scored by heading at goal.

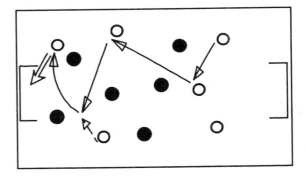

4. Head soccer

Two full-sized goals are placed 20 metres apart facing each other. Two equal teams compete against each other in a small-sided game. The ball can only be played by the head. If the ball is played by any other part of the body or drops to the ground then there is a change of possession. There are no offsides and teams can play with or without goalkeepers.

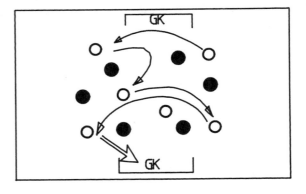

2.2 DECEPTIVE DRIBBLING AND FEINTING

At this level, deceptive dribbling and feinting techniques learnt in previous levels are reinforced.

Superstar Rivelino, well balanced and in control of the ball for Brazil

2.3 TECHNICAL–TACTICAL PROGRAM ELEMENTS

The overhead (scissors) volley kick

Today's game requires the player to become more mobile and elastic than ever before. With less time and space available the player often does not have the time to make that extra touch with the ball. As a result the overhead (scissors) volley kick has become a common element that is used in today's games.

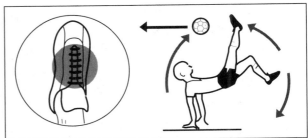

This technique would have to rate as one of the most spectacular and exciting kicks in attack and defence. The technique involves the player facing the opposite direction of the intended kick with eyes fixed on the ball. As the ball arrives the kicking foot is bent and acts as the supporting leg, maintaining body balance while the other leg moves to meet the ball. The hands now move to the ball. As the supporting leg leaves the ground the other leg has a sudden downward swing allowing the supporting leg to follow through and strike the ball. The bent hands now swing downward with the palms facing the ground. This allows a cushioning effect as it is the hands that make first contact with the ground followed by the bottom and finally the legs.

There are times when the player is unable to get completely under the ball and as a result must strike the ball using the side (scissors) volley kick. The technique here is exactly the same only the landing is on the side and on 1 hand only.

COMMON FAULTS — CORRECTIONS

1. The eyes are not fixed on the ball but on where the player is going to land. This fear of hurting oneself is corrected by exercising in a sand pit or on mats.
2. The hands do not go to meet the ball and move vertically to face the ground the moment the ball is struck.
3. There is no sudden downward swing at all to allow the supporting leg to move through and strike the ball.
4. There is no snap of the knee joint; the ankle joint is not hard and locked when striking the ball.
5. The palms of the hands do not face and make contact with the ground first.
6. The arms are straight and not bent to cushion the fall.

1. Introductory part of the coaching session

1.1 Basic running and then static exercises for flexibility without the ball

1.4 Individual corrective technical–tactical coaching .....

2. Main part of the coaching session

2.3 Technical–tactical program element

 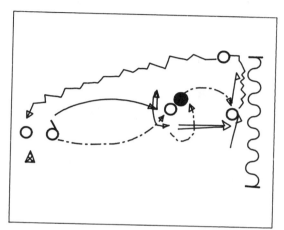

2.4 Technical–tactical shooting element

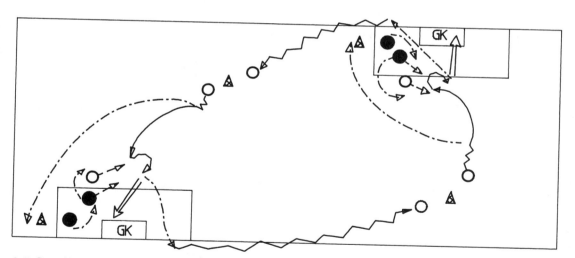

2.5 Small pitch or full pitch soccer ....

3. Concluding part of the coaching session

3.1 Summary of the coaching session

Kicking with the toe, heel and knee

Kicking with the toe: This was a technique used in the early days of soccer to kick the ball. There is less surface area when kicking with the toe than any other part of the foot and this simply means less control and accuracy. In today's modern game accuracy plays a more important role than the distance the ball is kicked. As a result kicking with the toes is of less significance. However there are situations in the game when kicking with the toe is quite useful and the only solution. One would be where the ball is caught in the water on a muddy pitch. The best way to kick the ball in this situation is with the toe. Here we are able to get under the horizontal axis with less water resistance with the toe than the instep. When there is not enough time and space to execute the intended technique, then it is of advantage to stretch out and play the ball with the toe. Another surprise kick with the toe that creates problems for the goalkeeper is when the ball is struck below the horizontal axis and over the ball. This type of kick rises quickly, 'wobbles' in the air and then suddenly dips down into goal.

Kicking with the heel: This type of kick is usually made as the attacking player is running forward and heel passing to his supporting player behind the ball. This type of pass puts the defending player in 2 minds. One is to press the ball and leave the player who played the ball free in space. The other is to press the player who played the ball and leave the receiving player free with the ball. Because of this surprise element the balance in defence can be broken and a goal-scoring situation created. With kicking with the heel the ball comes in contact with the heel bone. The technique involves the player stepping over the ball and playing it back with the heel. The pass can be made with the ball between the legs or when the ball is to the side where 1 leg crosses over the other to execute the pass.

Kicking with the knee: When the arriving ball bounces or arrives on the full, in front of the player, then a quick pass can be made with the use of the knee (patella). This pass is very uncommon in the game but can be used in tight situations as an urgent pass or clearance. For such a kick to be taken the ball is at a very uncomfortable height between the shins and the thigh. This makes it impossible for the foot to quickly make contact with the ball. As a result the knee moves to kick the ball.

COMMON FAULTS — CORRECTIONS

With all 3 techniques the faults are very similar.
1. Eyes are not fixed on the ball.
2. Hands are not wide for balance.
3. The kicking joint is not locked but loose and relaxed.
4. There is no follow through of movement after the kick.
5. The supporting leg is not bent in order to lower the centre of gravity and maintain body balance.

1. Introductory part of the coaching session

2. Main part of the coaching session

2.3 Technical–tactical program element

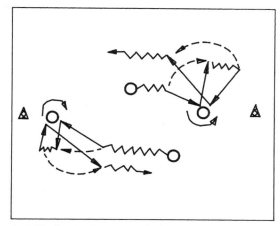 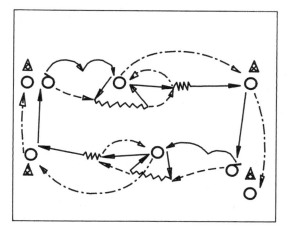

2.4 Technical–tactical shooting element

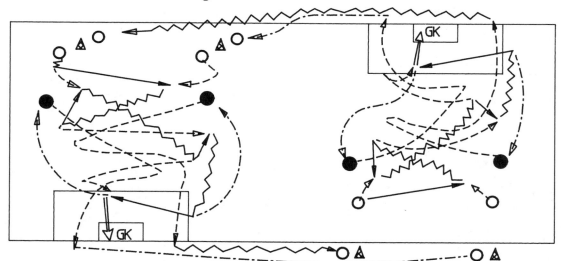

3. Concluding part of the coaching session

3.1 Summary of the coaching session

The diving header

The diving header will occur when the ball is in front of the player between the waist and the shoulder. In this situation the player has no time to control the ball and is in a difficult position for playing it with the foot. The diving header can be used in attack or defence, usually with the player running to meet the ball. The technique involves the player 'lunging' or diving at the ball with the hands bent in front of the body with the palms facing the ground.

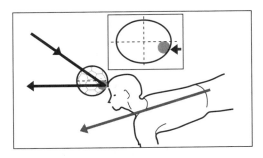

The hands must be placed in such a manner as they make contact with the ground first and allow a cushioned landing. The eyes are fixed on the ball with the neck muscles moving the head to meet the ball. At the moment of contact the muscles lock the neck joints into place to enable the middle or side zone of the head to be hard and not loose. At the moment of contact the body of the player should be near horizontal in flight with the ground.

The introductory exercises with this element should be done on sand or on a mat without the ball and once the technical execution is correct then introduce the ball.

COMMON FAULTS — CORRECTIONS

1. The player takes her eyes off the ball and looks to where it will land. The player here is more concerned about not hurting herself with the fall than heading the ball. The player should return to the introductory exercises on sand or on a mat without the ball.
2. The hands are not bent with palms facing the ground to cushion the fall.
3. The player does not make contact with the ground with both hands first but twists to fall on her side.
4. The neck muscles are loose and relaxed on contact and not locked and hard.
5. The player just falls allowing the ball to meet the head instead of diving to the ball.
6. The body is not horizontal to the ground at the moment of contact.

1. Introductory part of the coaching session
   1.1 Basic running and then static exercises for flexibility
      without the ball ....*refer to page 271*
   1.2 Active exercises for flexibility with/without the ball ....*refer to page 272*
   1.3 Juggling the ball ....*refer to page 275*
   1.4 Individual corrective technical–tactical coaching

2. Main part of the coaching session
   2.1 Helpful tactical games ....*refer to page 276*
   2.2 Deceptive dribbling and feinting techniques ....*reinforce*
   2.3 Technical–tactical program element

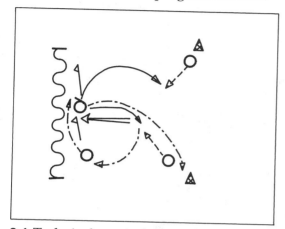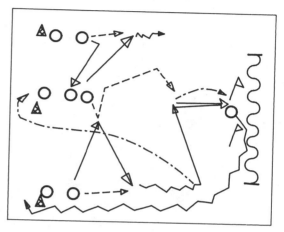

   2.4 Technical–tactical shooting element

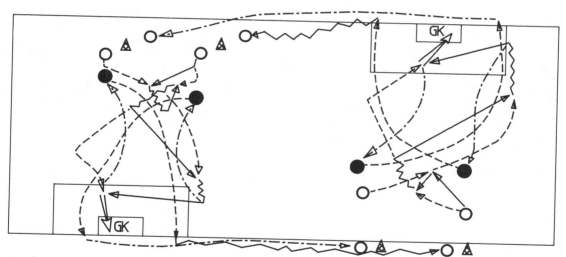

   2.5 Small pitch or full pitch soccer ....*refer to page 314*
3. Concluding part of the coaching session
   3.1 Summary of the coaching session

Intercepting the pass

For most of the game the attacking player will lose possession by interception of the pass or by a successful tackle. This element does not require any special technical quality of execution from the defender but rather the tactical ability to know the precise moment to jump forward and intercept the pass from the player she is marking. For this type of action the player must have excellent starting ability to explosively move between the ball and the attacking player before she receives.

To be successful in intercepting the pass it is important how the defending player positions herself in relation to the attacking player. Most defenders 'set up' the attacking player before the interception. For example, give the attacking player with the ball a little extra space to encourage her to make the pass, then at the moment the ball is about to be passed quickly move in and take possession. The precise moment to move in for the interception is the moment when the attacking player has the leg bent to play the ball.

There are advantages and disadvantages with the use of this technical–tactical element. The advantage is that, if executed correctly, the defending team gains possession and creates the extra man in attack with a 2:1 situation. This can be seen in the photos below.

If incorrectly executed, the attacking team gains the extra player in attack creating a 2:1 situation. This can be seen in the photos below.

COMMON FAULTS — CORRECTIONS

1. The timing of the interception is too early or too late, in both cases resulting in an unsuccessful interception.
2. Legs are not bent to lower the centre of gravity and have the body in a position to use the explosive strength to intercept.
3. Hands are not wide for balance.
4. Eyes are not fixed on the ball.
5. No feint movement away to encourage the pass.

1. Introductory part of the coaching session

1.1 Basic running and then static exercises for flexibility
without the ball .... *refer to page 271*

1.2 Active exercises for flexibility with/without the ball .... *refer to page 272*

1.3 Juggling the ball .... *refer to page 275*

1.4 Individual corrective technical–tactical coaching

2. Main part of the coaching session

2.1 Helpful tactical games .... *refer to page 276*

2.2 Deceptive dribbling and feinting techniques .... *reinforce*

2.3 Technical–tactical program element

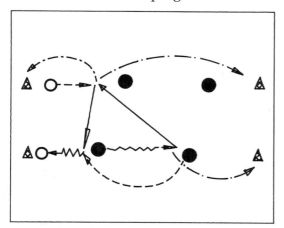 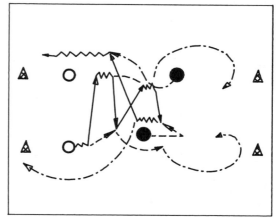

2.4 Technical–tactical shooting element

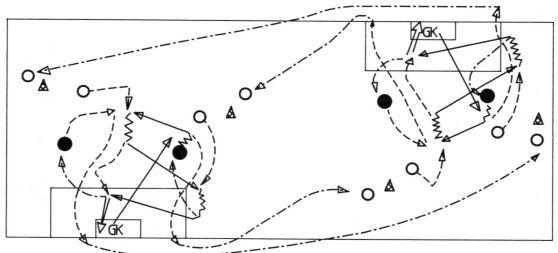

2.5 Small pitch or full pitch soccer .... *refer to page 314*

3. Concluding part of the coaching session

3.1 Summary of the coaching session

Basic combinations — 3:0

As with the previous levels these combinations represent the basic shape of the co-operation between 3 players and the basis for collective play. With passing between each other the players are able to communicate. The better the communication with the ball the better the chances of having a successful team.

The execution of the same type of pass and player movement will not be deceptive enough to outsmart the defender and in the majority of cases the passes will be intercepted and possession lost. This is why several combinations must be practised and this way the players can adapt to the given situation. When making passes, even in the 3:0 situations, players must be encouraged to disguise their intentions in order to catch the defending players off balance.

An important factor is the quality of the pass. A good player will be familiar with the qualities of his supporting player — his strengths and weaknesses — before delivering the pass.

Modern soccer demands the all round technical–tactical and physical quality of the player. Because of this priority in the game emphasis has to be given to the versatility of the player and the concept of play and not to the specialisation of the player in a specific function or position. As a result all the players must complete the attacking function of basic combinations of 3:0.

1. Introductory part of the coaching session

1.1 Basic running and then static exercises for flexibility
    without the ball .... *refer to page 271*
1.2 Active exercises for flexibility with/without the ball .... *refer to page 272*
1.3 Juggling the ball .... *refer to page 275*
1.4 Individual corrective technical–tactical coaching

2. Main part of the coaching session

2.1 Helpful tactical games .... *refer to page 276*
2.2 Deceptive dribbling and feinting techniques .... *reinforce*
2.3 Technical–tactical program element

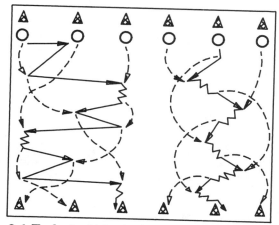
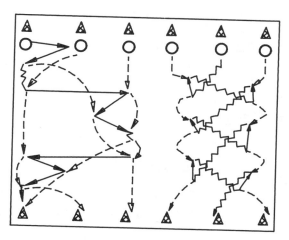

2.4 Technical–tactical shooting element

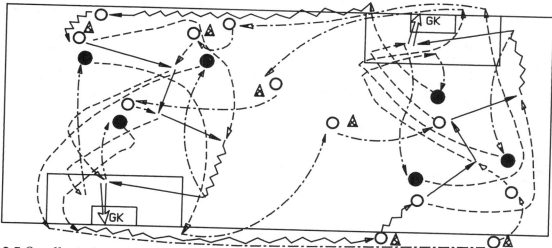

2.5 Small pitch or full pitch soccer .... *refer to page 314*

3. Concluding part of the coaching session

3.1 Summary of the coaching session

Basic combinations — 3:2

As with the previous levels these combinations represent the basic shape of the co-operation between 3 players and the basis for collective play. With passing between each other the players are able to communicate. The better the communication with the ball the better the chances of having a successful team.

The only change to the previous 3:0 combinations is that 2 token defenders are included in the exercises to create situations that the players are going to experience in the game. When making passes, even in the 3:2 situations, attacking players must be encouraged to disguise their intentions and to make a habit of catching the defending players off balance.

Another important factor is the quality of the pass. A good player will be familiar with the qualities of his supporting player — his strengths and weaknesses — before delivering the pass.

Modern soccer demands the all round technical–tactical and physical quality of the player. Because of this priority in the game emphasis has to be given to the versatility of the player and the concept of play and not to the specialisation of the player for a specific function or position. As a result all the players must complete the attacking function of basic combinations of 3:2.

1. Introductory part of the coaching session

1.1 Basic running and then static exercises for flexibility without the ball .... *refer to page 271*

1.2 Active exercises for flexibility with/without the ball .... *refer to page 272*

1.3 Juggling the ball .... *refer to page 275*

1.4 Individual corrective technical–tactical coaching

2. Main part of the coaching session

2.1 Helpful tactical games .... *refer to page 276*

2.2 Deceptive dribbling and feinting techniques .... *reinforce*

2.3 Technical–tactical program element

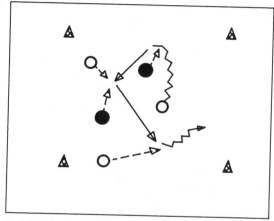 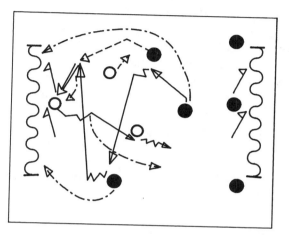

2.4 Technical–tactical shooting element

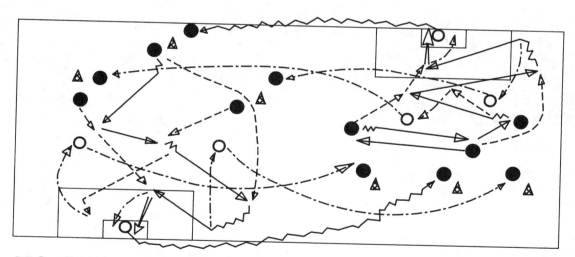

2.5 Small pitch or full pitch soccer .... *refer to page 314*

3. Concluding part of the coaching session

3.1 Summary of the coaching session

Team technical–tactical playing patterns — attack

In the observation of teams one is able to observe the different patterns of play. For example, some teams prefer the slow build up, playing the ball wide, while others prefer the long pass direct to the target players and so on.

When the coach analyses her team she then goes about implementing patterns of play in attack and defence that will best suit her players and not the opponent. The pattern must represent the long-term objective. With all technical–tactical elements the coach works to the team's strengths and to the opponent's weaknesses.

Players will develop certain habits from an early age. It is important that the habits learnt in the technical–tactical soccer development program are continued right through to the elements of playing patterns in attack.

It is clear that if young players practise without direction and correction they will develop bad habits that will be almost impossible to correct at senior level. The establishing of playing patterns is just 1 part in the development of the youth that will make him or her a complete player who meets the demands of today's modern game.

Establishing and practising patterns of play is hard work but there is no other way to get the players to understand player or ball movement in specific situations. It should be emphasised that the players should express their individuality and creativity within the basic framework of the playing patterns.

While practising the playing patterns in attack the player should always have the creative mind operating and imagine that he is in the real situation. He should be looking to create space with the deceptive runs. If the individual player is able to create space then he has also created time. Space and time are the necessary ingredients whereby players can demonstrate their abilities.

The great Diego Maradona beats 2 Australian defenders in a 1994 World Cup qualifier

The gradual progression in teaching basic technical–tactical playing patterns is as follows:

1. Talk to the players about the pattern you are going to introduce and its role in the game.

2. The players exercise the pattern without pressure and without a ball. There is correction from the coach.

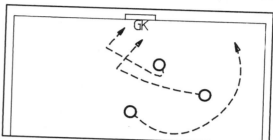

3. The players exercise the pattern without pressure and with a ball. The movements are linked to specific psychomotor skills that the player will need in the game.

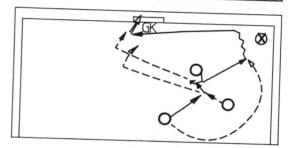

4. The players exercise the pattern with token pressure and with a ball.

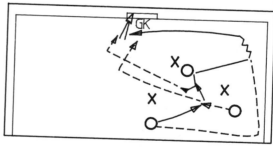

5. The players exercise the pattern with full pressure and with a ball. It is in these situations that the player is encouraged to express his individuality and creativity within the basic pattern of play framework.

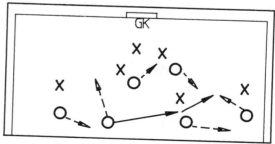

The following exercises are examples of basic technical–tactical playing patterns in attack.

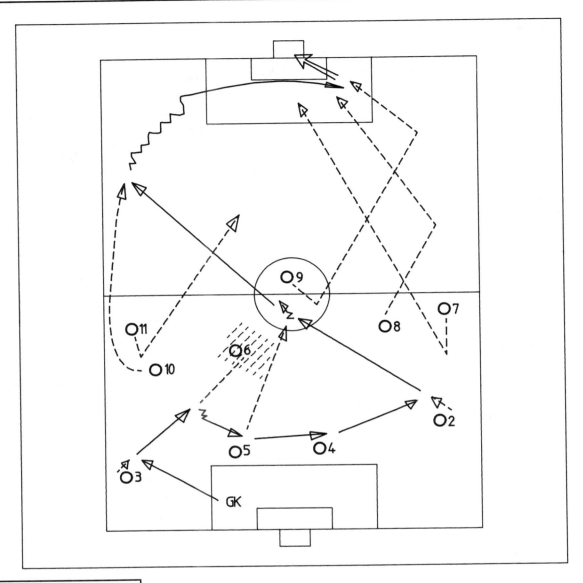

SWITCH OF PLAY

03 receives the ball from GK. The ball is played to 06, moving to the ball to create space behind him. The ball is played across the back to 02 who makes a 1-touch pass to 05 moving into the space created by 06. 010 overlaps 011 into a space behind the right full back and receives the switch of play pass from 05. 010 gets behind the defenders and puts in a cross for the supporting players to attack with their diagonal runs.

This pattern is to be exercised:
1. player without the ball — without pressure
2. player with the ball — without pressure
3. player with the ball — with token pressure
4. player with the ball — with full pressure

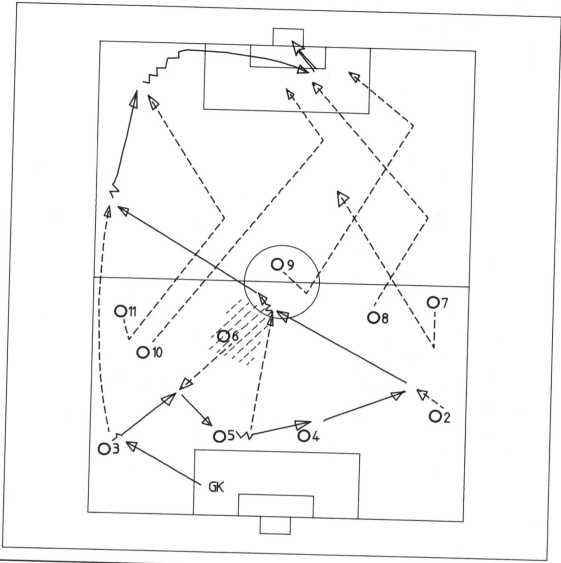

OVERLAPPING FULL BACK

03 wide, receives the ball from GK. The ball is played to 06 who is moving to the ball, creating space in the middle of the field. The ball is played back to 05 and 04 to draw the attacking players deep and out of position. 02 receives the pass from 04 who makes the pass into the space created by 06 for 05. During this time 011 and 010 have moved off the left side, taking defending players, creating space for the overlap. From behind the ball 03 makes the surprise sprint and overlaps into space on to the pass from 05 and finishes with a cross for the supporting players to attack.

The pattern is to be exercised:
1. player without the ball — without pressure
2. player with the ball — without pressure
3. player with the ball — with token pressure
4. player with the ball — with full pressure

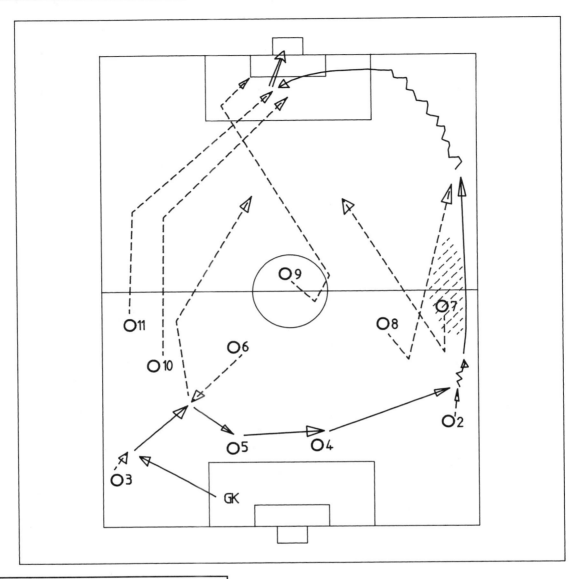

BALL PLAYED UP THE FLANK

03 receives the ball from GK and plays to 06, moving to the ball. The ball is then played with 1 touch to 05, 04 to 02. Both 07 and 08 move to the ball, creating space down the right side of the field behind the defending team. 08 quickly changes direction, sprinting at a diagonal up the line on to the pass from 02. 08 gets behind the defenders and puts in a cross for the supporting players to attack.

This pattern is to be exercised:

1. player without the ball — without pressure
2. player with the ball — without pressure
3. player with the ball — with token pressure
4. player with the ball — with full pressure

SITUATIONAL GROUP TRAINING — ATTACK

In these situational group training elements 1 group attacks a goal while the other group defends. The exercise is completed with a shot at goal or loss of possession. The groups then alternate so that the defending team becomes the attacking team while the attacking team now defends their goal. These group exercises can be 2:2, 3:3, 4:4, etc. or 3:2, 4:3, 5:4, etc. Goalkeepers do not alternate but defend their goals. The emphasis here is on specific attacking elements.

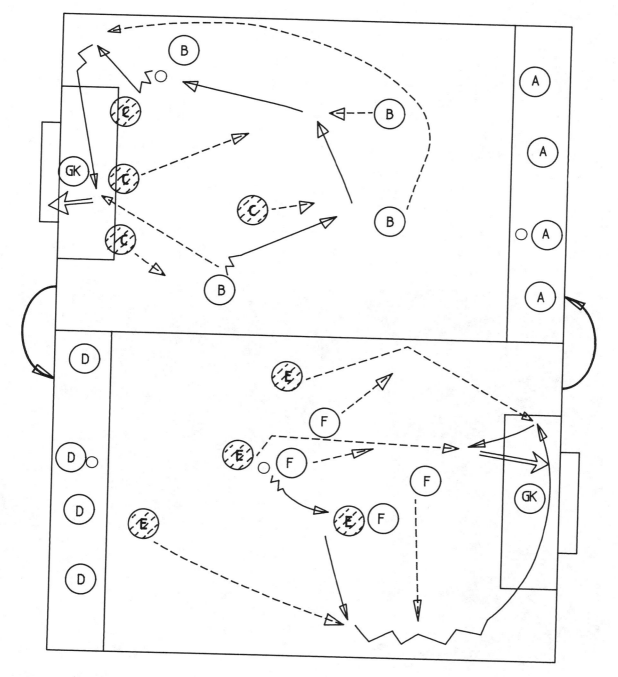

Team technical–tactical playing patterns — defence

As with playing patterns in attack the coach must implement playing patterns in defence. The patterns may vary from playing a zone, pressing in the opponent's half, combined zone and so on.

When the coach analyses his team he then goes about implementing patterns of play in attack and defence that will best suit his players. The pattern must represent the long-term objective. With all technical–tactical elements the coach works to the team's strengths and to the opponent's weaknesses.

Players will develop certain habits from an early age. It is important that the habits learnt in the technical–tactical soccer development program are continued right through to the elements of playing patterns in defence.

It is clear that if young players practise without direction and correction they will develop bad habits that will be almost impossible to correct at senior level. The establishing of playing patterns in defence is just one part in the development of the youth that will make him or her a complete player who meets the demands of today's modern game.

Establishing and practising patterns of play is hard work but there is no other way to get the players to understand player or ball movement in specific situations. It should be emphasised that the players should express their individuality and creativity within the basic framework of the playing patterns.

While practising the playing patterns in defence the player should always have his head up looking for solutions in advance and looking to reduce space for the attacking players. He should always have the creative mind operating as if it were the real situation. If he is able to reduce space he then has also reduced time for the attacking player. Space and time are the necessary ingredients whereby players can demonstrate their abilities.

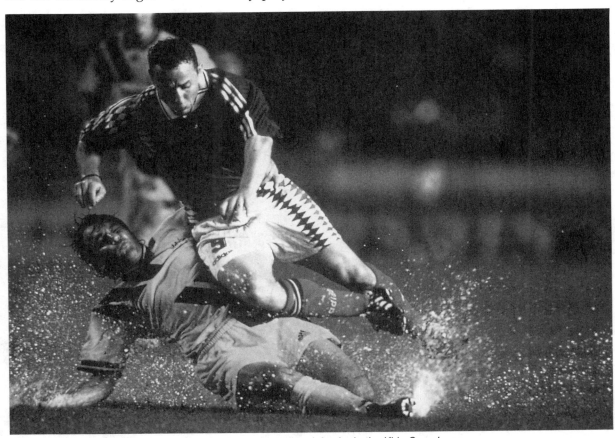

French goalscoring machine Papin is tackled by an Australian defender in the Kirin Cup, Japan

The gradual progression in teaching basic technical–tactical playing patterns is as follows:

1. Talk to the players about the pattern you are going to introduce and its role in the game.

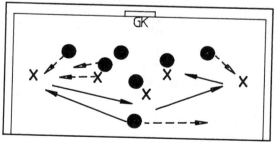

2. The players exercise the pattern without pressure and without a ball. There is correction from the coach.

3. The players exercise the pattern without pressure and with a ball. The movements are linked to specific psychomotor skills that the player will need in the game.

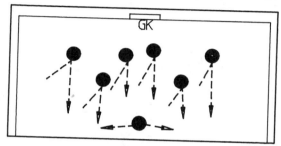

4. The players exercise the pattern with token pressure and with a ball.

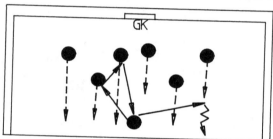

5. The players exercise the pattern with full pressure and with a ball. It is in these situations that the player is encouraged to express his individuality and creativity within the basic pattern of play framework.

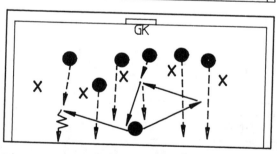

The following exercises are examples of basic technical–tactical playing patterns in defence.

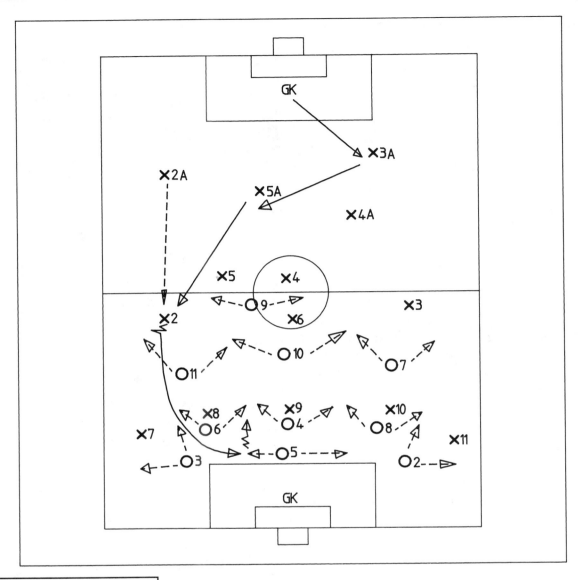

PLAYING THE ZONE

Team X starts the pattern from their goalkeeper with a slow build-up.

Team 0 recover quickly behind the ball into their half and set up the zone in the last quarter. Team X is not pressured in their half and is given space and time to play the ball. Player 09 plays a zone between X5 and X4, preventing either of them coming forward with the ball. As team X comes forward team 0 have all the passing angles and playing space reduced to a minimum. Following a successful interception by 05, team 0 is now able to go for goal on a counter attack and use the created space behind the defending X team.

The pattern is to be exercised:
1. player without the ball — without pressure
2. player with the ball — without pressure
3. player with the ball — with token pressure
4. player with the ball — with full pressure

PRESSING THE PLAYER FROM A ZONE FORMATION

Team 0 recovers behind the ball into a zone. At the moment the ball is played back to a supporting X player the pressing of the player is applied. Together 05, 010 and 09 apply a changeover press with GK moving out of the penalty area and taking up the role of sweeper. In a very short time, before a second touch of the ball is made by X5, all X players are in a pressing of the player situation with 09 forcing X5 into a hurried pass. From this situation team 0 manages to gain possession and go on to the counter attack.

This pattern is to be exercised:
1. player without the ball — without pressure
2. player with the ball — without pressure
3. player with the ball — with token pressure
4. player with the ball — with full pressure

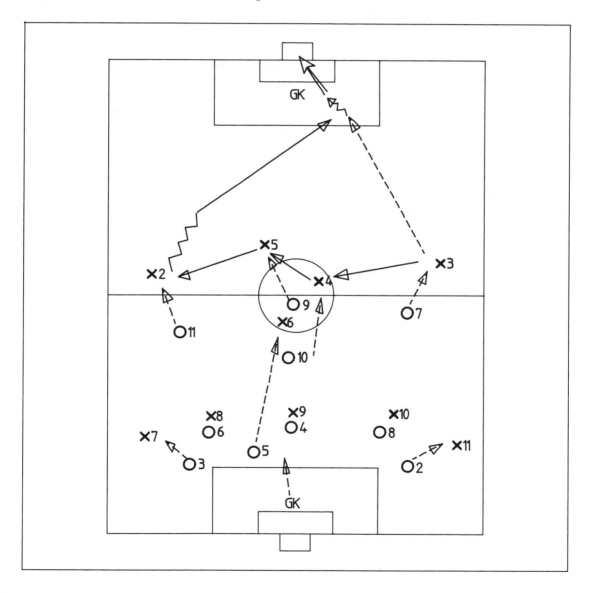

PRESSING THE BALL IN THE OPPONENT'S FRONT HALF

Player X3 is given space to receive a pass from GK. At the moment the ball is about to be played the pressing of the ball commences by 07. At the same time 09 prevents a return pass to GK while 011 closes the passing angle from X3 to X4 and X5. The only player to have free space in this pressing situation is X2. It is very unlikely that X3 would make a pass to X2 across the goal area in this pressing situation. When team 0 gains possession they then attack the opponent's goal.

This pattern is to be exercised:
1. player without the ball — without pressure
2. player with the ball — without pressure
3. player with the ball — with token pressure
4. player with the ball — with full pressure

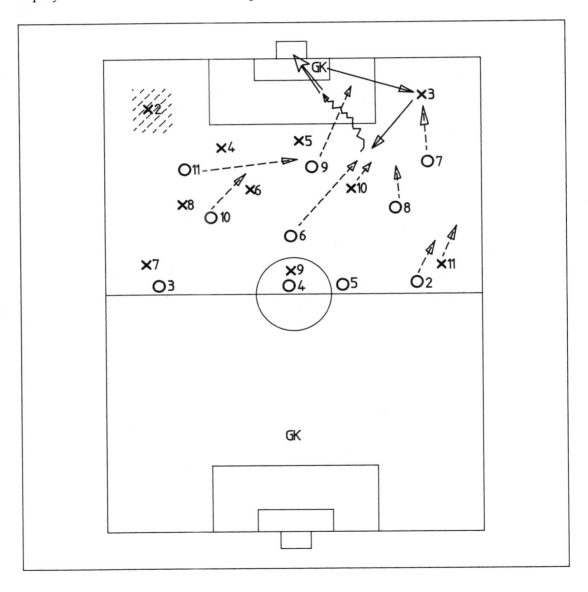

UMBRO

SITUATIONAL GROUP TRAINING — DEFENCE

In these situational group training elements 1 group attacks a goal while the other group defends. The exercise is completed with a shot at goal or loss of possession. The groups then alternate so that the defending team becomes the attacking team while the attacking team now defends their goal. These group exercises can be 2:2, 3:3, 4:4, etc. or 3:2, 4:3, 5:4, etc. Goalkeepers do no alternate but defend their goals. The emphasis here is on specific defending elements.

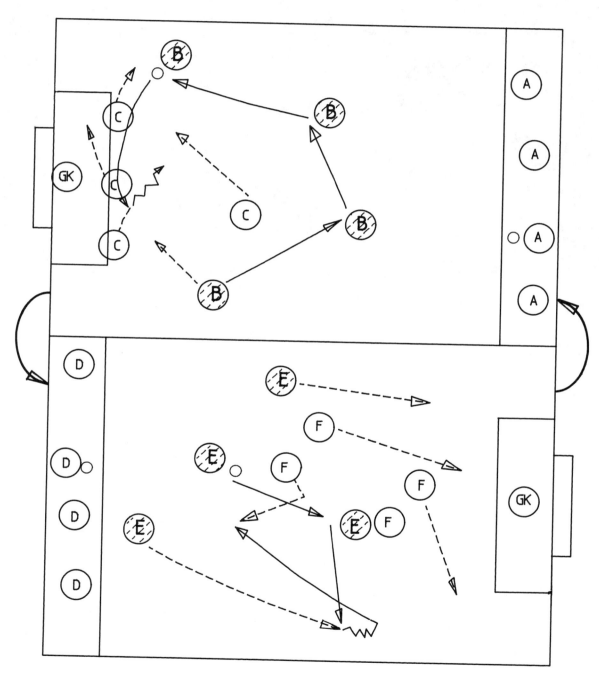

Superstar Paolo Rossi, top goalscorer for Italy at the 1982 World Cup finals in Spain

Set play — attacking situations

Almost 50% of goals in today's modern game are the direct result of well rehearsed set plays. Whenever the referee has stopped the game, because of a foul or the ball passing over the line, all players have to wait for play to restart. The team that gets the restart has a big advantage in that:

1. no defending player can tackle before the ball has been played;
2. all defending players must stand at least 10 yards from the ball;
3. the attacking players all have time to be in position before the ball is kicked;
4. the attacking players know in advance what set pattern is going to be played.

The selection of which set piece to apply will depend to a great extent on the general tactical plan and playing conditions. This would include the playing surface (bumpy, hard, soft, muddy), the weather (windy, wet, raining, sunny), etc. Set play in attacking situations would represent:

1. free kick with defending players in a wall
2. free kick without defending players in a wall
3. corner
4. throw- in
5. penalty kick

1. FREE KICK WITH DEFENDING PLAYERS IN A WALL

A free kick can be either direct or indirect. The direct free kick is where a direct shot can be taken at goal while an indirect free kick is where the ball must be played by another player before it is in play. This is represented by the referee raising his hand in the air. In these situations the defenders will form a wall to prevent the direct shot at goal. As a result the attacking players have to be precise and deceptive to catch the defending team off balance. Usually there are 3 or more players around the ball. This often confuses the defenders about who is actually going to execute the move. This disguise is often quite successful.

The disadvantage of the wall is that it blocks the direct path of the ball to the goal. The great advantage is that the players in the wall cannot mark any of the attacking players. The following 4 combinations can be used as examples.

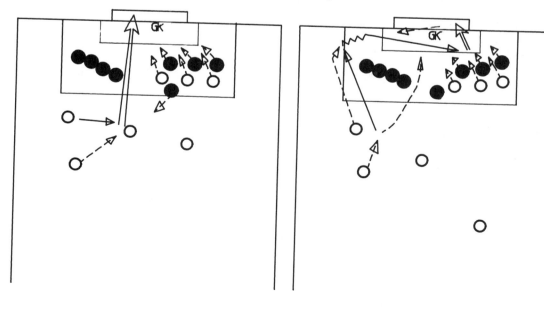

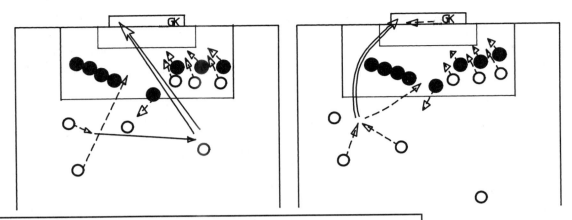

2. FREE KICK WITHOUT DEFENDING PLAYERS IN A WALL

There are many free kicks given from out wide on the wings. These positions do not provide a serious threat to goal and as a result there is no necessity for the defending team to put up a wall. The great disadvantage with the wall is that those players in it are out of the game, giving the opposition the extra players in attack.

The free kicks taken from out wide are more service balls than direct shots at goal. Here, as with all the other set moves, precision and organisation is essential. The following 4 combinations can be used as examples.

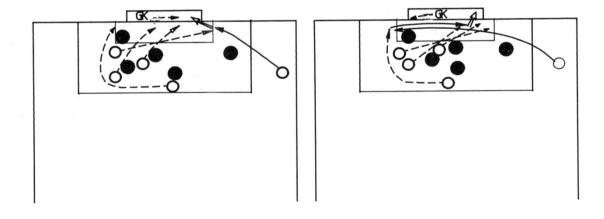

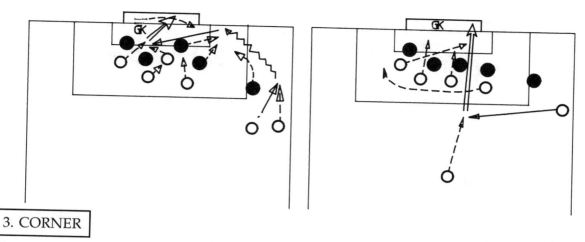

3. CORNER

There are many different combinations that can be used when taking a corner kick. The corner kick can be taken with an outswinging or inswinging ball, near or far post or short with the co-operation of 2 players. Whatever the solution the attacking team always works to its strengths and to the opponent's weaknesses. The following 4 combinations can be used as examples.

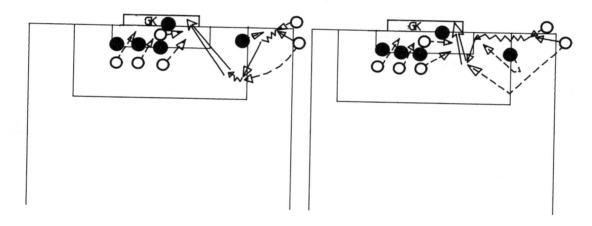

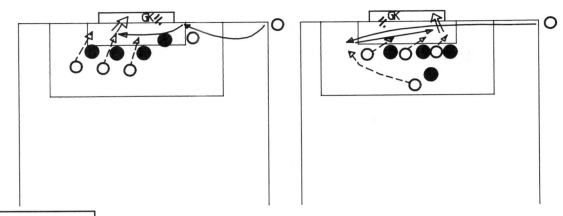

4. THROW-IN

The aim of every team is to maintain possession after the throw-in. The majority of players are more relaxed at defending throw-ins, so a mobile player moving into space on to the throw can cause quite a bit of damage and throw the defence completely off balance. The supporting player must also know that she can receive the ball from a throw-in and not be offside.

The priority, when taking a throw-in, should be:

1. Throw to the unmarked supporting player.
2. Throw up the line to a player moving into space.
3. Throw square to a supporting player.
4. Throw back to a supporting player.

The long throw to the supporting player at the near post is particularly dangerous and goal-threatening. The target player has to be tall and have good heading qualities. Here the aim is to draw the goalkeeper out of position, to near post, with the target player heading over the goalkeeper into the goalmouth. The following 4 combinations can be used as examples.

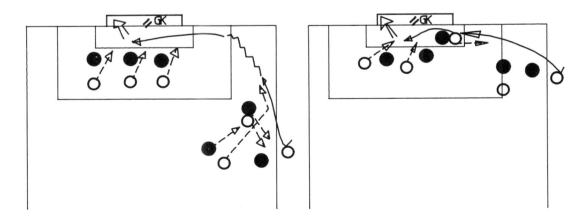

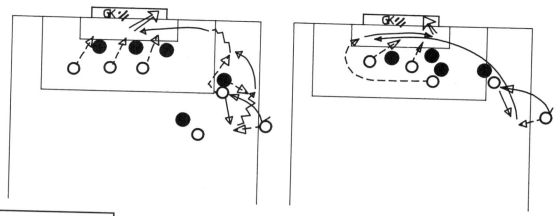

5. PENALTY KICK

A penalty is a direct free kick taken by 1 attacking player at the opponent's goal defended by the goalkeeper. A penalty results from a foul in the 18 yard goalkeeper area.

A well taken penalty is almost impossible to save. The ideal kick is the 1 taken hard and accurately. Some players, however, prefer to concentrate on accuracy while others concentrate on power.

The usual practice with players taking penalties is as follows:

1. Place the ball on the spot and make certain it will remain still.

2. Make up your mind as to placement or power.

3. Do not let any distractions influence or change your mind.

4. Face the ball, concentrate, then move smoothly up to the ball and execute the penalty.

The penalty kick will vary from player to player. The following 2 combinations can be used as examples.

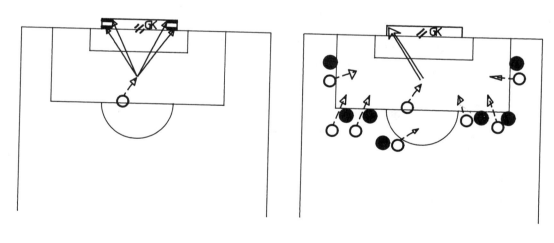

Set play — defending situations

As with attacking situations the defending situations from set play also involve:

1. formation of the wall
2. free kicks
3. corner
4. throw-in
5. penalty kick

As almost 50% of goals are scored from set play the same can be said for the defence. However, a better organised and disciplined team, in these situations, will increase the percentage substantially in favour of the defence from set play.

The difficulty in defending set play is that the attacking team can place a large number of players in front of the ball in planned attacking positions and the defending player must stand at least 10 yards from the ball and not apply any ball pressure until it is kicked.

1. FORMATION OF THE WALL

If the awarded free kick represents a direct danger to the goal, the defending players will form a wall. The wall is usually made up of 4 players but this number will be determined by the goalkeeper. The theory is usually the more acute the angle to goal the less players required in the wall.

The wall should be set in position by the goalkeeper by lining up the first defender in the wall with the remaining wall players falling into line. The first defender in the wall faces the goal where the goalkeeper lines him up with the ball. Once satisfied, the first defender is instructed to turn 180° to face the ball with the other wall members falling into place. The tallest player blocks the near angle to the smaller players. While careful consideration is given to the wall height, the players who have better tackling and pressing abilities are left to mark space and players, while the remainder are placed in the wall.

If the wall is not formed correctly then the attacking player will take advantage by having a direct shot through the 'hole'. Otherwise he will be forced to swerve the ball around or over the wall or make a short pass for a supporting player to strike.

The 'live wall' is put in place to block the near angle to goal while the goalkeeper blocks the far angle. The goalkeeper should be in the middle of the goal, behind the wall, with a view of the ball.

Once in place the wall must not move or break until the shot or pass is taken. The following 2 combinations can be used as examples.

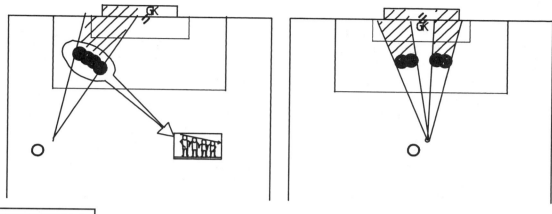

2. FREE KICKS

Defence from free kicks from the side are similar to the corner kick situation, only more dangerous as the attacking angle at goal is greater.

Depending on the distance from goal and the quality of the attacking player, the goalkeeper may decide to place 1 or even 2 defending players in front of the ball to form a wall to block or distract the player from finding his target.

In the scoring quarter of the field the defensive pattern in such situations will be either pressing the player without the ball or zone or combined zone defence and when the ball is kicked, pressing the player moving to strike the ball.

Free kicks are more effective if taken quickly, with the sole purpose of catching the defenders off balance. The quicker the defenders get behind the ball and take up their positions the more difficult it will be for the attacking team to penetrate the defence. The following 2 combinations can be used as examples.

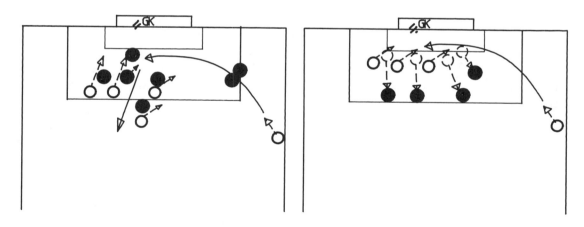

3. CORNER

The defence from a corner kick is very similar to that of a free kick.

A defending player should always stand 10 yards from the ball near the base line. The 2 simple reasons for this are: to try and disturb the concentration of the attacking player about to kick the ball and be in a position to block or intercept a pass.

Usually the goalkeeper will have 2 defenders taking up positions at the goal posts. The 2 players usually do not have the height and defensive heading abilities of the other players. Their job is to protect the goal when the goalkeeper leaves it.

The defensive pattern with corners can vary from pressing the man without the ball, zone or combined zone defence and pressing the player about to strike the ball.

There is a tendency today for the whole team to be in the penalty area, excluding 1 player at half way and the defending player 10 yards from the ball. The pattern here is to clear the ball and everyone sprints to half way with the nearest player to the ball pressing the ball. This way, if the defending team gains possession they go on the counter attack or if the opposing player plays the ball forward his team is caught in the offside trap. The following 2 combinations can serve as examples.

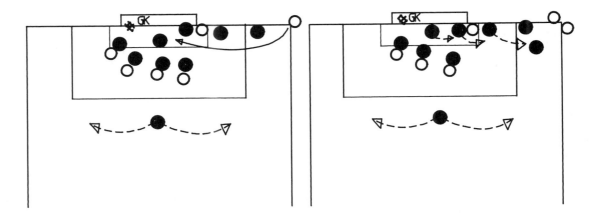

4. THROW-IN

The greatest problem in defence from throw-ins is the lack of concentration and discipline of the defending team when pressuring the opponent.

A well taken throw-in can create a goalscoring opportunity. Many games have been lost because of poor defensive abilities in this area.

Unless specific tactical reasons are given, I see no reason why all attacking players from a throw-in should be pressured. Usually defending players will pressure the attacking players near the ball and on the field of play, but rarely is the thrower pressured. As a result the thrower receives the ball back and is able to play the ball into space or to a player and maintain possession and attack.

It must be stressed that in these situations all players, including the thrower, are to be marked, tracked and pressured goalside into making a mistake. As a result possession will be lost.

In the front quarter some teams prefer to take the long throw to the near post. This throw is aimed at drawing the goalkeeper out of position with the target player heading the ball into the goal mouth, creating an ideal scoring opportunity. To defend this set play the target player should be pressured from in front and behind, with all other players pressing the attacking players goalside in the penalty area. The following 2 combinations can serve as examples.

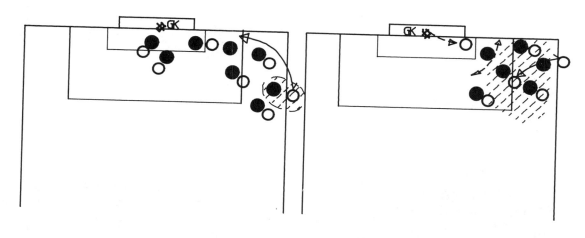

5. PENALTY

A well taken penalty kick is almost impossible to save as the reaction speed is simply not quick enough to move the body parts into position behind the ball.

The only possible way to save a set play penalty kick is either to know the kicking habits of the player concerned or for the penalty kick to be inaccurate. Knowing the habit, the goalkeeper simply makes up her mind which way she will dive before the kick is taken.

Some goalkeepers purposely stand slightly off centre in goal to provoke the penalty taker to aim for that side. Others sway and make other movements to distract the player and increase the pressure before the kick.

Australia scores from a penalty against Argentina at the Sydney Football Stadium

Superstar Zico, one of the all-time greats of Brazilian soccer

2.5 SMALL PITCH OR FULL PITCH SOCCER

Every coaching session, at this level, should end with a small-sided game on a small pitch; however, there will be times when a coaching session will end with or consist of a full-sided game. But it is the small-sided situations that the young players enjoy most. They are in constant contact with the ball, enabling the technical–tactical and physical skills to be put into practice.

The aim when playing small-sided games is simply to attack the opponent's goal in the phase of attack and defend your goal in the phase of defence. The phase of attack is that moment your team gains possession, while the phase of defence is the moment the team has lost possession.

This is called soccer tactics — the art by which the player's technical and physical qualities are used to achieve the best possible result.

Tactics can be divided into 3 distinct categories:

1. *Individual tactics:* pressing the player, pressing the ball, creating space, dribbling, feinting, receiving, heading, passing, shooting, etc.
2. *Group tactics:* the mobility and interchange of players, the recovery behind the ball of the front attacking line, defending the goal, counter attacking, offside tactics, co-operation with the goalkeeper, playing wide or through the middle, etc.
3. *Team tactics:* keeping possession, slow build up, long direct penetrating passes, playing the high ball, keeping the ball low, switch of play, recovering behind the ball into a zone, pressing on all parts of the field, etc.

Team tactics used by the coach will also be determined by many factors that may include the way the opponent plays, state of the playing surface, the team's position in the competition, phase of the game, the weather, etc.

The technical–tactical elements in the phase of attack are:

1. *Mobility:* the ability to move with or without the ball to create playing space.
2. *Penetration:* the ability to get past or behind defenders, with or without the ball.
3. *Width and depth:* the ability to create playing space across and along the field of play.
4. *Switch of play:* the ability to draw defenders out of position and exploit space on the opposite side.

The technical–tactical elements in the phase of defence are:

1. *Balance:* the ability to limit the creation of space, penetration and passing angles.
2. *Pressing the player without the ball:* the ability to reduce the time and playing space an attacking player will have when receiving the ball.
3. *Pressing the ball:* the ability to reduce the time and space the attacking player will have to receive, pass, dribble or shoot at goal.
4. *Zone and combined zone formations:* the ability to recover goalside of the ball, cover an area, and press any player entering that zone.

> **Note: It is necessary for coaches, coaching at all levels, to understand the technical–tactical elements in the phase of attack and defence. In level 5 greater emphasis is placed on tactical and physical development.**

Order of coaching technical–tactical elements in attack and defence

The following technical–tactical elements in attack and defence are to be applied and reinforced at each level.

	TE–TA *elements in attack*				**TE–TA** *elements in defence*			
	Number 1	*Number 2*	*Number 3*	*Number 4*	*Number 1*	*Number 2*	*Number 3*	*Number 4*
Level 1 (5 to 8 years)	Unlimited touches with the ball Playing for fun				Unlimited touches with the ball Playing for fun			
Level 2 (9 to 10 years)	Mobility Maximum 3 touches Reinforce level 1				Balance Reinforce level 1			
Level 3 (11 to 12 years)	Mobility Maximum 2 touches Reinforce levels 1 and 2	Penetration			Balance Reinforce levels 1 and 2	Pressing the player without the ball		
Level 4 (13 to 14 years)	Mobility Maximum 1 touch Reinforce levels 1 to 3	Penetration Reinforce level 3	Width and depth		Balance Reinforce levels 1 to 3	Pressing the player without the ball Reinforce level 3	Pressing the ball	
Level 5 (15 to 16 years)	Mobility Maximum 1 touch Reinforce levels 1 to 4	Penetration Reinforce levels 3 and 4	Width and depth Reinforce level 4	Switch of play	Balance Reinforce levels 1 to 4	Pressing the player without the ball Reinforce levels 3 and 4	Pressing the ball Reinforce level 4	Zone and combined zone defence
Level 6 (17+ years)	Mobility Maximum 1 touch Reinforce levels 1 to 5	Penetration Reinforce levels 3 to 5	Width and depth Reinforce levels 4 and 5	Switch of play Reinforce level 5	Balance Reinforce levels 1 to 5	Pressing the player without the ball Reinforce levels 3 to 5	Pressing the ball Reinforce levels 4 and 5	Zone and combined zone defence Reinforce level 5

Technical–tactical elements in attack

SWITCH OF PLAY

Switch of play is the ability to draw defenders out of position and exploit space on the opposite side. It is common for defending players to retreat into a zone and reduce the working space the attacking team has with the ball.

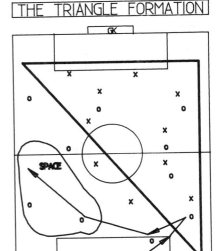

In the majority of defensive play one will find the 'triangle' formation. At the top will be the player either pressuring or delaying the attacking player, while behind will be the supporting defenders creating the base. These supporting defending players are restricting the passing and angles of support of the attacking team. It is in this situation that the attacking player, at the top of the triangle, is able to play the ball across the field of play into free space for a switch of play. This movement immediately draws players from the base to reduce the attacking space. As a result an imbalance is created which could result in a goalscoring opportunity. In today's modern game all attacking players in front of the ball are pressed by defenders to reduce their time and space with the ball; it is very rare to have any player pressed behind the ball.

With this quick switch of play element, it is the players behind the ball who are encouraged to go forward and exploit the space on the opposite side of play.

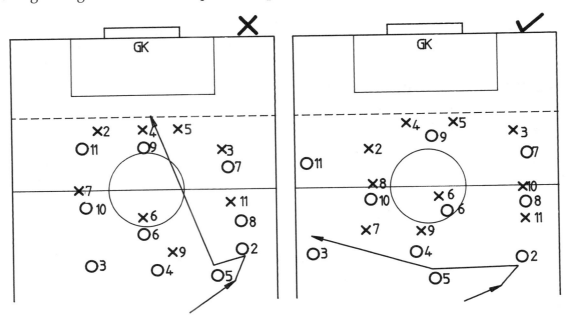

Technical–tactical elements in defence

ZONE AND COMBINED ZONE DEFENCE

Zone and combined zone defence is the ability to recover goalside of the ball, cover an area, and press any player entering that zone.

With zone formations the defending players must quickly recover behind the ball, mark a zone, and restrict space and passing angles that an attacking player can play in.

There are several ways to play in the zone defence:

1. When the attacking player enters the defender's zone, then pressing the player is applied with the attacking player followed everywhere in the back quarter. The disadvantage here is that the mobile attacking player will create space for other players to use in the zone.

2. When the attacking player enters the defender's zone, pressing applies only within the zone. The defending player does not leave his zone. When 2 attacking players enter the zone the defender is at a disadvantage as a 2:1 situation has developed.

3. Play a player zone and, when the attacking player enters the zone area, adopt a pressing of the ball or pressing of the player.

When playing these formations, players retreat behind the ball towards their own goal but face the attack. By not committing oneself and being beaten in a 1:1, this can be an extremely effective way of delaying the attacking players and reducing the space they can use in the front quarter.

The combined zone defence is preferred by many teams where the zone defence is combined with pressing the player or the ball. If the opponents have a very skilful and match-winning player then 1 player will have the role of marking him out of the game while the rest of the team simply play zone.

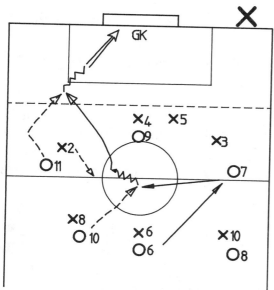

Team X fail to get behind the ball into a zone formation. O10 gets goal side of X8 and receives the pass from O7, creating a 2:1 with O11 against X2. O11 passes the ball to strike at goal

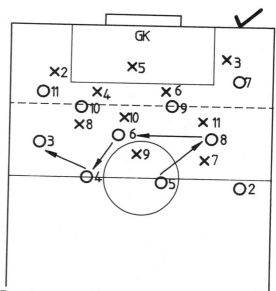

Team X successfully gets behind the ball, into a zone and restricts space and passing angles for the attacking team

The laws of the game

1. *The field of play*
   Length — 100 to 130 yards
   Width — 50 to 100 yards
   The goal area — 6×20 yards
   The penalty area — 18×44 yards
   The corner area — 1 yard
   The goals — shall be 8 yards apart joined by a horizontal cross-bar 8 feet high
   The centre circle — shall have a radius of 10 yards

2. *The ball* — shall be a size 5 and of leather

3. *Number of players* — a match shall be played by 2 teams consisting of not more than 11 players each; each team includes a goalkeeper

4. *Referees and linesmen* — a referee and linesmen shall be appointed to officiate at each game

5. *Duration* — 45 minutes each way with 10 minutes for half-time

6. *The start of play* — before or after goals are scored, play is started by a player taking a place kick at the centre. All defending players must be in their half and outside the circle

7. *The ball out of play* — when it has wholly crossed the goal line or touch line, when in the air or on the ground

8. *Offside* — the offside law shall apply at this level

9. *Fouls and misconduct* — the player is penalised by awarding a free kick

10. *Free kicks* — all free kicks can result in a direct or indirect shot at goal. All opposing players shall be at least 10 yards from the ball

11. *Penalty kicks* — the penalty kick is taken 12 yards from the goal line

12. *Throw-in* — at the point where the ball crossed the line the throw is taken with both hands behind the head and with both feet on the ground

13. *Goal kick* — at the side where the ball crossed the line the ball is placed in the goal area and kicked into play

14. *Corner kick* — if the ball passes over the goal line, excluding the goals, and is last played by the defending team, then a player from the attacking team takes a free kick from the corner of the field

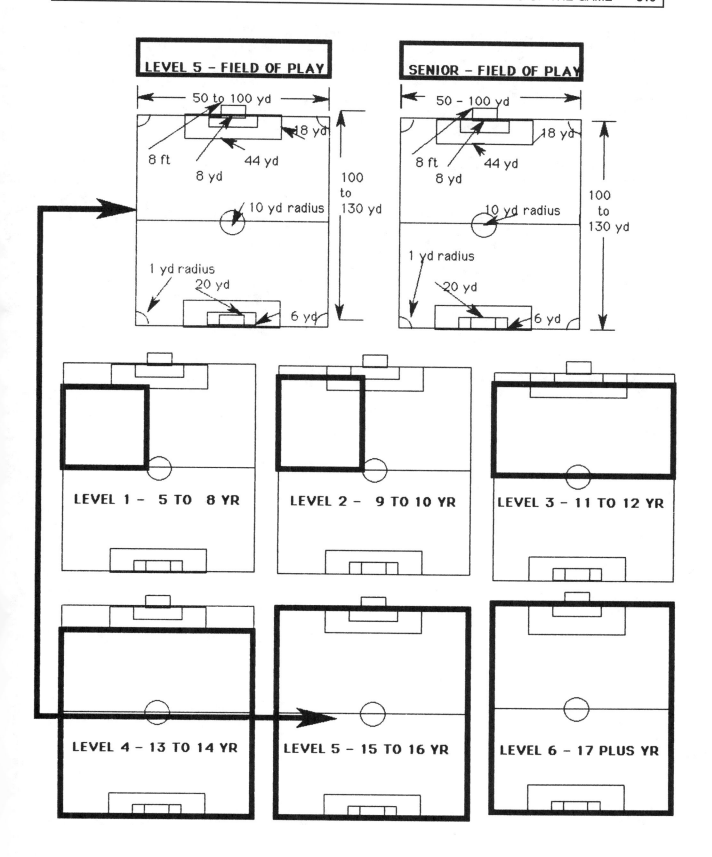

LEVEL 5 – FIELD OF PLAY

50 to 100 yd

18 yd
8 ft
44 yd
8 yd
100 to 130 yd
10 yd radius
1 yd radius
20 yd
6 yd

SENIOR – FIELD OF PLAY

50 – 100 yd

18 yd
8 ft
44 yd
8 yd
100 to 130 yd
10 yd radius
1 yd radius
20 yd
6 yd

LEVEL 1 – 5 TO 8 YR

LEVEL 2 – 9 TO 10 YR

LEVEL 3 – 11 TO 12 YR

LEVEL 4 – 13 TO 14 YR

LEVEL 5 – 15 TO 16 YR

LEVEL 6 – 17 PLUS YR

UMBRO

Superstar Diego Maradona scoring one of the greatest goals ever seen in soccer in the 1986 World Cup in Mexico

technical–tactical elements

Active exercises for flexibility with/without the ball

Group exercises no. 1

As with the static exercises, these active exercises are also designed to prepare the body for the coaching session and to enhance performance.

1.

2.

3.

4.

5.

6.

Group exercises no. 2

As with the static exercises, these active exercises are also designed to prepare the body for the coaching session and to enhance performance.

1.

2.

3.

4.

5.

6.

Group exercises no. 3

As with the static exercises, these active exercises are also designed to prepare the body for the coaching session and enhance performance.

1.

2.

3.

4.

5.

6.

Juggling the ball

Juggling the ball is simply keeping the ball off the ground, playing it with all parts of the body except from the arms to the hands.

There is no better exercise for young players than juggling the ball to get universal feeling and confidence with the ball.

When juggling, it is necessary to be relaxed and have good body balance.

Juggling the ball is an important introductory part of each coaching session.

1. Juggling with the use of the shoulder

2. Juggling and catching the ball on the back of the neck

3. Juggling with the use of the heel

Helpful tactical games

1. Head volleyball

The area on which the game is played is the size of a volleyball court with a net 2.5 metres high. The game is started with a serve, throwing the ball and heading over the net from behind the base line. Points can only be won while the team has service. The ball can be headed a maximum of 4 times before passing over the net. The ball is dead if it hits the ground or is played with any other part of the body.

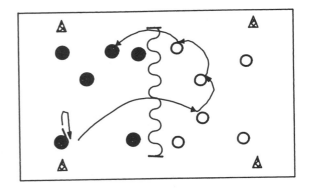

2. Play in your zone

Each player must play in his zone. Goals can only be scored from zone 1 and zone 3. In zone 1 and zone 3 each attacking team has an extra player advantage. In zone 2, 1 player gives an attacking advantage for both teams. The ball can be passed between the zones to supporting players but a goal can only be scored from the end zones.

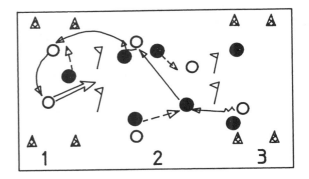

3. All up in attack

Teams play 2 or 1 touch in a small-sided game across the soccer field. All members of the attacking side must move up and support play in the opponent's half. Only if all attacking players are in the opponent's half, and a goal is scored, does it count. The team with the most number of goals wins.

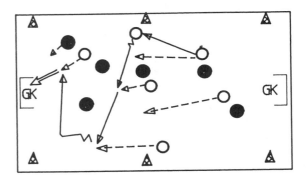

4. Soccer with 1 goal

The team in possession attacks and the team without possession defends. The goalkeeper plays for both teams with a goal being scored from any part of the pitch. The basic rule is that when a team gains possession of the ball it must be dribbled or passed over the 30 metre line before an attack can be mounted at goal. The normal rules of soccer apply. The team with the most number of goals wins.

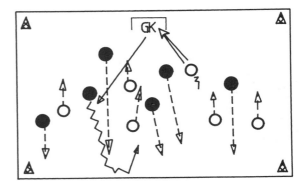

Deceptive dribbling and feinting techniques
The following represent the 5 deceptive dribbling and feinting techniques to be executed in level 4.

1. Double run over the ball

2. Roll out, in and away

3. Roll to the side and roll back

4. Flick the ball with the outside of the instep out of a tackle

5. Run over 1–2 pass

Technical–tactical program elements

Changing direction and speed

1. Introductory part of the coaching session

1.1 Basic running and then static exercises for flexibility
without the ball .... *refer to page 271*
1.2 Active exercises for flexibility with/without the ball .... *refer to page 272*
1.3 Juggling the ball .... *refer to page 275*
1.4 Individual corrective technical–tactical coaching

2. Main part of the coaching session

2.1 Helpful tactical games ....
2.2 Deceptive dribbling and feinting techniques .... *refer to page 276*
2.3 Technical–tactical program element .... *reinforce*

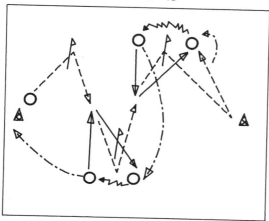
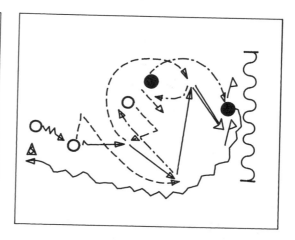

2.4 Technical–tactical shooting element

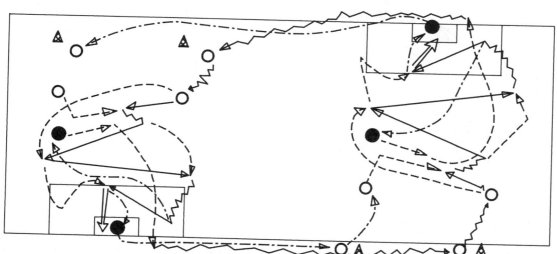

2.5 Small pitch or full pitch soccer .... *refer to page 314*

3. Concluding part of the coaching session

3.1 Summary of the coaching session

Chipping the ball

1. Introductory part of the coaching session

1.1 Basic running and then static exercises for flexibility
without the ball .... *refer to page 271*

1.2 Active exercises for flexibility with/without the ball .... *refer to page 272*

1.3 Juggling the ball .... *refer to page 275*

1.4 Individual corrective technical–tactical coaching

2. Main part of the coaching session

2.1 Helpful tactical games .... *refer to page 276*

2.2 Deceptive dribbling and feinting techniques .... *reinforce*

2.3 Technical–tactical program element

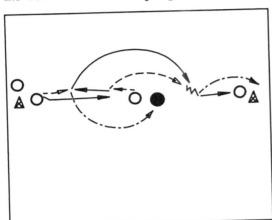
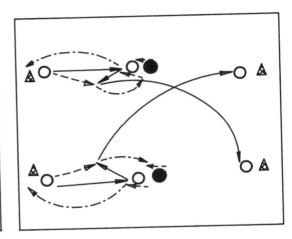

2.4 Technical–tactical shooting element

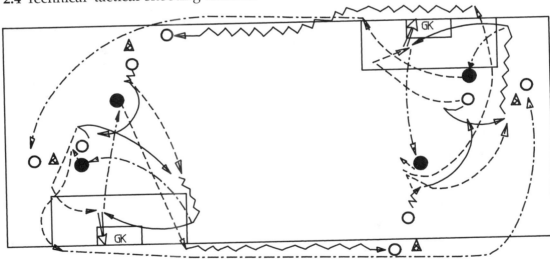

2.5 Small pitch or full pitch soccer .... *refer to page 314*

3. Concluding part of the coaching session

3.1 Summary of the coaching session

Full volley kick (front side)

1. Introductory part of the coaching session

1.1 Basic running and then static exercises for flexibility
without the ball .... *refer to page 271*
1.2 Active exercises for flexibility with/without the ball ...... *refer to page 272*
1.3 Juggling the ball .... *refer to page 275*
1.4 Individual corrective technical–tactical coaching

2. Main part of the coaching session

2.1 Helpful tactical games .... *refer to page 276*
2.2 Deceptive dribbling and feinting techniques .... *reinforce*
2.3 Technical–tactical program element

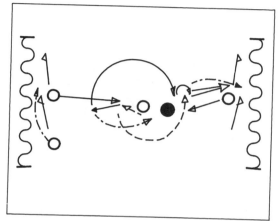 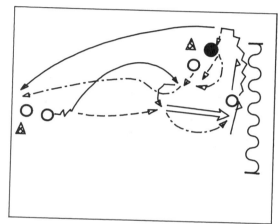

2.4 Technical–tactical shooting element

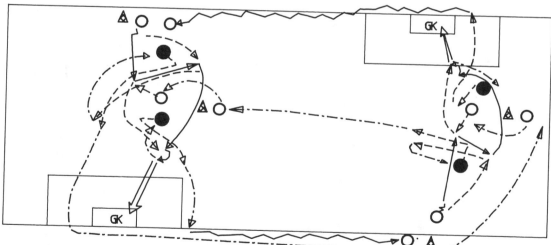

2.5 Small pitch or full pitch soccer .... *refer to page 314*

3. Concluding part of the coaching session

3.1 Summary of the coaching session

Half volley kick (front side)

1. Introductory part of the coaching session
    1.1 Basic running and then static exercises for flexibility
    without the ball .... *refer to page 271*
    1.2 Active exercises for flexibility with/without the ball .... *refer to page 272*
    1.3 Juggling the ball .... *refer to page 275*
    1.4 Individual corrective technical–tactical coaching

2. Main part of the coaching session
    2.1 Helpful tactical games .... *refer to page 276*
    2.2 Deceptive dribbling and feinting techniques .... *reinforce*
    2.3 Technical–tactical program element

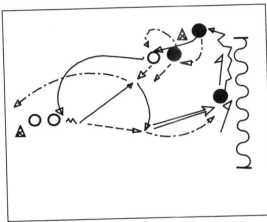 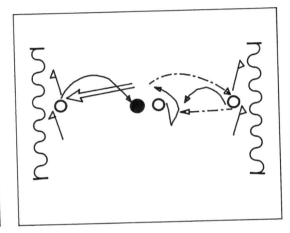

    2.4 Technical–tactical shooting element

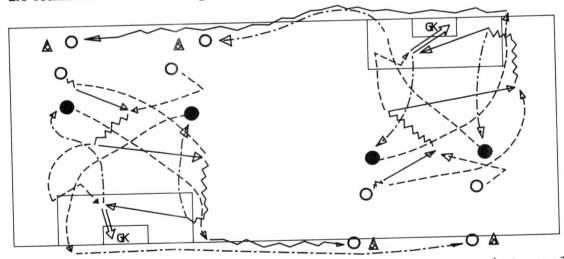

    2.5 Small pitch or full pitch soccer .... *refer to page 314*

3. Concluding part of the coaching session
    3.1 Summary of the coaching session

Receiving (amortisation) with the head

1. Introductory part of the coaching session
1.1 Basic running and then static exercises for flexibility
without the ball ....*refer to page 271*
1.2 Active exercises for flexibility with/without the ball ....*refer to page 272*
1.3 Juggling the ball ....*refer to page 275*
1.4 Individual corrective technical–tactical coaching

2. Main part of the coaching session
2.1 Helpful tactical games ....*refer to page 276*
2.2 Deceptive dribbling and feinting techniques ....*reinforce*
2.3 Technical–tactical program element

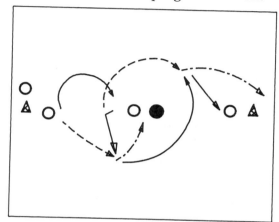
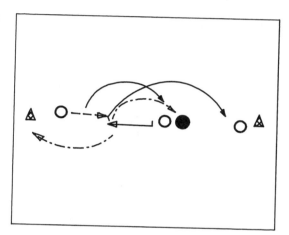

2.4 Technical–tactical shooting element

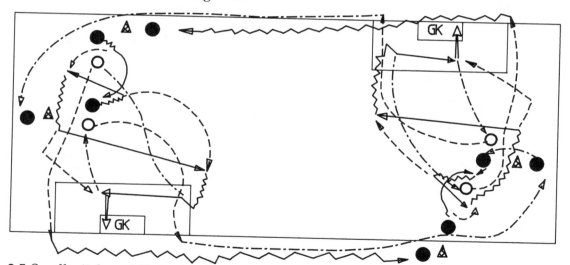

2.5 Small pitch or full pitch soccer ....*refer to page 314*

3. Concluding part of the coaching session
3.1 Summary of the coaching session

Receiving (trapping) with the stomach/chest

1. Introductory part of the coaching session

1.1 Basic running and then static exercises for flexibility
without the ball ....*refer to page 271*

1.2 Active exercises for flexibility with/without the ball ....*refer to page 272*

1.3 Juggling the ball ....*refer to page 275*

1.4 Individual corrective technical–tactical coaching

2. Main part of the coaching session

2.1 Helpful tactical games ....*refer to page 276*

2.2 Deceptive dribbling and feinting techniques ....*reinforce*

2.3 Technical–tactical program element

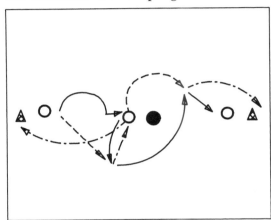 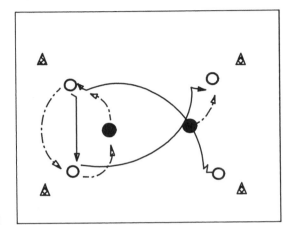

2.4 Technical–tactical shooting element

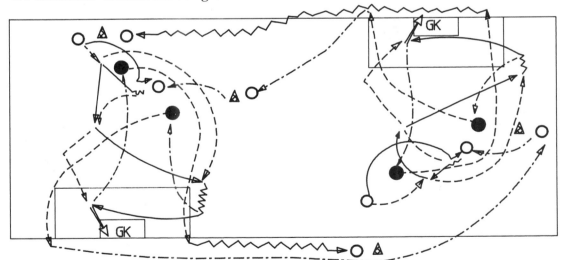

2.5 Small pitch or full pitch soccer ....*refer to page 314*

3. Concluding part of the coaching session

3.1 Summary of the coaching session

Heading with the side zone of the forehead

1. Introductory part of the coaching session
    1.1 Basic running and then static exercises for flexibility
    without the ball ....*refer to page 271*
    1.2 Active exercises for flexibility with/without the ball ....*refer to page 272*
    1.3 Juggling the ball ....*refer to page 275*
    1.4 Individual corrective technical–tactical coaching

2. Main part of the coaching session
    2.1 Helpful tactical games ....*refer to page 276*
    2.2 Deceptive dribbling and feinting techniques ....*reinforce*
    2.3 Technical–tactical program element

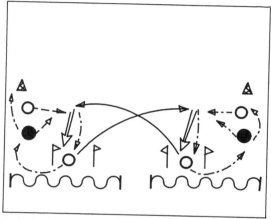
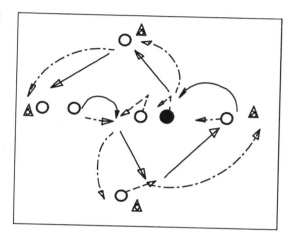

    2.4 Technical–tactical shooting element

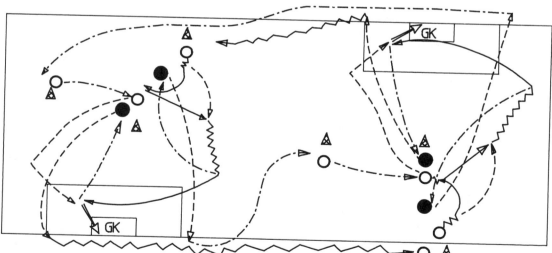

    2.5 Small pitch or full pitch soccer ....*refer to page 314*

3. Concluding part of the coaching session
    3.1 Summary of the coaching session

The shoulder charge

1. Introductory part of the coaching session
    1.1 Basic running and then static exercises for flexibility
       without the ball .... *refer to page 271*
    1.2 Active exercises for flexibility with/without the ball .... *refer to page 272*
    1.3 Juggling the ball .... *refer to page 275*
    1.4 Individual corrective technical–tactical coaching

2. Main part of the coaching session
    2.1 Helpful tactical games .... *refer to page 276*
    2.2 Deceptive dribbling and feinting techniques .... *reinforce*
    2.3 Technical–tactical program element

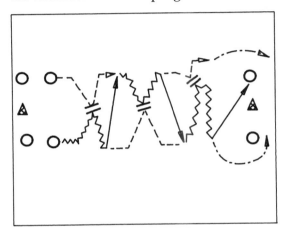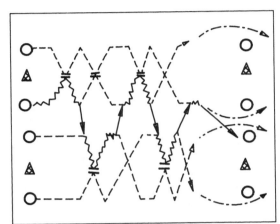

    2.4 Technical–tactical shooting element

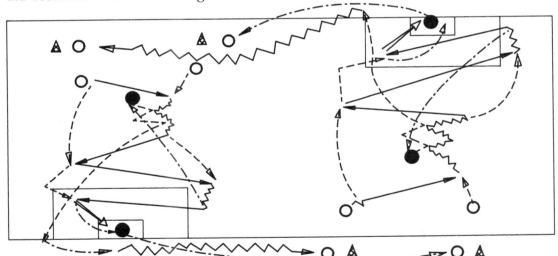

    2.5 Small pitch or full pitch soccer .... *refer to page 314*

3. Concluding part of the coaching session
    3.1 Summary of the coaching session

Basic combinations — 2:2

1. Introductory part of the coaching session

1.1 Basic running and then static exercises for flexibility without the ball .... *refer to page 271*
1.2 Active exercises for flexibility with/without the ball .... *refer to page 272*
1.3 Juggling the ball .... *refer to page 275*
1.4 Individual corrective technical–tactical coaching

2. Main part of the coaching session

2.1 Helpful tactical games .... *refer to page 276*
2.2 Deceptive dribbling and feinting techniques .... *reinforce*
2.3 Technical–tactical program element

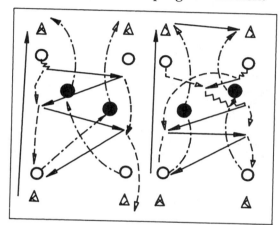 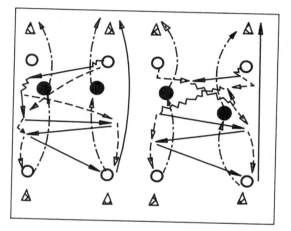

2.4 Technical–tactical shooting element

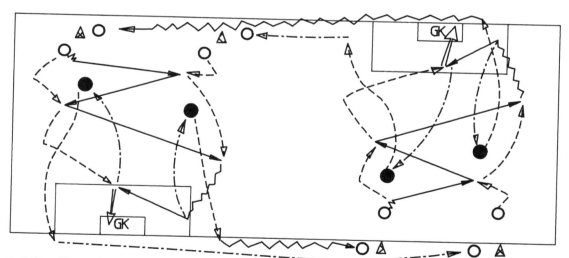

2.5 Small pitch or full pitch soccer .... *refer to page 314*

3. Concluding part of the coaching session

3.1 Summary of the coaching session

Superstar Michel Platini with 2 soccer legends — Pele and Maradona

technical–tactical elements

Juggling the ball

Juggling the ball is simply keeping the ball off the ground, playing it with all parts of the body except from the arms to the hands.

There is no better exercise for young players than juggling the ball to get universal feeling and confidence with the ball.

When juggling, it is necessary to be relaxed and have good body balance.

Juggling the ball is an important introductory part of each coaching session.

1. Juggling with the use of the outside of the foot

2. Juggling with the use of the chest

3. Juggling with the use of the head

Kicking the ball with the outside of the instep

1. Introductory part of the coaching session

1.4 Individual corrective technical–tactical coaching

2. Main part of the coaching session

2.2 Deceptive dribbling and feinting techniques .... *reinforce*
2.3 Technical–tactical program element

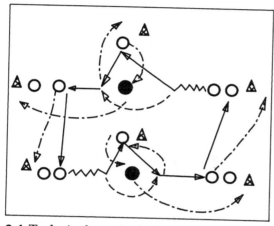
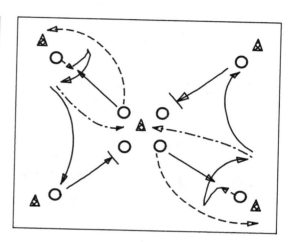

2.4 Technical–tactical shooting element

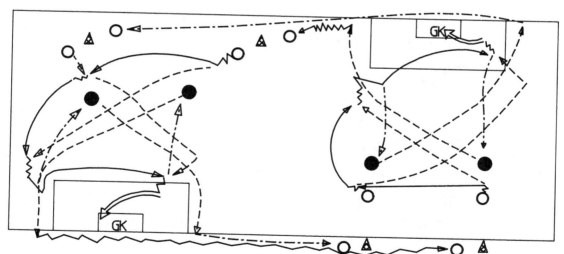

3. Concluding part of the coaching session

3.1 Summary of the coaching session

The wall pass — 1–2 pass

1. Introductory part of the coaching session
1.1 Basic running and then static exercises for flexibility
without the ball ....*refer to page 271*
1.2 Active exercises for flexibility with/without the ball ....*refer to page 272*
1.3 Juggling the ball ....*refer to page 275*
1.4 Individual corrective technical–tactical coaching

2. Main part of the coaching session
2.1 Helpful tactical games ....*refer to page 276*
2.2 Deceptive dribbling and feinting techniques ....*reinforce*
2.3 Technical–tactical program element

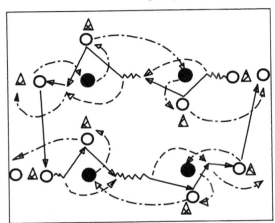 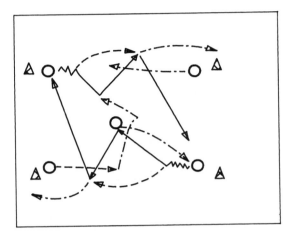

2.4 Technical–tactical shooting element

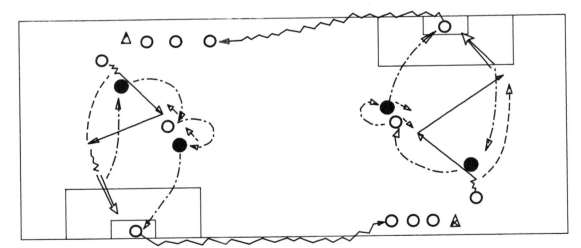

2.5 Small pitch or full pitch soccer ....*refer to page 314*

3. Concluding part of the coaching session
3.1 Summary of the coaching session

Receiving (amortisation) with the thigh

1. Introductory part of the coaching session

1.1 Basic running and then static exercises for flexibility
without the ball ....*refer to page 271*

1.2 Active exercises for flexibility with/without the ball ....*refer to page 272*

1.3 Juggling the ball ....*refer to page 275*

1.4 Individual corrective technical–tactical coaching

2. Main part of the coaching session

2.1 Helpful tactical games ....*refer to page 276*

2.2 Deceptive dribbling and feinting techniques ....*reinforce*

2.3 Technical–tactical program element

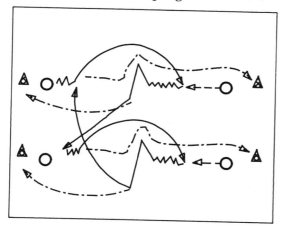 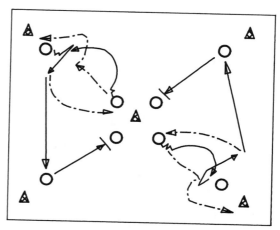

2.4 Technical–tactical shooting element

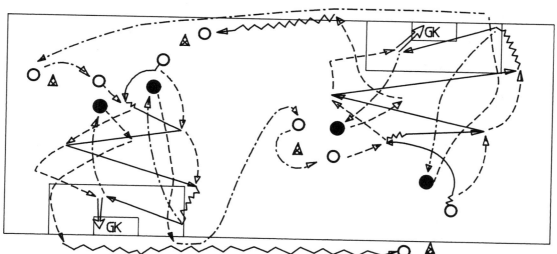

2.5 Small pitch or full pitch soccer ....*refer to page 314*

3. Concluding part of the coaching session

3.1 Summary of the coaching session

Receiving (amortisation) with the chest

1. Introductory part of the coaching session

1.1 Basic running and then static exercises for flexibility
without the ball ....*refer to page 271*
1.2 Active exercises for flexibility with/without the ball ....*refer to page 272*
1.3 Juggling the ball ....*refer to page 275*
1.4 Individual corrective technical–tactical coaching

2. Main part of the coaching session

2.1 Helpful tactical games ....*refer to page 276*
2.2 Deceptive dribbling and feinting techniques ....*reinforce*
2.3 Technical–tactical program element

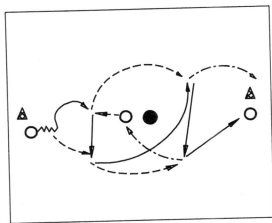 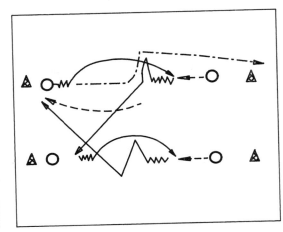

2.4 Technical–tactical shooting element

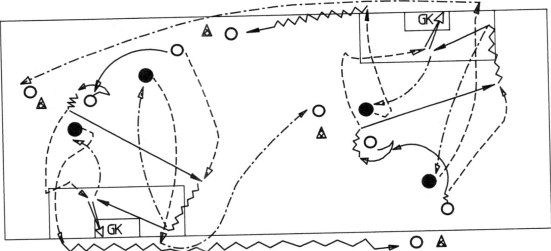

2.5 Small pitch or full pitch soccer ....*refer to page 314*

3. Concluding part of the coaching session

3.1 Summary of the coaching session

Receiving (trapping) with the outside of the instep

1. Introductory part of the coaching session

1.1 Basic running and then static exercises for flexibility without the ball .... *refer to page 271*

1.2 Active exercises for flexibility with/without the ball .... *refer to page 272*

1.3 Juggling the ball .... *refer to page 275*

1.4 Individual corrective technical–tactical coaching

2. Main part of the coaching session

2.1 Helpful tactical games .... *refer to page 276*

2.2 Deceptive dribbling and feinting techniques .... *reinforce*

2.3 Technical–tactical program element

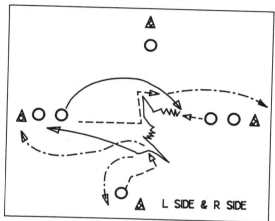
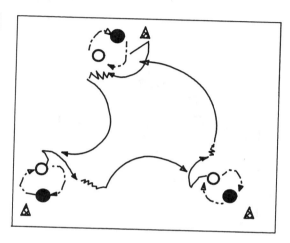

2.4 Technical–tactical shooting element

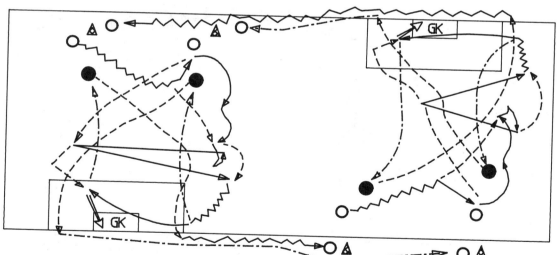

2.5 Small pitch or full pitch soccer .... *refer to page 314*

3. Concluding part of the coaching session

3.1 Summary of the coaching session

Heading with the middle zone of the forehead

1. Introductory part of the coaching session
    1.1 Basic running and then static exercises for flexibility
       without the ball .... *refer to page 271*
    1.2 Active exercises for flexibility with/without the ball .... *refer to page 272*
    1.3 Juggling the ball .... *refer to page 275*
    1.4 Individual corrective technical–tactical coaching

2. Main part of the coaching session
    2.1 Helpful tactical games .... *refer to page 276*
    2.2 Deceptive dribbling and feinting techniques .... *reinforce*
    2.3 Technical–tactical program element

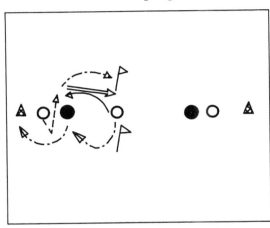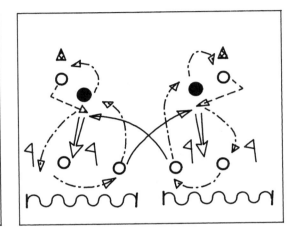

    2.4 Technical–tactical shooting element

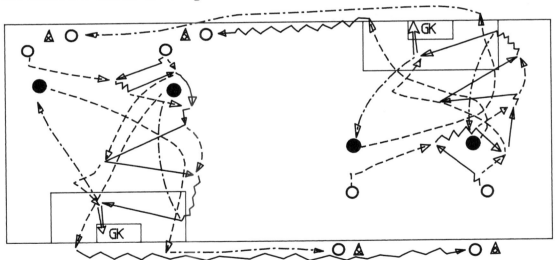

    2.5 Small pitch or full pitch soccer .... *refer to page 314*

3. Concluding part of the coaching session
    3.1 Summary of the coaching session

The sliding–straddle tackle

1. Introductory part of the coaching session

1.1 Basic running and then static exercises for flexibility
without the ball .... *refer to page 271*
1.2 Active exercises for flexibility with/without the ball .... *refer to page 272*
1.3 Juggling the ball .... *refer to page 275*
1.4 Individual corrective technical–tactical coaching

2. Main part of the coaching session

2.1 Helpful tactical games .... *refer to page 276*
2.2 Deceptive dribbling and feinting techniques .... *reinforce*
2.3 Technical–tactical program element

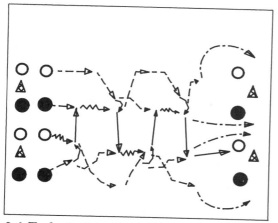
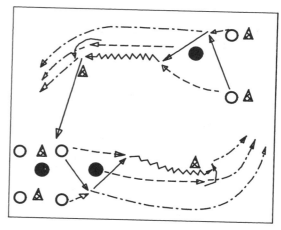

2.4 Technical–tactical shooting element

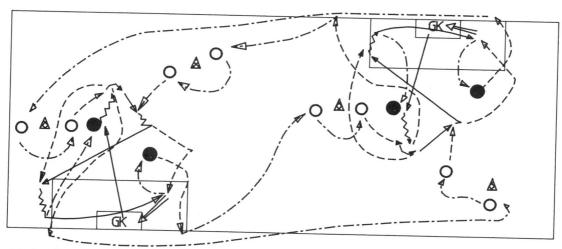

2.5 Small pitch or full pitch soccer .... *refer to page 314*

3. Concluding part of the coaching session

3.1 Summary of the coaching session

Basic combinations — 2:0

1. Introductory part of the coaching session
    1.1 Basic running and then static exercises for flexibility
    without the ball .... *refer to page 271*
    1.2 Active exercises for flexibility with/without the ball .... *refer to page 272*
    1.3 Juggling the ball .... *refer to page 275*
    1.4 Individual corrective technical–tactical coaching

2. Main part of the coaching session
    2.1 Helpful tactical games .... *refer to page 276*
    2.2 Deceptive dribbling and feinting techniques .... *reinforce*
    2.3 Technical–tactical program element

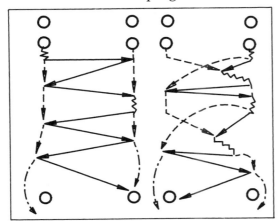 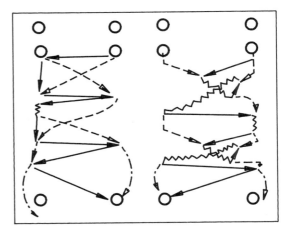

    2.4 Technical–tactical shooting element

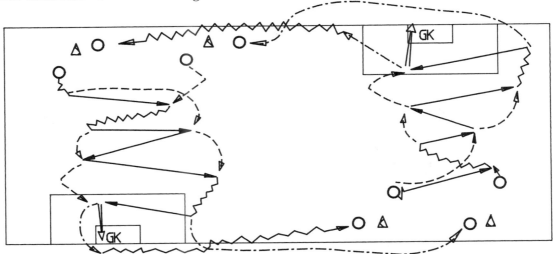

    2.5 Small pitch or full pitch soccer .... *refer to page 314*

3. Concluding part of the coaching session
    3.1 Summary of the coaching session

Basic combinations — 2:1

1. Introductory part of the coaching session

1.1 Basic running and then static exercises for flexibility
without the ball .... *refer to page 271*
1.2 Active exercises for flexibility with/without the ball .... *refer to page 272*
1.3 Juggling the ball .... *refer to page 275*
1.4 Individual corrective technical–tactical coaching

2. Main part of the coaching session

2.1 Helpful tactical games .... *refer to page 276*
2.2 Deceptive dribbling and feinting techniques .... *reinforce*
2.3 Technical–tactical program element

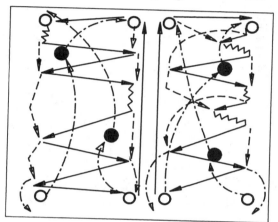 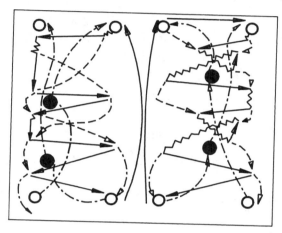

2.4 Technical–tactical shooting element

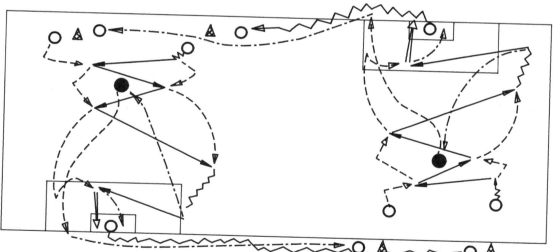

2.5 Small pitch or full pitch soccer .... *refer to page 314*

3. Concluding part of the coaching session

3.1 Summary of the coaching session

UMBRO

Superstar Lothar Matthaus moves between 2 Holland defenders in the European championship

technical–tactical elements

Juggling the ball

Juggling the ball is simply keeping the ball off the ground, playing it with all parts of the body except from the arms to the hands.

There is no better exercise for young players than juggling the ball to get universal feeling and confidence with the ball.

When juggling, it is necessary to be relaxed and have good body balance.

Juggling the ball is an important introductory part of each coaching session.

1. Juggling with the use of the instep

2. Juggling with the use of the thigh

3. Juggling with the use of the inside of the foot

Helpful tactical games

1. Soccer handball

1 team attacks and 1 team defends until a
goal is scored or possession lost. Players
interpass by throwing the ball with a
maximum of 1 step with the ball. The
attacking player with the ball must play a
1–2 pass and switch to another team
player. Goals can only be scored by
throwing the ball through the small goals.
There are no outs or offside.

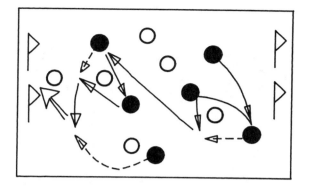

2. Piggy in the middle — 3:1

3 players, in a marked grid, keep
possession of the ball away from the
defending player in the middle. The
defending player in the middle tries to
intercept the ball being passed. If the ball
is intercepted, the defending player
changes places with the attacking player
who lost possession.

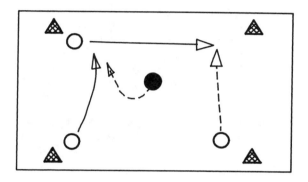

3. Soccer with 4 goals

Each team has 2 goals to attack and 2
goals to defend. There are no goalkeepers,
no offside and no outs. Goals can only be
scored from shooting from inside the grid.

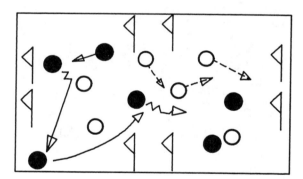

4. Hit your coloured marker

The playing area is covered with 2
different types of coloured markers, evenly
distributed. The players must hit any 1 of
their markers to score a goal. There are no
outs and offside. Teams must defend their
coloured marker.

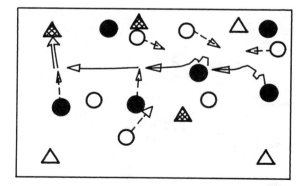

Deceptive dribbling and feinting techniques

The following represent the 15 deceptive dribbling and feinting techniques to be executed in level 2.

1. Cutting the ball back inside

2. Cutting the ball back under the bottom

3. Scissors 1 way and go the other way

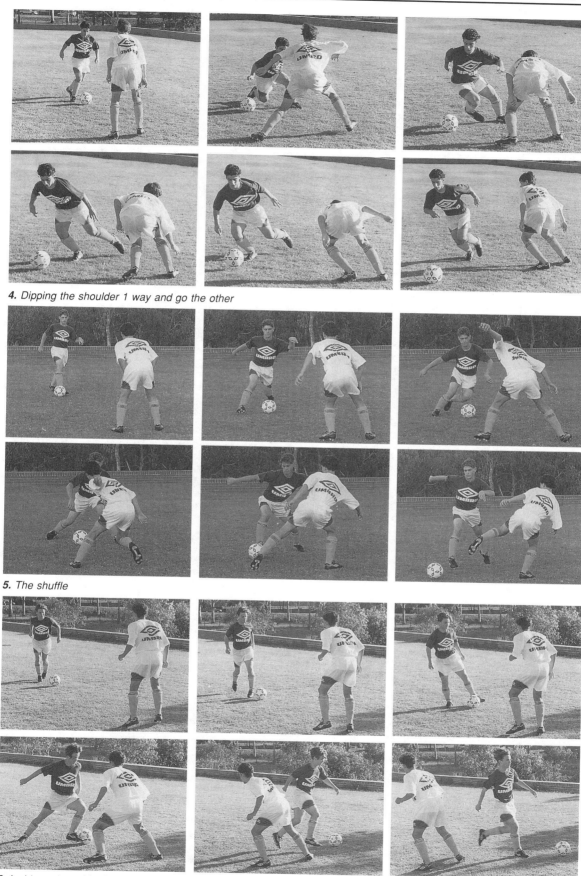

4. *Dipping the shoulder 1 way and go the other*

5. *The shuffle*

6. *Inside and outside the instep*

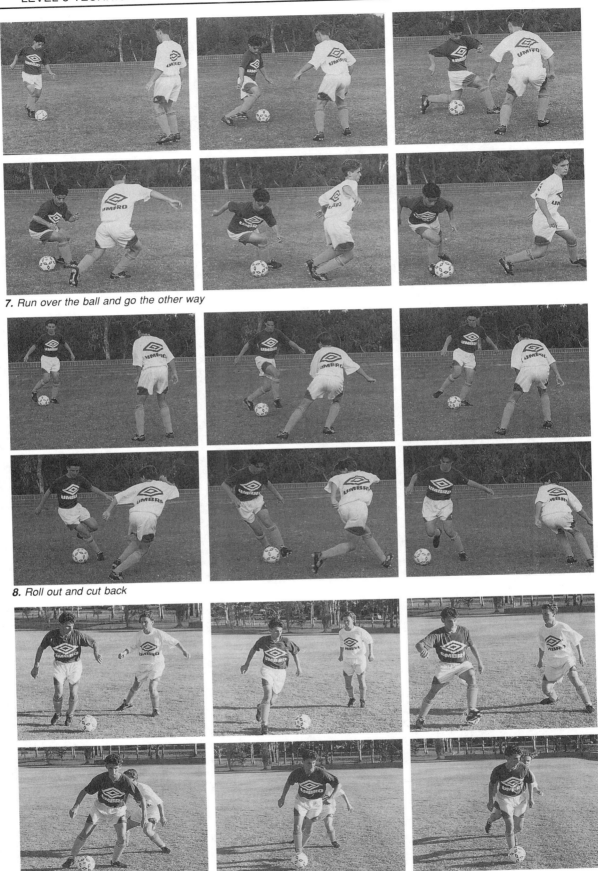

7. Run over the ball and go the other way

8. Roll out and cut back

9. Scissors 1 way and go the same way

10. *Dummy kick and roll back*

11. *Placing the ball between the legs*

12. *Dummy heel pass*

13. *Cross over heel pass*

14. *Roll under the bottom and change direction*

15. *Overhead heel of the ball*

Technical–tactical program elements

Basic running and sprinting technique

1. Introductory part of the coaching session
1.1 Basic running and then static exercises for flexibility
without the ball .... *refer to page 271*
1.2 Active exercises for flexibility with/without the ball .... *refer to page 272*
1.3 Juggling the ball .... *refer to page 275*
1.4 Individual corrective technical–tactical coaching

2. Main part of the coaching session
2.1 Helpful tactical games .... *refer to page 276*
2.2 Deceptive dribbling and feinting techniques .... *reinforce*
2.3 Technical–tactical program element

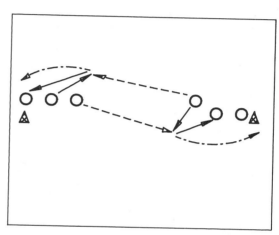

2.4 Technical–tactical shooting element

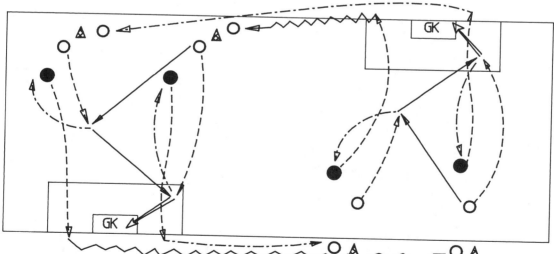

2.5 Small pitch or full pitch soccer .... *refer to page 314*

3. Concluding part of the coaching session
3.1 Summary of the coaching session

The start technique (forward side)

1. Introductory part of the coaching session

1.1 Basic running and then static exercises for flexibility
without the ball ....*refer to page 271*
1.2 Active exercises for flexibility with/without the ball ....*refer to page 272*
1.3 Juggling the ball ....*refer to page 275*
1.4 Individual corrective technical–tactical coaching

2. Main part of the coaching session

2.1 Helpful tactical games ....*refer to page 276*
2.2 Deceptive dribbling and feinting techniques ....*reinforce*
2.3 Technical–tactical program element

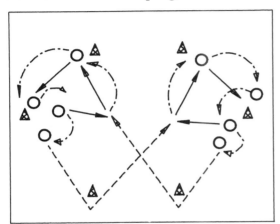 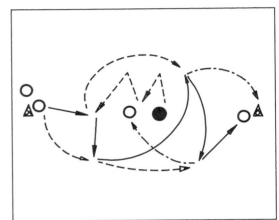

2.4 Technical–tactical shooting element

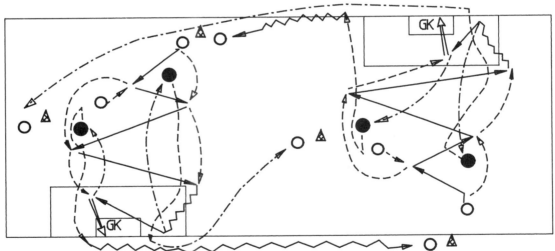

2.5 Small pitch or full pitch soccer ....*refer to page 314*

3. Concluding part of the coaching session

3.1 Summary of the coaching session

Dribbling with the full instep

1. Introductory part of the coaching session

1.1 Basic running and then static exercises for flexibility
without the ball ....*refer to page 271*
1.2 Active exercises for flexibility with/without the ball ....*refer to page 272*
1.3 Juggling the ball ....*refer to page 275*
1.4 Individual corrective technical–tactical coaching

2. Main part of the coaching session

2.1 Helpful tactical games ....*refer to page 276*
2.2 Deceptive dribbling and feinting techniques ....*reinforce*
2.3 Technical–tactical program element

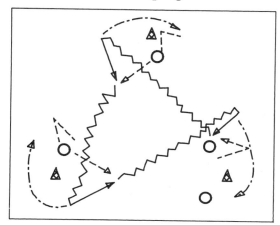
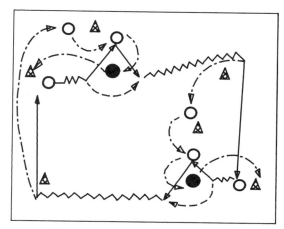

2.4 Technical–tactical shooting element

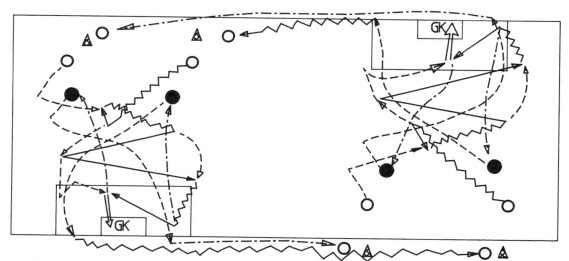

2.5 Small pitch or full pitch soccer ....*refer to page 314*

3. Concluding part of the coaching session

3.1 Summary of the coaching session

Dribbling with the sole of the foot

1. Introductory part of the coaching session

2. Main part of the coaching session

2.3 Technical–tactical program element

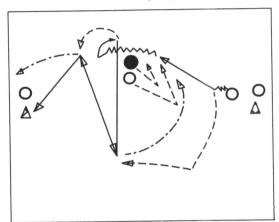 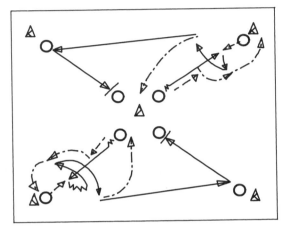

2.4 Technical–tactical shooting element

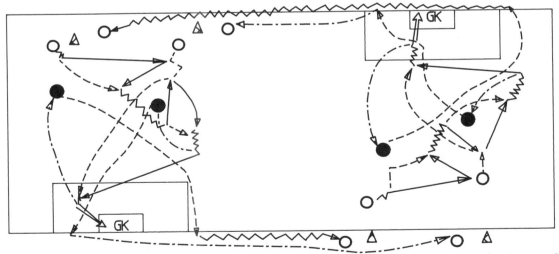

3. Concluding part of the coaching session

3.1 Summary of the coaching session

Kicking the ball with the full instep

1. Introductory part of the coaching session

1.1 Basic running and then static exercises for flexibility
without the ball .... *refer to page 271*

1.2 Active exercises for flexibility with/without the ball .... *refer to page 272*

1.3 Juggling the ball .... *refer to page 275*

1.4 Individual corrective technical–tactical coaching

2. Main part of the coaching session

2.1 Helpful tactical games .... *refer to page 276*

2.2 Deceptive dribbling and feinting techniques .... *reinforce*

2.3 Technical–tactical program element

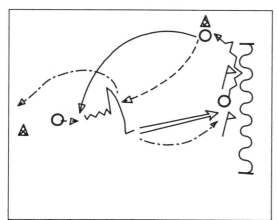 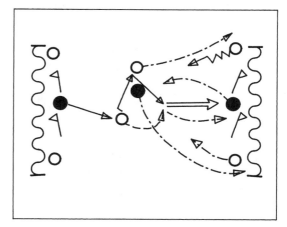

2.4 Technical–tactical shooting element

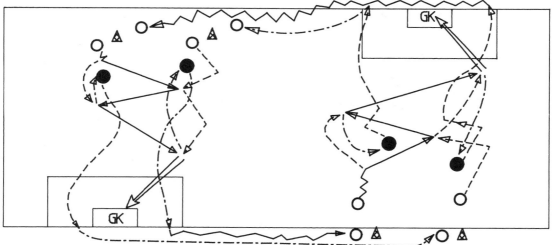

2.5 Small pitch or full pitch soccer .... *refer to page 314*

3. Concluding part of the coaching session

3.1 Summary of the coaching session

Kicking the ball with the inside of the foot

1. Introductory part of the coaching session

1.1 Basic running and then static exercises for flexibility
without the ball .... *refer to page 271*
1.2 Active exercises for flexibility with/without the ball .... *refer to page 272*
1.3 Juggling the ball .... *refer to page 275*
1.4 Individual corrective technical–tactical coaching

2. Main part of the coaching session

2.1 Helpful tactical games .... *refer to page 276*
2.2 Deceptive dribbling and feinting techniques .... *reinforce*
2.3 Technical–tactical program element

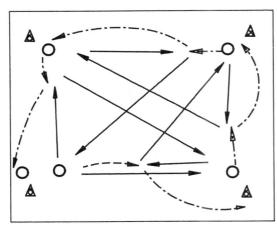 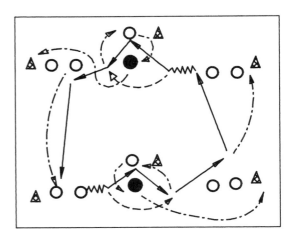

2.4 Technical–tactical shooting element

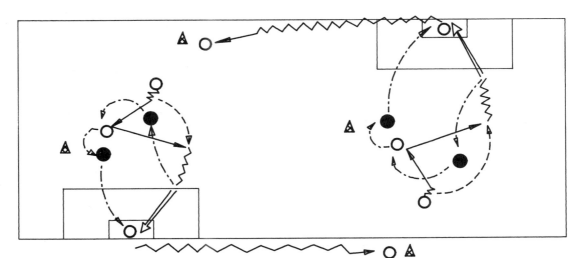

2.5 Small pitch or full pitch soccer .... *refer to page 314*

3. Concluding part of the coaching session

3.1 Summary of the coaching session

Receiving (amortisation) with the inside of the foot

1. Introductory part of the coaching session

1.1 Basic running and then static exercises for flexibility
without the ball ....*refer to page 271*
1.2 Active exercises for flexibility with/without the ball ....*refer to page 272*
1.3 Juggling the ball ....*refer to page 275*
1.4 Individual corrective technical–tactical coaching

2. Main part of the coaching session

2.1 Helpful tactical games ....*refer to page 276*
2.2 Deceptive dribbling and feinting techniques ....*reinforce*
2.3 Technical–tactical program element

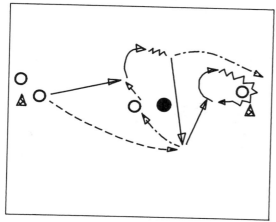
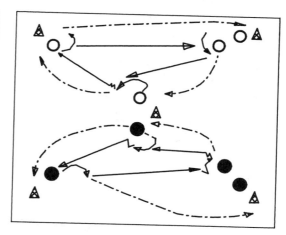

2.4 Technical–tactical shooting element

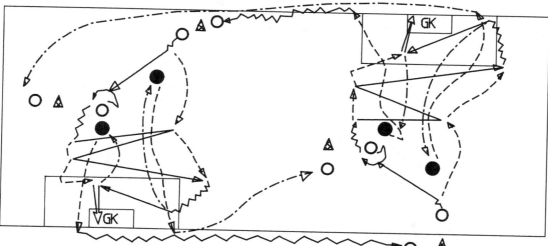

2.5 Small pitch or full pitch soccer ....*refer to page 314*

3. Concluding part of the coaching session

3.1 Summary of the coaching session

Receiving (amortisation) with the full instep

1. Introductory part of the coaching session

1.1 Basic running and then static exercises for flexibility
without the ball .... *refer to page 271*

1.2 Active exercises for flexibility with/without the ball .... *refer to page 272*

1.3 Juggling the ball .... *refer to page 275*

1.4 Individual corrective technical–tactical coaching

2. Main part of the coaching session

2.1 Helpful tactical games .... *refer to page 276*

2.2 Deceptive dribbling and feinting techniques .... *reinforce*

2.3 Technical–tactical program element

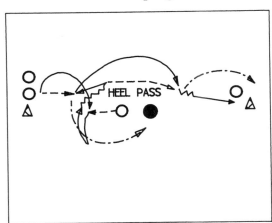 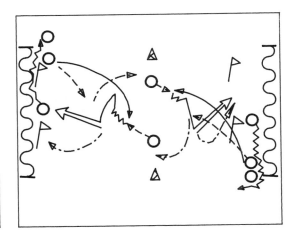

2.4 Technical–tactical shooting element

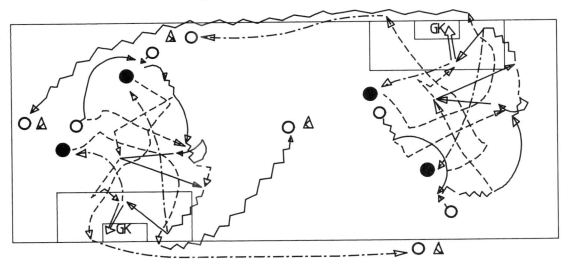

2.5 Small pitch or full pitch soccer .... *refer to page 314*

3. Concluding part of the coaching session

3.1 Summary of the coaching session

Receiving (trapping) with the inside of the foot

1. Introductory part of the coaching session

1.1 Basic running and then static exercises for flexibility
without the ball ....*refer to page 271*

1.2 Active exercises for flexibility with/without the ball ....*refer to page 272*

1.3 Juggling the ball ....*refer to page 275*

1.4 Individual corrective technical–tactical coaching

2. Main part of the coaching session

2.1 Helpful tactical games ....*refer to page 276*

2.2 Deceptive dribbling and feinting techniques ....*reinforce*

2.3 Technical–tactical program element

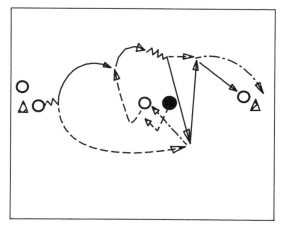 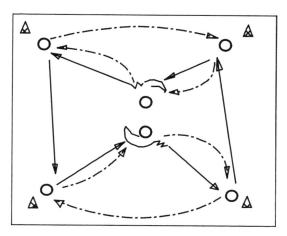

2.4 Technical–tactical shooting element

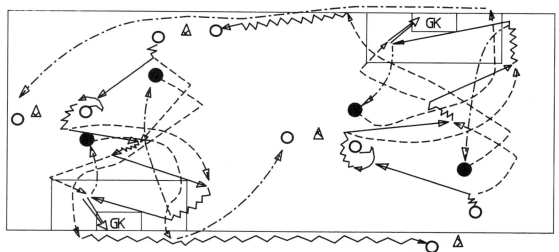

2.5 Small pitch or full pitch soccer ....*refer to page 314*

3. Concluding part of the coaching session

3.1 Summary of the coaching session

Receiving (trapping) with the sole of the foot

1. Introductory part of the coaching session
1.1 Basic running and then static exercises for flexibility
without the ball ....*refer to page 271*
1.2 Active exercises for flexibility with/without the ball ....*refer to page 272*
1.3 Juggling the ball ....*refer to page 275*
1.4 Individual corrective technical–tactical coaching

2. Main part of the coaching session
2.1 Helpful tactical games ....*refer to page 276*
2.2 Deceptive dribbling and feinting techniques ....*reinforce*
2.3 Technical–tactical program element

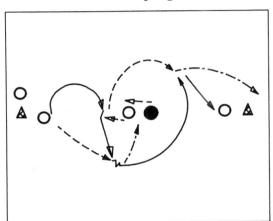
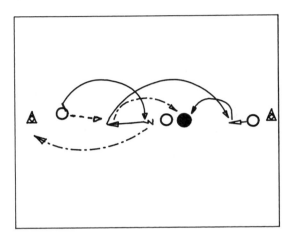

2.4 Technical–tactical shooting element

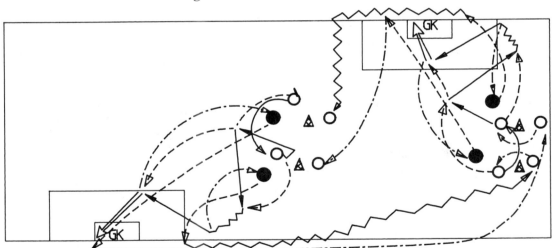

2.5 Small pitch or full pitch soccer ....*refer to page 314*

3. Concluding part of the coaching session
3.1 Summary of the coaching session

The delay and basic block tackle

1. Introductory part of the coaching session

1.1 Basic running and then static exercises for flexibility
without the ball ....*refer to page 271*

1.2 Active exercises for flexibility with/without the ball ....*refer to page 272*

1.3 Juggling the ball ....*refer to page 275*

1.4 Individual corrective technical–tactical coaching

2. Main part of the coaching session

2.1 Helpful tactical games ....*refer to page 276*

2.2 Deceptive dribbling and feinting techniques ....*reinforce*

2.3 Technical–tactical program element

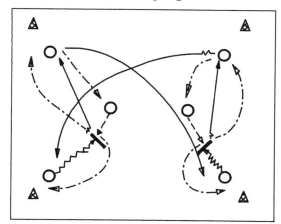 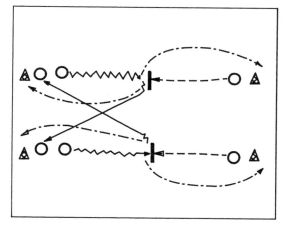

2.4 Technical–tactical shooting element

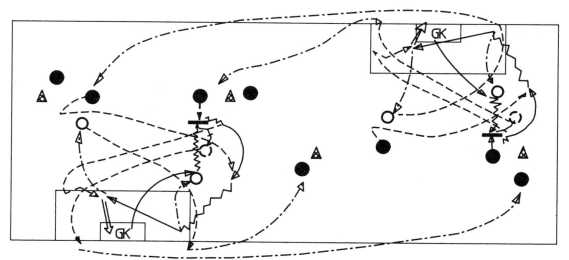

2.5 Small pitch or full pitch soccer ....*refer to page 314*

3. Concluding part of the coaching session

3.1 Summary of the coaching session

Basic combinations — 1:1

1. Introductory part of the coaching session

1.4 Individual corrective technical–tactical coaching

2. Main part of the coaching session

2.3 Technical–tactical program element

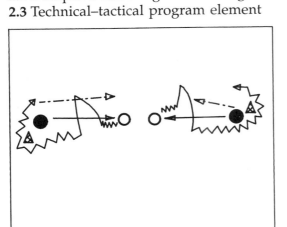 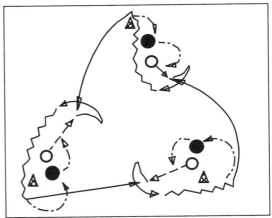

2.4 Technical–tactical shooting element

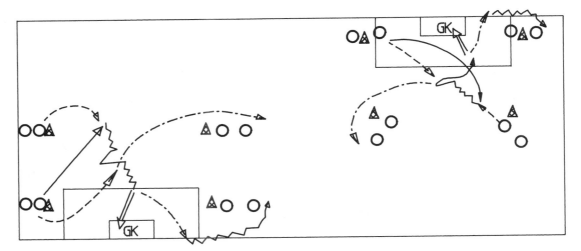

3. Concluding part of the coaching session

3.1 Summary of the coaching session

technical–tactical elements

Agility in the air and on the ground

Trampoline

The basic bounce: *can be used as a warm-up activity. The body and arms should be straight with head erect. At the top of the bounce, the legs are straight with toes pointing down. On the downward bounce flex the legs, hitting the mat with flat feet shou. width*

The seat drop: *from the basic bounce position raise the legs to a horizontal position, moving arms forward and upwards. From her drop back on to the mat into the seat position and bounce back vertical*

The tuck jump: *at the top of the bounce clasp the shins, bringing knees to the chest. Tuck in the elbows with eyes fixed on the ce. end of the trampoline. The heels are against the seat while the t are pointing downward*

The closed pike jump: *from the basic bounce bring the legs straight with toes pointing to a horizontal position. Bend the body forward at the hips with the hands straight with the legs*

The half pirouette: *on the bounce, raise 1 arm above the head while bending the other at 90° across the chest. Twist the body 180° around its vertical axis*

The split pike jump: *the split pike is similar to the closed pike jump except that both legs and arms are stretched apart during the bounce*

The pirouette: *this is similar to the half pirouette but twist a full 360° instead of 180°*

FLOOR

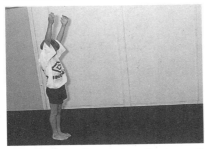

The forward roll: *crouch on the toes with hands on the mat shoulder width apart. Place the chin to the chest, lift the hips and kick off the mat and overbalance. Roll over to the crouch position*

The backward roll: *squat on the mat with elbows bent and palms facing up. Curl the body and rock back, lowering the seat to the mat. Roll back and swing the feet over the head, rolling into a squat*

The mule kick: *place the hands on the mat shoulder width apart. All the weight is taken by the hands with a kick of 1 leg followed by the other high in the air*

The crouch balance: *place the hands on the mat shoulder width apart, palms down. Kick both legs high in the air, bent together while balancing on the hands in the crouch position*

The twist crouch: *the player stands with 1 foot forward, bends and places hands flat on the mat. Travelling sideways, the legs are bent and together, twisting at the hips*

BALANCE BEAM

Walking forward   *Walking backwards*

Walking through hoops   *Bouncing a ball*

Balancing objects   *Picking up objects*

Catching a ball   *Walking over objects*

Hopping

MINI-TRAMPOLINE/VAULTING BOX

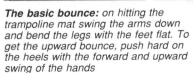

The basic bounce: *on hitting the trampoline mat swing the arms down and bend the legs with the feet flat. To get the upward bounce, push hard on the heels with the forward and upward swing of the hands*

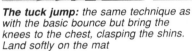

The tuck jump: *the same technique as with the basic bounce but bring the knees to the chest, clasping the shins. Land softly on the mat*

The closed pike jump: *following the bounce bring the legs straight and to a horizontal position. Bend the body at the hips with the hands pointing down the shins*

The split pike jump: *the technique with this element is the same as with the closed pike jump, only the legs and arms are stretched apart*

The side vault: *from the mini-trampoline bounce place the hands on either side of the box. Twist the body to 1 side with a soft landing side-on to the box*

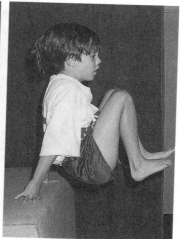

The bent leg squat vault: *following the bounce the stretched out arms touch the box while the legs are bent and close to the chest. The upper extremity is leaning forward. The legs straighten for a soft landing*

Phase 2: 7 to 8 years

TRAMPOLINE — Reinforce basic elements: 5 to 6 years

Swivel hips: *from a basic bounce, go into a seat drop. At the top of the bounce do a half twist and drop into another seat drop*

FLOOR — Reinforce basic elements: 5 to 6 years

The dive roll: *dive forward, stretching the body to land on the hands. Tuck the chin to the chest. Roll over the shoulders and on to the back*

BALANCE BEAM — Reinforce basic elements: 5 to 6 years

Inclined bench balances   *See-saw*   *Passing over arms*

Mini-trampoline/vaulting box

Straddle vault: *following the bounce, lean forward and straighten the legs, keeping them apart with toes pointed. Extend the hands quickly so that they make contact with the apparatus and the body can straddle over it. Land on 2 feet, hands wide*

Forward dive roll: *leap forward with the body and arms stretched. The hands make contact first with the mat, softening the fall, the chin tucked into the chest and knees likewise. Staying curled, roll to your feet*

Forward somersault: *from the forward bounce, clasp the shins by the hands with the chin tucked into the chest. With the quick rotation spin into the somersault, opening out before coming to the vertical axis*

UMBRO

Trampoline

Floor

Balance beam

Mini-trampoline/vaulting box

Superstar Ruud Gullit beats off another challenge in the European Championship

technical–tactical development program

Core learning areas in the soccer development program

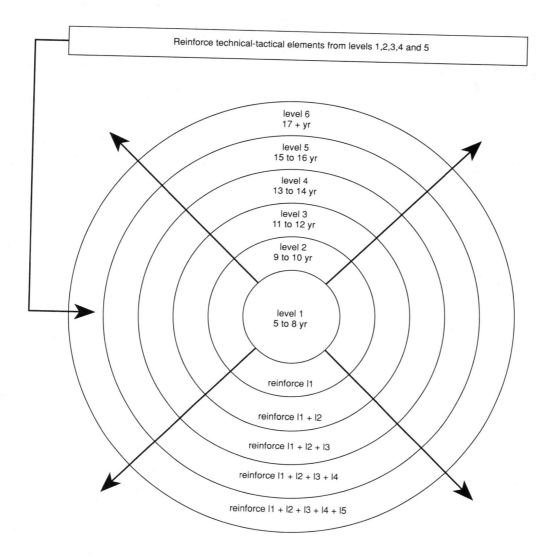

Reinforce technical-tactical elements from levels 1,2,3,4 and 5

level 6
17 + yr

level 5
15 to 16 yr

level 4
13 to 14 yr

level 3
11 to 12 yr

level 2
9 to 10 yr

level 1
5 to 8 yr

reinforce l1

reinforce l1 + l2

reinforce l1 + l2 + l3

reinforce l1 + l2 + l3 + l4

reinforce l1 + l2 + l3 + l4 + l5

Technical–tactical program

Element	Level 1 (5–8 yr)	Level 2 (9–10 yr)	Level 3 (11–12 yr)	Level 4 (13–14 yr)	Level 5 (15–16 yr)	Level 6 (17+ yr)
Agility in the air and on the ground	1	Reinforce	Reinforce	Reinforce	Reinforce	Reinforce
Basic running and sprinting technique		1	Reinforce	Reinforce	Reinforce	Reinforce
The start technique (forward side)		2	Reinforce	Reinforce	Reinforce	Reinforce
Jumping with 1 and 2 feet			1	Reinforce	Reinforce	Reinforce
Changing direction and speed				1	Reinforce	Reinforce
Dribbling with the full instep		3	Reinforce	Reinforce	Reinforce	Reinforce
Dribbling with the sole of the foot		4	Reinforce	Reinforce	Reinforce	Reinforce
Dribbling with the outside of the instep			2	Reinforce	Reinforce	Reinforce
Dribbling with the inside of the instep			3	Reinforce	Reinforce	Reinforce
Deceptive dribbling and feinting (15 tricks)		5	Reinforce	Reinforce	Reinforce	Reinforce
Deceptive dribbling and feinting (10 tricks)			4	Reinforce	Reinforce	Reinforce
Deceptive dribbling and feinting (5 tricks)				2	Reinforce	Reinforce
Juggling the ball (individual)		6	Reinforce	Reinforce	Reinforce	Reinforce
Juggling the ball (partner)			5	Reinforce	Reinforce	Reinforce
Juggling the ball (group)				3	Reinforce	Reinforce
Kicking the ball with the full instep		7	Reinforce	Reinforce	Reinforce	Reinforce
Kicking the ball with the inside of the foot		8	Reinforce	Reinforce	Reinforce	Reinforce
Kicking the ball with the inside of the instep			6	Reinforce	Reinforce	Reinforce
Kicking the ball with the outside of the instep			7	Reinforce	Reinforce	Reinforce
The wall pass — 1–2 pass			8	Reinforce	Reinforce	Reinforce
Chipping the ball				4	Reinforce	Reinforce
Full volley kick (front side)				5	Reinforce	Reinforce
Half volley kick (front side)				6	Reinforce	Reinforce
Overhead (scissors) volley kick					1	Reinforce
Kicking with the toe, heel and knee					2	Reinforce
Receiving (amortisation) — inside of the foot		9	Reinforce	Reinforce	Reinforce	Reinforce
Receiving (amortisation) with the full instep		10	Reinforce	Reinforce	Reinforce	Reinforce
Receiving (amortisation) with the thigh			9	Reinforce	Reinforce	Reinforce
Receiving (amortisation) with the chest			10	Reinforce	Reinforce	Reinforce
Receiving (amortisation) with the head				7	Reinforce	Reinforce
Receiving (trapping) — inside of the foot		11	Reinforce	Reinforce	Reinforce	Reinforce
Receiving (trapping) with the sole of the foot		12	Reinforce	Reinforce	Reinforce	Reinforce
Receiving (trapping) with the outside of the instep			11	Reinforce	Reinforce	Reinforce
Receiving (trapping) with the stomach/chest				8	Reinforce	Reinforce
Heading with the middle zone of the forehead			12	Reinforce	Reinforce	Reinforce
Heading with the side zone of the forehead				9	Reinforce	Reinforce
The diving header					3	Reinforce
The delay and basic block tackle		13	Reinforce	Reinforce	Reinforce	Reinforce
The sliding–straddle tackle			13	Reinforce	Reinforce	Reinforce
The shoulder charge				10	Reinforce	Reinforce
Intercepting the pass					4	Reinforce
Basic combinations — 1:1		14	Reinforce	Reinforce	Reinforce	Reinforce
Basic combinations — 2:0			14	Reinforce	Reinforce	Reinforce
Basic combinations — 2:1			15	Reinforce	Reinforce	Reinforce
Basic combinations — 2:2				11	Reinforce	Reinforce
Basic combinations — 3:0					5	Reinforce
Basic combinations — 3:2					6	Reinforce
Helpful tactical games		15	Reinforce	Reinforce	Reinforce	Reinforce
Kicking at goal		16	Reinforce	Reinforce	Reinforce	Reinforce
Heading at goal			16	Reinforce	Reinforce	Reinforce
Team technical–tactical playing patterns — attack					7	Reinforce
Team technical–tactical playing patterns — defence					8	Reinforce
Set play — attacking situations					9	Reinforce
Set play — defending situations					10	Reinforce
Small pitch soccer — TE–TA elements	2	Reinforce	Reinforce	Reinforce	Reinforce	Reinforce
Full pitch soccer — TE–TA elements				12	Reinforce	Reinforce
	2	16	16	12	10	0

Total soccer development program elements = 56 elements

Time allocation for the 110 minute coaching session

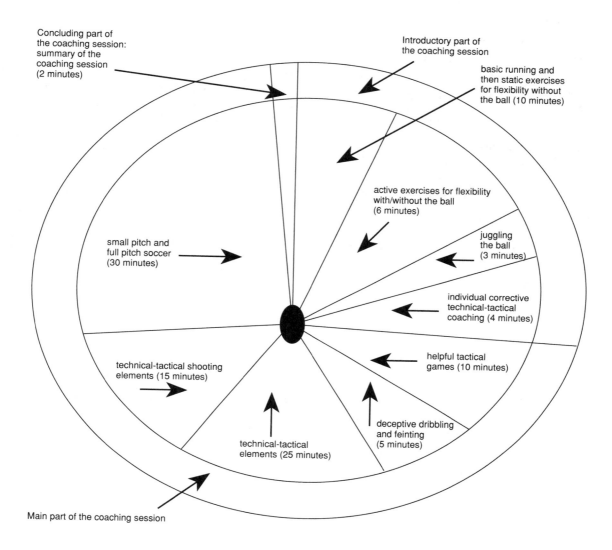

Concluding part of the coaching session: summary of the coaching session (2 minutes)

Introductory part of the coaching session

basic running and then static exercises for flexibility without the ball (10 minutes)

active exercises for flexibility with/without the ball (6 minutes)

juggling the ball (3 minutes)

small pitch and full pitch soccer (30 minutes)

individual corrective technical-tactical coaching (4 minutes)

helpful tactical games (10 minutes)

technical-tactical shooting elements (15 minutes)

deceptive dribbling and feinting (5 minutes)

technical-tactical elements (25 minutes)

Main part of the coaching session

Structure of the practical coaching session — 110 minutes

1. Introductory part of the coaching session

1.4 Individual corrective technical–tactical coaching (4 minutes)

2. Main part of the coaching session

3. Concluding part of the coaching session

3.1 Summary of the coaching session (2 minutes)

Total practical coaching time = 110 minutes

1. Introductory part of the coaching session

1.1 STATIC EXERCISES FOR FLEXIBILITY WITHOUT THE BALL

These exercises are designed to prepare the body in order to prevent injury and to enhance performance. A sustained stretch of 15 seconds or longer is preferable.

1. Thigh (quadriceps): opposite hand holds the instep

2. Calf (gastrocnemius): feet pointing forward. Back straight, lunge forward, heel down

3. Inner thigh (adductors): push knees towards the ground

4. Back of thigh (hamstrings): knee is straight

5. Back of thigh (outside hamstrings): foot turned out, taken across the body (lateral hamstring)

6. Back of thigh (inside hamstrings): foot turned in, placed away from the body (medial hamstring)

7. Outer thigh (iliotibial band): step behind and stretch with leg straight. Rotate away

8. Buttocks (gluteals): both buttocks on the ground, back straight. Press knee and turn

9. Stomach (abdominals): hips remain on the ground

10. Back (erector spinae): curl and hold into a ball

11. Side (latissimus dorsi): hand over hand, raise the hips and stretch

12. Neck (trapezius sternomastoid): stretch forward, back and to the sides

1.2 ACTIVE EXERCISES FOR FLEXIBILITY WITH/WITHOUT THE BALL

Group exercises no. 1

As with the static exercises, these active exercises are also designed to prepare the body for the coaching session and to enhance performance.

1.

2.

3.

4.

5.

6.

Group exercises no. 2

As with the static exercises, these active exercises are also designed to prepare the body for the coaching session and to enhance performance.

1.

2.

3.

4.

5.

6.

Group exercises no. 3

As with the static exercises, these active exercises are also designed to prepare the body for the coaching session and to enhance performance.

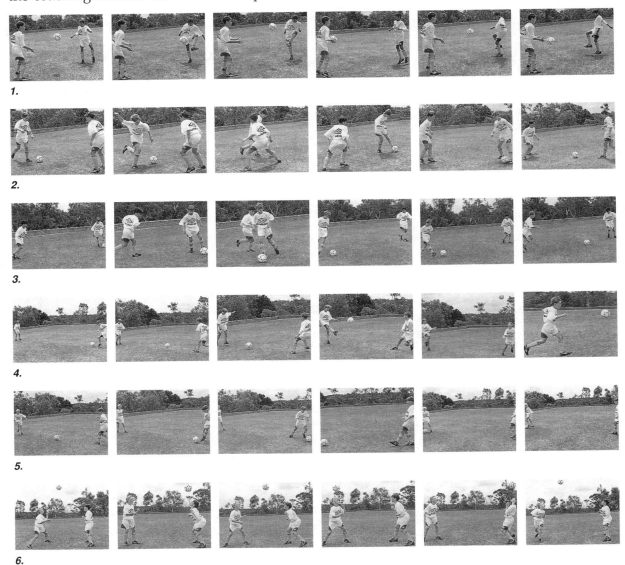

1.

2.

3.

4.

5.

6.

Group exercises no. 4

As with the static exercises, these active exercises are also designed to prepare the body for the coaching session and to enhance performance.

1.

2.

3.

4.

5.

6.

Group exercises no. 5

As with the static exercises, these active exercises are also designed to prepare the body for the coaching session and to enhance performance.

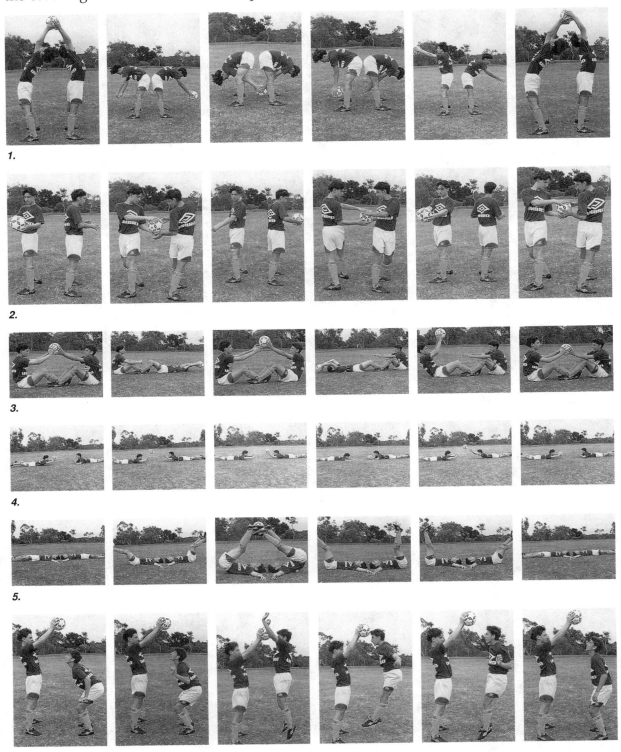

1.

2.

3.

4.

5.

6.

Group exercises no. 6

As with the static exercises, these active exercises are also designed to prepare the body for the coaching session and to enhance performance.

1.

2.

3.

4.

5.

6.

1.3 JUGGLING THE BALL

Juggling the ball is simply keeping the ball off the ground, playing it with all parts of the body except from the arms to the hands.

There is no better exercise for young players than juggling the ball to get universal feeling and confidence with the ball.

When juggling, it is necessary to be relaxed and have good body balance.

Juggling the ball is an important introductory part of each coaching session.

All elements of juggling from the previous levels must be reinforced as progression is made from individual, partner and group juggling.

1. Juggling individually

2. Juggling with a partner

3. Juggling with a group

2. Main part of the coaching session

2.1 HELPFUL TACTICAL GAMES

1. Switch of play and width game

Two teams play across the width of the field, each with goalkeepers. The attacking team must play and switch the ball from 1 side line to the other and then play the ball between a marker and the side line before a shot can be taken at goal. The ball can pass between any marker and the side line by either a pass or dribble. A goal can only count if the attacking team did not lose possession after the ball passed the outer markers.

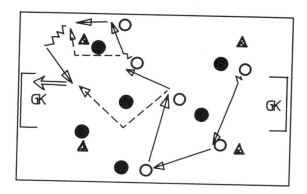

2. Horseback soccer

Two equal teams play small-sided soccer without goalkeepers. The jockey is carried on the back of the 'horse' and must not interfere in the game by obstructing others. The rider changes with the horse when the horse gets tired. There are no offsides and throw-ins are taken with a pass.

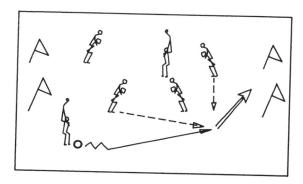

3. One touch — head to score

Two equal teams play across the field of play with or without goalkeepers. The attacking players are allowed a maximum of just 1 touch of the ball. A goal can only be scored by heading at goal.

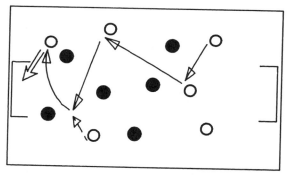

4. Head soccer

Two full-sized goals are placed 20 metres apart facing each other. Two equal teams compete against each other in a small-sided game. The ball can only be played by the head. If the ball is played by any other part of the body or drops to the ground then there is a change of possession. There are no offsides and teams can play with or without goalkeepers.

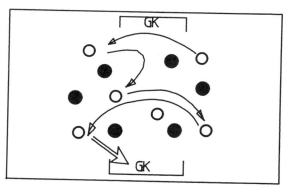

5. Head volleyball

The area on which the game is played is the size of a volleyball court with a net 2.5 metres high. The game is started with a serve, throwing the ball and heading over the net from behind the base line. Points can only be won while the team has service. The ball can be headed a maximum of 3 times before passing over the net. The ball is dead if it hits the ground or is played with any other part of the body.

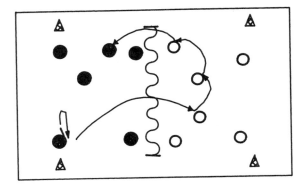

6. Play in your zone

Each player must play in his zone. Goals can only be scored from zone 1 and zone 3. In zone 1 and zone 3 each attacking team has an extra player advantage. In zone 2, 1 player gives an atacking advantage for both teams. The ball can be passed between the zones to supporting players but a goal can only be scored from the end zones.

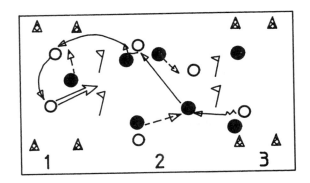

7. All up in attack

Teams play 2 or 1 touch in a small-sided game across the soccer field. All members of the attacking side must move up and support play in the opponent's half. Only if all attacking players are in the opponent's half, and a goal is scored, does it count.

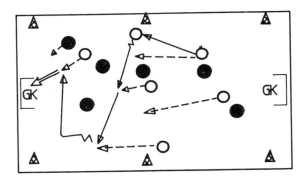

8. Soccer with 1 goal

The team in possession attacks and the team without possession defends. The goalkeeper plays for both teams with a goal being scored from any part of the pitch. The basic rule is that when a team gains possession of the ball it must be dribbled or passed over the 25 metre line before an attack can be mounted at goal. The normal rules of soccer apply.

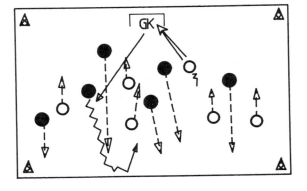

9. Parallel 4-goal soccer

One team attacks either 1 of the opponent's goals or defends its own. There are no offsides but corners are taken. The team can have goalkeepers or play without.

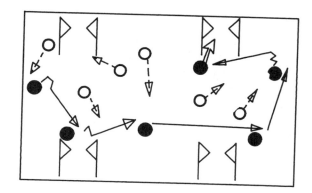

10. Soccer tennis

The ball is served from the bottom right corner behind the base line. The ball must pass over the net on the full and bounce in the opponent's court before being played. The ball can be played a maximum of 2 times in succession by the same player, before passing or playing directly over the net. The net height is above the hips or below the shoulders.

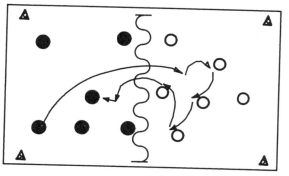

11. Mini-competition — 4:4, 3:3, 2:2

Four or 6 teams are selected to play in an organised mini-competition. There are no outs and a goal can only be scored from the front of the goal. Games are played equal time, with each team playing one another once. The team with the most number of points is declared winner.

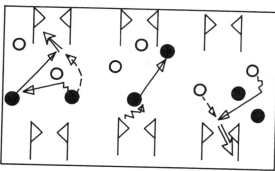

12. Medicine balls as goals

Two medicine balls are placed 20 metres apart. Two teams compete against each other in a game of small-sided soccer. There are no outs, with the goal being scored by hitting the medicine ball from any angle. There are no offsides.

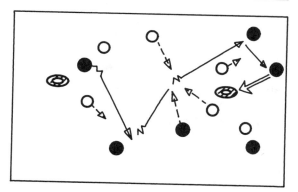

13. *Soccer handball*

One team attacks and 1 team defends until a goal is scored or possession lost. Players interpass by throwing the ball with the hand with a maximum of 1 step with the ball. The attacking player with the ball must play a 1–2 pass and switch to another team player. Goals can only be scored by throwing the ball through the small goals. There are no outs or offside.

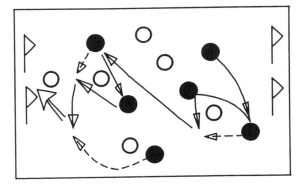

14. *Piggy in the middle — 3:1*

Three players, in a marked grid, keep possession of the ball away from the defending player in the middle. The defending player in the middle tries to intercept the ball being passed. If the ball is intercepted the defending player changes places with the attacking player who lost possession.

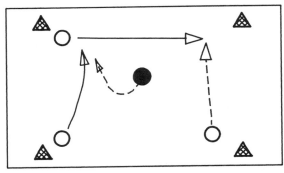

15. *Soccer with 4 goals*

Each team has 2 goals to attack and 2 goals to defend. There are no goalkeepers, no offside and no outs. Goals can only be scored from shooting from inside the grid.

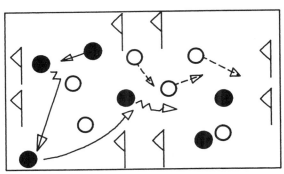

16. *Hit your coloured marker*

The playing area is covered with 2 different types of coloured markers, evenly distributed. The players must hit any 1 of their markers to score a goal. There are no outs and offside. Teams must defend their coloured marker.

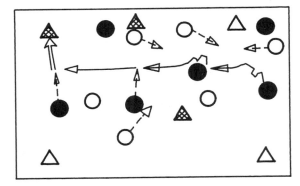

2.2 DECEPTIVE DRIBBLING AND FEINTING

At this level, deceptive dribbling and feinting techniques learnt in previous levels are reinforced.

2.3 TECHNICAL–TACTICAL PROGRAM ELEMENTS TO BE REINFORCED

Element	Level 1 Page	Level 2 Page	Level 3 Page	Level 4 Page	Level 5 Page
Agility in the air and on the ground	20	82	162	256	380
Basic running and sprinting technique		50	148	243	367
The start technique (forward side)		52	149	244	368
Jumping with 1 and 2 feet			106	221	345
Changing direction and speed				190	329
Dribbling with the full instep		54	150	245	369
Dribbling with the sole of the foot		56	151	246	370
Dribbling with the outside of the instep			108	222	346
Dribbling with the inside of the instep			110	223	347
Deceptive dribbling and feinting (15 tricks)		44	142	238	362
Deceptive dribbling and feinting (10 tricks)			103	218	342
Deceptive dribbling and feinting (5 tricks)				188	327
Juggling the ball (individual)		39	140	236	360
Juggling the ball (partner)			98	216	340
Juggling the ball (group)				183	325
Kicking the ball with the full instep		58	152	247	371
Kicking the ball with the inside of the foot		60	153	248	372
Kicking the ball with the inside of the instep			112	224	348
Kicking the ball with the outside of the instep			114	225	349
The wall pass — 1–2 pass			116	226	350
Chipping the ball				192	330
Full volley kick (front side)				194	331
Half volley kick (front side)				196	332
Overhead (scissors) volley kick					278
Kicking with the toe, heel and knee					280
Receiving (amortisation) with the inside of the foot		62	154	249	373
Receiving (amortisation) with the full instep		64	155	250	374
Receiving (amortisation) with the thigh			118	227	351
Receiving (amortisation) with the chest			120	228	352
Receiving (amortisation) with the head				198	333
Receiving (trapping) with the inside of the foot		66	156	251	375
Receiving (trapping) with the sole of the foot		68	157	252	376
Receiving (trapping) with the outside of the instep			122	229	353
Receiving (trapping) with the stomach/chest				200	334
Heading with the middle zone of the forehead			124	230	354
Heading with the side zone of the forehead				202	335
The diving header					282
The delay and basic block tackle		70	158	253	377
The sliding–straddle tackle			126	231	355
The shoulder charge				204	336
Intercepting the pass					
Basic combinations — 1:1					284
Basic combinations — 2:0		72	159	254	378
Basic combinations — 2:1			128	232	356
Basic combinations — 2:2			130	233	357
Basic combinations — 3:0				206	337
Basic combinations — 3:2					286
Helpful tactical games					288
Kicking at goal		40	141	237	276
Heading at goal		43	102	187	187
Team technical–tactical playing patterns — attack			124	230	335
Team technical–tactical playing patterns — defence					290
Set play — attacking situations					296
Set play — defending situations					303
Small pitch soccer — TE–TA elements	29	74	132	208	308
Full pitch soccer — TE–TA elements				208	314

Note: In level 6 coaches are to refer to the above elements and pages for reinforced coaching sessions.

Superstar Marco Van Basten, one of the greatest goalscorers in world soccer

2.5 SMALL PITCH OR FULL PITCH SOCCER

Every coaching session, at this level, should end with a small-sided game on a small pitch; however, there will be times when a coaching session will end with or consist of a full-sided game. But it is the small-sided situations that the young players enjoy most. They are in constant contact with the ball, enabling the technical-tactical and physical skills to be put into practice.

The aim when playing small-sided games is simply to attack the opponent's goal in the phase of attack and defend your goal in the phase of defence. The phase of attack is that moment your team gains possession, while the phase of defence is the moment the team has lost possession.

This is called soccer tactics — the art by which the player's technical and physical qualities are used to achieve the best possible result.

Tactics can be divided into 3 distinct categories:

1. *Individual tactics:* pressing the player, pressing the ball, creating space, dribbling, feinting, receiving, heading, passing, shooting, etc.
2. *Group tactics:* the mobility and interchange of players, the recovery behind the ball of the front attacking line, defending the goal, counter attacking, offside tactics, co-operation with the goalkeeper, playing wide or through the middle, etc.
3. *Team tactics:* keeping possession, slow build up, long direct penetrating passes, playing the high ball, keeping the ball low, switch of play, recovering behind the ball into a zone, pressing on all parts of the field, etc.

Team tactics used by the coach will also be determined by many factors that may include the way the opponents play, state of the playing surface, the team's position in the competition, phase of the game, the weather, etc.

The technical–tactical elements in the phase of attack are:

1. *Mobility:* the ability to move with or without the ball to create playing space.
2. *Penetration:* the ability to get past or behind defenders, with or without the ball.
3. *Width and depth:* the ability to create playing space across and along the field of play.
4. *Switch of play:* the ability to draw defenders out of position and exploit space on the opposite side.

The technical–tactical elements in the phase of defence are:

1. *Balance:* the ability to limit the creation of space, penetration and passing angles.
2. *Pressing the player without the ball:* the ability to reduce the time and playing space an attacking player will have when receiving the ball.
3. *Pressing the ball:* the ability to reduce the time and space the attacking player will have to receive, pass, dribble or shoot at goal.
4. *Zone and combined zone formations:* the ability to recover goal side of the ball, cover an area, and press any player entering that zone.

> **Note: It is necessary for coaches, coaching at all levels, to understand the technical–tactical elements in the phases of attack and defence. In level 6 all the soccer development program's technical–tactical elements are to be reinforced, maintaining the level of excellence in execution.**

Order of coaching technical–tactical elements in attack and defence

The following technical–tactical elements in attack and defence are to be applied and reinforced at each level.

TE–TA *elements in attack*				**TE–TA** *elements in defence*			
Number 1	*Number 2*	*Number 3*	*Number 4*	*Number 1*	*Number 2*	*Number 3*	*Number 4*
Level 1 (5 to 8 years) Unlimited touches with the ball Playing for fun				Unlimited touches with the ball Playing for fun			
Level 2 (9 to 10 years) Mobility Maximum 3 touches Reinforce level 1				Balance Reinforce level 1			
Level 3 (11 to 12 years) Mobility Maximum 2 touches Reinforce levels 1 and 2	Penetration			Balance Reinforce levels 1 and 2	Pressing the player without the ball		
Level 4 (13 to 14 years) Mobility Maximum 1 touch Reinforce levels 1 to 3	Penetration Reinforce level 3	Width and depth		Balance Reinforce levels 1 to 3	Pressing the player without the ball Reinforce level 3	Pressing the ball	
Level 5 (15 to 16 years) Mobility Maximum 1 touch Reinforce levels 1 to 4	Penetration Reinforce levels 3 and 4	Width and depth Reinforce level 4	Switch of play	Balance Reinforce levels 1 to 4	Pressing the player without the ball Reinforce levels 3 and 4	Pressing the ball Reinforce level 4	Zone and combined zone defence
Level 6 (17+ years) Mobility Maximum 1 touch Reinforce levels 1 to 5	Penetration Reinforce levels 3 to 5	Width and depth Reinforce levels 4 and 5	Switch of play Reinforce level 5	Balance Reinforce levels 1 to 5	Pressing the player without the ball Reinforce levels 3 to 5	Pressing the ball Reinforce levels 4 and 5	Zone and combined zone defence Reinforce level 5

The laws of the game

1. *The field of play*
   Length — 100 to 130 yards
   Width — 50 to 100 yards
   The goal area — 6×20 yards
   The penalty area — 18×44 yards
   The corner area — 1 yard
   The goals — shall be 8 yards apart joined by a horizontal cross-bar 8 feet high
   The centre circle — shall have a radius of 10 yards

2. *The ball* — shall be a size 5 and of leather

3. *Number of players* — a match shall be played by 2 teams consisting of not more than 11 players each; each team includes a goalkeeper

4. *Referees and linesmen* — a referee and linesmen shall be appointed to officiate at each game

5. *Duration* — 45 minutes each way with 10 minutes for half-time

6. *The start of play* — before or after goals are scored, play is started by a player taking a place kick at the centre. All defending players must be in their half and outside the circle

7. *The ball out of play* — when it has wholly crossed the goal line or touch line, when in the air or on the ground

8. *Offside* — the offside law shall apply at this level

9. *Fouls and misconduct* — the player is penalised by awarding a free kick

10. *Free kicks* — all free kicks can result in a direct or indirect shot at goal. All opposing players shall be at least 10 yards from the ball

11. *Penalty kicks* — the penalty kick is taken 12 yards from the goal line

12. *Throw-in* — at the point where the ball crossed the line the throw is taken with both hands behind the head and with both feet on the ground

13. *Goal kick* — at the side where the ball crossed the line the ball is placed in the goal area and kicked into play

14. *Corner kick* — if the ball passes over the goal line, excluding the goals, and is last played by the defending team, then a player from the attacking team takes a free kick from the corner of the field

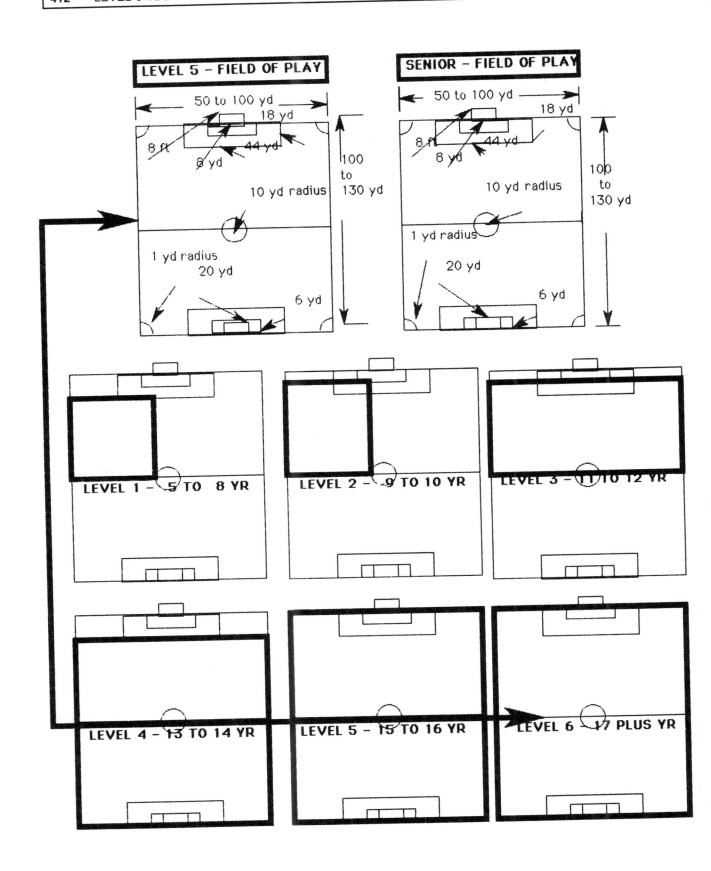

LEVEL 5 – FIELD OF PLAY

50 to 100 yd
18 yd
8 ft
44 yd
8 yd
10 yd radius
100 to 130 yd
1 yd radius
20 yd
6 yd

SENIOR – FIELD OF PLAY

50 to 100 yd
18 yd
8 ft
8 yd
44 yd
10 yd radius
100 to 130 yd
1 yd radius
20 yd
6 yd

LEVEL 1 – 5 TO 8 YR

LEVEL 2 – 9 TO 10 YR

LEVEL 3 – 11 TO 12 YR

LEVEL 4 – 13 TO 14 YR

LEVEL 5 – 15 TO 16 YR

LEVEL 6 – 17 PLUS YR

Superstar Roberto Baggio, one of the most exciting players in the world, scores for Italy in the World Cup USA '94

Soccer development program

LEVEL 1: 5 TO 8 YEARS

Players in level 1 are 5 to 6 and 7 to 8 years of age.
Coaching sessions in this level are to be limited to 1 session per week, with a small pitch game on the weekends.
The program is only for 3 terms of the year, with the 4th term comprising a free choice of activity away from organised coaching.

5 to 6 years

TERM 1

WEEK NO.	TECHNICAL–TACTICAL PROGRAM — LEVEL 1	PAGE NO.
1	**Gymnastics** *Trampoline* — The basic bounce, The seat drop, The tuck jump *Floor* — The forward roll, The backward roll, The mule kick or **Helpful tactical games** **Small pitch soccer**	20 22 28 29
2	**Gymnastics** *Balance beam* — Walking forward, Walking backwards, Walking through hoops, Bouncing a ball *Mini-trampoline/vaulting box* — The basic bounce, The tuck jump, The closed pike jump or **Helpful tactical games** **Small pitch soccer**	23 24 28 29
3	**Gymnastics** *Trampoline* — The closed pike jump, The half pirouette, The split pike jump, The pirouette *Floor* — The crouch balance, The twist crouch or **Helpful tactical games** **Small pitch soccer**	21 22 23 28 29
4	**Gymnastics** *Balance beam* — Balancing objects, Picking up objects, Catching a ball, Walking over objects, Hopping *Mini-trampoline/vaulting box* — The split pike jump, The side vault, The bent leg squat vault or **Helpful tactical games** **Small pitch soccer**	23 24 25 28 29
5	**Gymnastics** *Trampoline* — The basic bounce, The seat drop, The tuck jump *Floor* — The forward roll, The backward roll, The mule kick or **Helpful tactical games** **Small pitch soccer**	20 22 28 29

WEEK NO.	TECHNICAL–TACTICAL PROGRAM — LEVEL 1	PAGE NO.
6	**Gymnastics** *Balance beam* — Walking forward, Walking backwards, Walking through hoops, Bouncing a ball *Mini-trampoline/vaulting box* — The basic bounce, The tuck jump, The closed pike jump or **Helpful tactical games** **Small pitch soccer**	23 24 28 29
7	**Gymnastics** *Trampoline* — The closed pike jump, The half pirouette, The split pike jump, The pirouette *Floor* — The crouch balance, The twist crouch or **Helpful tactical games** **Small pitch soccer**	21 22 23 28 29
8	**Gymnastics** *Balance beam* — Balancing objects, Picking up objects, Catching a ball, Walking over objects, Hopping *Mini-trampoline/vaulting box* — The split pike jump, The side vault, The bent leg squat vault or **Helpful tactical games** **Small pitch soccer**	23 24 25 28 29
9	**Gymnastics** *Trampoline* — The basic bounce, The seat drop, The tuck jump *Floor* — The forward roll, The backward roll, The mule kick or **Helpful tactical games** **Small pitch soccer**	20 22 28 29
10	**Gymnastics** *Balance beam* — Walking forward, Walking backwards, Walking through hoops, Bouncing a ball *Mini-trampoline/vaulting box* — The basic bounce, The tuck jump, The closed pike jump or **Helpful tactical games** **Small pitch soccer**	23 24 28 29

TERM 2

WEEK NO.	TECHNICAL–TACTICAL PROGRAM — LEVEL 1	PAGE NO.
1	**Gymnastics** *Trampoline* — The closed pike jump, The half pirouette, The split pike jump, The pirouette *Floor* — The crouch balance, The twist crouch or **Helpful tactical games** **Small pitch soccer**	21 22 23 28 29
2	**Gymnastics** *Balance beam* — Balancing objects, Picking up objects, Catching a ball, Walking over objects, Hopping *Mini-trampoline/vaulting box* — The split pike jump, The side vault, The bent leg squat vault or **Helpful tactical games** **Small pitch soccer**	23 24 25 28 29
3	**Gymnastics** *Trampoline* — The basic bounce, The seat drop, The tuck jump *Floor* — The forward roll, The backward roll, The mule kick or **Helpful tactical games** **Small pitch soccer**	20 22 28 29
4	**Gymnastics** *Balance beam* — Walking forward, Walking backwards, Walking through hoops, Bouncing a ball *Mini-trampoline/vaulting box* — The basic bounce, The tuck jump, The closed pike jump or **Helpful tactical games** **Small pitch soccer**	23 24 28 29
5	**Gymnastics** *Trampoline* — The closed pike jump, The half pirouette, The split pike jump, The pirouette *Floor* — The crouch balance, The twist crouch or **Helpful tactical games** **Small pitch soccer**	21 22 23 28 29

WEEK NO.	TECHNICAL–TACTICAL PROGRAM — LEVEL 1	PAGE NO.

6	**Gymnastics**
	Balance beam — Balancing objects, Picking up objects,
	   Catching a ball, Walking over objects, Hopping
	Mini-trampoline/vaulting box — The split pike jump, The side vault, The bent leg
	   squat vault
	or
	Helpful tactical games
	Small pitch soccer
		23
		24
		
		25
		
		28
		29

7	**Gymnastics** *Trampoline* — The basic bounce, The seat drop, The tuck jump *Floor* — The forward roll, The backward roll, The mule kick or **Helpful tactical games** **Small pitch soccer**	20 22 28 29

8	**Gymnastics**
	Balance beam — Walking forward, Walking backwards, Walking through hoops,
	   Bouncing a ball
	Mini-trampoline/vaulting box — The basic bounce, The tuck jump, The closed pike
	   jump
	or
	Helpful tactical games
	Small pitch soccer
		23
		
		24
		
		28
		29

9	**Gymnastics**
	Trampoline — The closed pike jump, The half pirouette, The split pike jump, The
	   pirouette
	Floor — The crouch balance,
	   The twist crouch
	or
	Helpful tactical games
	Small pitch soccer
		21
		22
		23
		
		28
		29

10	**Gymnastics**
	Balance beam — Balancing objects, Picking up objects,
	   Catching a ball, Walking over objects, Hopping
	Mini-trampoline/vaulting box — The split pike jump, The side vault, The bent leg
	   squat vault
	or
	Helpful tactical games
	Small pitch soccer
		23
		24
		
		25
		
		28
		29

TERM 3

WEEK NO.	TECHNICAL–TACTICAL PROGRAM — LEVEL 1	PAGE NO.
1	**Gymnastics** *Trampoline* — The basic bounce, The seat drop, The tuck jump *Floor* — The forward roll, The backward roll, The mule kick or **Helpful tactical games** **Small pitch soccer**	20 22 28 29
2	**Gymnastics** *Balance beam* — Walking forward, Walking backwards, Walking through hoops, Bouncing a ball *Mini-trampoline/vaulting box* — The basic bounce, The tuck jump, The closed pike jump or **Helpful tactical games** **Small pitch soccer**	23 24 28 29
3	**Gymnastics** *Trampoline* — The closed pike jump, The half pirouette, The split pike jump, The pirouette *Floor* — The crouch balance, The twist crouch or **Helpful tactical games** **Small pitch soccer**	21 22 23 28 29
4	**Gymnastics** *Balance beam* — Balancing objects, Picking up objects, Catching a ball, Walking over objects, Hopping *Mini-trampoline/vaulting box* — The split pike jump, The side vault, The bent leg squat vault or **Helpful tactical games** **Small pitch soccer**	23 24 25 28 29
5	**Gymnastics** *Trampoline* — The basic bounce, The seat drop, The tuck jump *Floor* — The forward roll, The backward roll, The mule kick or **Helpful tactical games** **Small pitch soccer**	20 22 28 29

WEEK NO.	TECHNICAL–TACTICAL PROGRAM — LEVEL 1	PAGE NO.
6	**Gymnastics** *Balance beam* — Walking forward, Walking backwards, Walking through hoops, Bouncing a ball *Mini-trampoline/vaulting box* — The basic bounce, The tuck jump, The closed pike jump or **Helpful tactical games** **Small pitch soccer**	23 24 28 29
7	**Gymnastics** *Trampoline* — The closed pike jump, The half pirouette, The split pike jump, The pirouette *Floor* — The crouch balance, The twist crouch or **Helpful tactical games** **Small pitch soccer**	21 22 23 28 29
8	**Gymnastics** *Balance beam* — Balancing objects, Picking up objects, Catching a ball, Walking over objects, Hopping *Mini-trampoline/vaulting box* — The split pike jump, The side vault, The bent leg squat vault or **Helpful tactical games** **Small pitch soccer**	23 24 25 28 29
9	**Gymnastics** *Trampoline* — The basic bounce, The seat drop, The tuck jump *Floor* — The forward roll, The backward roll, The mule kick or **Helpful tactical games** **Small pitch soccer**	20 22 28 29
10	**Gymnastics** *Balance beam* — Walking forward, Walking backwards, Walking through hoops, Bouncing a ball *Mini-trampoline/vaulting box* — The basic bounce, The tuck jump, The closed pike jump or **Helpful tactical games** **Small pitch soccer**	23 24 28 29

7 to 8 years

TERM 1

WEEK NO.	TECHNICAL–TACTICAL PROGRAM — LEVEL 1	PAGE NO.
1	**Gymnastics** *Trampoline* — Swivel hips Reinforce 5 and 6 years *Floor* — The dive roll Reinforce 5 and 6 years or **Helpful tactical games** **Small pitch soccer**	26 20 26 22 28 29
2	**Gymnastics** *Balance beam* — Inclined bench balances Reinforce 5 and 6 years *Mini-trampoline/vaulting box* — Straddle vault, Forward dive roll Reinforce 5 and 6 years or **Helpful tactical games** **Small pitch soccer**	26 23 27 24 28 29
3	**Gymnastics** *Trampoline* — Swivel hips Reinforce 5 and 6 years *Floor* — The dive roll Reinforce 5 and 6 years or **Helpful tactical games** **Small pitch soccer**	26 20 26 22 28 29
4	**Gymnastics** *Balance beam* — The see-saw, Passing over arms Reinforce 5 and 6 years *Mini-trampoline/vaulting box* — Forward somersault Reinforce 5 and 6 years or **Helpful tactical games** **Small pitch soccer**	26 23 27 24 28 29
5	**Gymnastics** *Trampoline* — Swivel hips Reinforce 5 and 6 years *Floor* — The dive roll Reinforce 5 and 6 years or **Helpful tactical games** **Small pitch soccer**	26 20 26 22 28 29

WEEK NO.	TECHNICAL–TACTICAL PROGRAM — LEVEL 1	PAGE NO.
6	**Gymnastics** *Balance beam* — Inclined bench balances Reinforce 5 and 6 years *Mini-trampoline/vaulting box* — Straddle vault, Forward dive roll Reinforce 5 and 6 years or **Helpful tactical games** **Small pitch soccer**	26 23 27 24 28 29
7	**Gymnastics** *Trampoline* — Swivel hips Reinforce 5 and 6 years *Floor* — The dive roll Reinforce 5 and 6 years or **Helpful tactical games** **Small pitch soccer**	26 20 26 22 28 29
8	**Gymnastics** *Balance beam* — The see-saw, Passing over arms Reinforce 5 and 6 years *Mini-trampoline/vaulting box* — Forward somersault Reinforce 5 and 6 years or **Helpful tactical games** **Small pitch soccer**	26 23 27 24 28 29
9	**Gymnastics** *Trampoline* — Swivel hips Reinforce 5 and 6 years *Floor* — The dive roll Reinforce 5 and 6 years or **Helpful tactical games** **Small pitch soccer**	26 20 26 22 28 29
10	**Gymnastics** *Balance beam* — Inclined bench balances Reinforce 5 and 6 years *Mini-trampoline/vaulting box* — Straddle vault, Forward dive roll Reinforce 5 and 6 years or **Helpful tactical games** **Small pitch soccer**	26 23 27 24 28 29

TERM 2

WEEK NO.	TECHNICAL–TACTICAL PROGRAM — LEVEL 1	PAGE NO.
1	**Gymnastics** *Trampoline* — Swivel hips Reinforce 5 and 6 years *Floor* — The dive roll Reinforce 5 and 6 years or **Helpful tactical games** **Small pitch soccer**	26 20 26 22 28 29
2	**Gymnastics** *Balance beam* — The see-saw, Passing over arms Reinforce 5 and 6 years *Mini-trampoline/vaulting box* — Forward somersault Reinforce 5 and 6 years or **Helpful tactical games** **Small pitch soccer**	26 23 27 24 28 29
3	**Gymnastics** *Trampoline* — Swivel hips Reinforce 5 and 6 years *Floor* — The dive roll Reinforce 5 and 6 years or **Helpful tactical games** **Small pitch soccer**	26 20 26 22 28 29
4	**Gymnastics** *Balance beam* — Inclined bench balances Reinforce 5 and 6 years *Mini-trampoline/vaulting box* — Straddle vault, Forward dive roll Reinforce 5 and 6 years or **Helpful tactical games** **Small pitch soccer**	26 23 27 24 28 29
5	**Gymnastics** *Trampoline* — Swivel hips Reinforce 5 and 6 years *Floor* — The dive roll Reinforce 5 and 6 years or **Helpful tactical games** **Small pitch soccer**	26 20 26 22 28 29

WEEK NO.	TECHNICAL–TACTICAL PROGRAM — LEVEL 1	PAGE NO.
6	**Gymnastics** *Balance beam* — The see-saw, Passing over arms Reinforce 5 and 6 years *Mini-trampoline/vaulting box* — Forward somersault Reinforce 5 and 6 years or **Helpful tactical games** **Small pitch soccer**	26 23 27 24 28 29
7	**Gymnastics** *Trampoline* — Swivel hips Reinforce 5 and 6 years *Floor* — The dive roll Reinforce 5 and 6 years or **Helpful tactical games** **Small pitch soccer**	26 20 26 22 28 29
8	**Gymnastics** *Balance beam* — Inclined bench balances Reinforce 5 and 6 years *Mini-trampoline/vaulting box* — Straddle vault, Forward dive roll Reinforce 5 and 6 years or **Helpful tactical games** **Small pitch soccer**	26 23 27 24 28 29
9	**Gymnastics** *Trampoline* — Swivel hips Reinforce 5 and 6 years *Floor* — The dive roll Reinforce 5 and 6 years or **Helpful tactical games** **Small pitch soccer**	26 20 26 22 28 29
10	**Gymnastics** *Balance beam* — The see-saw, Passing over arms Reinforce 5 and 6 years *Mini-trampoline/vaulting box* — Forward somersault Reinforce 5 and 6 years or **Helpful tactical games** **Small pitch soccer**	26 23 27 24 28 29

TERM 3

WEEK NO.	*TECHNICAL–TACTICAL PROGRAM — LEVEL 1*	*PAGE NO.*
1	**Gymnastics** *Trampoline* — Swivel hips Reinforce 5 and 6 years *Floor* — The dive roll Reinforce 5 and 6 years or **Helpful tactical games** **Small pitch soccer**	26 20 26 22 28 29
2	**Gymnastics** *Balance beam* — Inclined bench balances Reinforce 5 and 6 years *Mini-trampoline/vaulting box* — Straddle vault, Forward dive roll Reinforce 5 and 6 years or **Helpful tactical games** **Small pitch soccer**	26 23 27 24 28 29
3	**Gymnastics** *Trampoline* — Swivel hips Reinforce 5 and 6 years *Floor* — The dive roll Reinforce 5 and 6 years or **Helpful tactical games** **Small pitch soccer**	26 20 26 22 28 29
4	**Gymnastics** *Balance beam* — The see-saw, Passing over arms Reinforce 5 and 6 years *Mini-trampoline/vaulting box* — Forward somersault Reinforce 5 and 6 years or **Helpful tactical games** **Small pitch soccer**	26 23 27 24 28 29
5	**Gymnastics** *Trampoline* — Swivel hips Reinforce 5 and 6 years *Floor* — The dive roll Reinforce 5 and 6 years or **Helpful tactical games** **Small pitch soccer**	26 20 26 22 28 29

WEEK NO.	TECHNICAL–TACTICAL PROGRAM — LEVEL 1	PAGE NO.
6	**Gymnastics** *Balance beam* — Inclined bench balances Reinforce 5 and 6 years *Mini-trampoline/vaulting box* — Straddle vault, Forward dive roll Reinforce 5 and 6 years or **Helpful tactical games** **Small pitch soccer**	26 23 27 24 28 29
7	**Gymnastics** *Trampoline* — Swivel hips Reinforce 5 and 6 years *Floor* — The dive roll Reinforce 5 and 6 years or **Helpful tactical games** **Small pitch soccer**	26 20 26 22 28 29
8	**Gymnastics** *Balance beam* — The see-saw, Passing over arms Reinforce 5 and 6 years *Mini-trampoline/vaulting box* — Forward somersault Reinforce 5 and 6 years or **Helpful tactical games** **Small pitch soccer**	26 23 27 24 28 29
9	**Gymnastics** *Trampoline* — Swivel hips Reinforce 5 and 6 years *Floor* — The dive roll Reinforce 5 and 6 years or **Helpful tactical games** **Small pitch soccer**	26 20 26 22 28 29
10	**Gymnastics** *Balance beam* — Inclined bench balances Reinforce 5 and 6 years *Mini-trampoline/vaulting box* — Straddle vault, Forward dive roll Reinforce 5 and 6 years or **Helpful tactical games** **Small pitch soccer**	26 23 27 24 28 29

LEVEL 2: 9 TO 10 YEARS

Players in level 2 are 9 to 10 years of age.

Tactics in this level must not be coached at the expense of techniques.

The program is for 4 terms of the year, with the 4th term comprising recreation and small pitch soccer.

TERM 1

WEEK NO.	TECHNICAL–TACTICAL PROGRAM — LEVEL 2	PAGE NO.
1	**Basic running and sprinting technique** Mobility in attack Balance in defence **Dribbling with the full instep** Mobility in attack Balance in defence	50 76 77 54 76 77
2	**The start technique (forward side)** Mobility in attack Balance in defence **Dribbling with the sole of the foot** Mobility in attack Balance in defence	52 76 77 56 76 77
3	**Kicking the ball with the full instep** Mobility in attack Balance in defence **Kicking the ball with the inside of the foot** Mobility in attack Balance in defence	58 76 77 60 76 77
4	**Receiving (amortisation) with the inside of the foot** Mobility in attack Balance in defence **Receiving (amortisation) with the full instep** Mobility in attack Balance in defence	62 76 77 64 76 77
5	**Receiving (trapping) with the inside of the foot** Mobility in attack Balance in defence **Receiving (trapping) with the sole of the foot** Mobility in attack Balance in defence	66 76 77 68 76 77

TERM 2

WEEK NO.	TECHNICAL–TACTICAL PROGRAM — LEVEL 2	PAGE NO.
1	**Receiving (trapping) with the inside of the foot** Mobility in attack Balance in defence **Receiving (trapping) with the sole of the foot** Mobility in attack Balance in defence	66 76 77 68 76 77
2	**The delay and basic block tackle** Mobility in attack Balance in defence **Basic combinations — 1:1** Mobility in attack Balance in defence	70 76 77 72 76 77
3	**Basic running and sprinting technique** Mobility in attack Balance in defence **Dribbling with the full instep** Mobility in attack Balance in defence	50 76 77 54 76 77
4	**The start technique (forward side)** Mobility in attack Balance in defence **Dribbling with the sole of the foot** Mobility in attack Balance in defence	52 76 77 56 76 77
5	**Kicking the ball with the full instep** Mobility in attack Balance in defence **Kicking the ball with the inside of the foot** Mobility in attack Balance in defence	58 76 77 60 76 77

Term 3

WEEK NO.	TECHNICAL–TACTICAL PROGRAM — LEVEL 2	PAGE NO.
1	**Kicking the ball with the full instep** Mobility in attack Balance in defence **Kicking the ball with the inside of the foot** Mobility in attack Balance in defence	58 76 77 60 76 77
2	**Receiving (amortisation) with the inside of the foot** Mobility in attack Balance in defence **Receiving (amortisation) with the full instep** Mobility in attack Balance in defence	62 76 77 64 76 77
3	**Receiving (trapping) with the inside of the foot** Mobility in attack Balance in defence **Receiving (trapping) with the sole of the foot** Mobility in attack Balance in defence	66 76 77 68 76 77
4	**The delay and basic block tackle** Mobility in attack Balance in defence **Basic combinations — 1:1** Mobility in attack Balance in defence	70 76 77 72 76 77
5	**Basic running and sprinting technique** Mobility in attack Balance in defence **Dribbling with the full instep** Mobility in attack Balance in defence	50 76 77 54 76 77

TERM 4

WEEK NO.	TECHNICAL–TACTICAL PROGRAM — LEVEL 2	PAGE NO.
1	Agility in the air and on the ground (reinforce level 1) Small pitch soccer	82 74
2	Agility in the air and on the ground (reinforce level 1) Small pitch soccer	82 74
3	Basketball Small pitch soccer	Basketball* 74
4	Basketball Small pitch soccer	Basketball* 74
5	Agility in the air and on the ground (reinforce level 1) Small pitch soccer	82 74
6	Agility in the air and on the ground (reinforce level 1) Small pitch soccer	82 74
7	Volleyball Small pitch soccer	Volleyball* 74
8	Volleyball Small pitch soccer	Volleyball* 74
9	Agility in the air and on the ground (reinforce level 1) Small pitch soccer	82 74
10	Agility in the air and on the ground (reinforce level 1) Small pitch soccer	82 74

*For the rules of volleyball and basketball, coaches should refer to the relevant coaching books.

LEVEL 3: 11 TO 12 YEARS

Players in level 3 are 11 to 12 years of age.

Tactics in this level must not be coached at the expense of techniques.

The program is for 4 terms of the year, with the 4th term comprising recreation and small pitch soccer.

TERM 1

WEEK NO.	TECHNICAL–TACTICAL PROGRAM — LEVEL 3	PAGE NO.
1	**Jumping with 1 and 2 feet** Penetration in attack Pressing the player without the ball in defence **Basic running and sprinting technique (reinforce level 2)** Mobility in attack Balance in defence	106 134 135 148 76 77
2	**Dribbling with the outside of the instep** Penetration in attack Pressing the player without the ball in defence **The start technique (forward side) (reinforce level 2)** Mobility in attack Balance in defence	108 134 135 149 76 77
3	**Dribbling with the inside of the instep** Penetration in attack Pressing the player without the ball in defence **Dribbling with the full instep (reinforce level 2)** Mobility in attack Balance in defence	110 134 135 150 76 77
4	**Kicking the ball with the inside of the instep** Penetration in attack Pressing the player without the ball in defence **Dribbling with the sole of the foot (reinforce level 2)** Mobility in attack Balance in defence	112 134 135 151 76 77
5	**Kicking the ball with the outside of the instep** Penetration in attack Pressing the player without the ball in defence **Kicking the ball with the full instep (reinforce level 2)** Mobility in attack Balance in defence	114 134 135 152 76 77

WEEK NO.	TECHNICAL–TACTICAL PROGRAM — LEVEL 3	PAGE NO.
6	**The wall pass — 1–2 pass** Penetration in attack Pressing the player without the ball in defence **Kicking the ball with the inside of the foot (reinforce level 2)** Mobility in attack Balance in defence	116 134 135 153 76 77
7	**Receiving (amortisation) with the thigh** Penetration in attack Pressing the player without the ball in defence **Receiving (amortisation) with the inside of the foot (reinforce level 2)** Mobility in attack Balance in defence	118 134 135 154 76 77
8	**Receiving (amortisation) with the chest** Penetration in attack Pressing the player without the ball in defence **Receiving (amortisation) with the full instep (reinforce level 2)** Mobility in attack Balance in defence	120 134 135 155 76 77
9	**Receiving (trapping) with the outside of the instep** Penetration in attack Pressing the player without the ball in defence **Receiving (trapping) with the inside of the foot (reinforce level 2)** Mobility in attack Balance in defence	122 134 135 156 76 77
10	**Heading with the middle zone of the forehead** Penetration in attack Pressing the player without the ball in defence **Receiving (trapping) with the sole of the foot (reinforce level 2)** Mobility in attack Balance in defence	124 134 135 157 76 77

Term 2

WEEK NO.	TECHNICAL–TACTICAL PROGRAM — LEVEL 3	PAGE NO.
1	**The sliding–straddle tackle** Penetration in attack Pressing the player without the ball in defence **The delay and basic block tackle (reinforce level 2)** Mobility in attack Balance in defence	126 134 135 158 76 77
2	**Basic combinations — 2:0** Penetration in attack Pressing the player without the ball in defence **Basic combinations — 1:1 (reinforce level 2)** Mobility in attack Balance in defence	128 134 135 159 76 77
3	**Basic combinations — 2:1** Penetration in attack Pressing the player without the ball in defence **Kicking the ball with the full instep (reinforce level 2)** Mobility in attack Balance in defence	130 134 135 152 76 77
4	**Jumping with 1 and 2 feet** Penetration in attack Pressing the player without the ball in defence **Basic running and sprinting technique (reinforce level 2)** Mobility in attack Balance in defence	106 134 135 148 76 77
5	**Dribbling with the outside of the instep** Penetration in attack Pressing the player without the ball in defence **The start technique (forward side) (reinforce level 2)** Mobility in attack Balance in defence	108 134 135 149 76 77

TERM 3

TERM 4

WEEK NO.	TECHNICAL–TACTICAL PROGRAM — LEVEL 3	PAGE NO.
1	Agility in the air and on the ground (reinforce level 2) Small pitch soccer	162 132
2	Agility in the air and on the ground (reinforce level 2) Small pitch soccer	162 132
3	Basketball Small pitch soccer	Ref. Basketball* 132
4	Basketball Small pitch soccer	Ref. Basketball* 132
5	Agility in the air and on the ground (reinforce level 2) Small pitch soccer	162 132
6	Agility in the air and on the ground (reinforce level 2) Small pitch soccer	162 132
7	Volleyball Small pitch soccer	Ref. Volleyball* 132
8	Volleyball Small pitch soccer	Ref. Volleyball* 132
9	Agility in the air and on the ground (reinforce level 2) Small pitch soccer	162 132
10	Agility in the air and on the ground (reinforce level 2) Small pitch soccer	162 132

*For the rules of volleyball and basketball, coaches should refer to the relevant coaching books.

LEVEL 4: 13 TO 14 YEARS

Players in level 4 are 13 to 14 years of age.
In this level, greater emphasis is placed on the tactical and physical development of the player.
The program is for 4 terms of the year, with the 4th term comprising recreation and small pitch soccer.

TERM 1

WEEK NO.	TECHNICAL–TACTICAL PROGRAM — LEVEL 4	PAGE NO.
1	**Changing direction and speed** Width and depth in attack Pressing the ball in defence **Jumping with 1 and 2 feet (reinforce level 3)** Penetration in attack Pressing the player without the ball in defence	190 210 211 221 134 135
2	**Chipping the ball** Width and depth in attack Pressing the ball in defence **Basic running and sprinting technique (reinforce level 2)** Mobility in attack Balance in defence	192 210 211 243 76 77
3	**Full volley kick (front side)** Width and depth in attack Pressing the ball in defence **Dribbling with the outside of the instep (reinforce level 3)** Penetration in attack Pressing the player without the ball in defence	194 210 211 222 134 135
4	**Half volley kick (front side)** Width and depth in attack Pressing the ball in defence **The start technique (forward side) (reinforce level 2)** Mobility in attack Balance in defence	196 210 211 244 76 77
5	**Receiving (amortisation) with the head** Width and depth in attack Pressing the ball in defence **Dribbling with the inside of the instep (reinforce level 3)** Penetration in attack Pressing the player without the ball in defence	198 210 211 223 134 135

WEEK NO.	TECHNICAL–TACTICAL PROGRAM — LEVEL 4	PAGE NO.
6	**Receiving (trapping) with the stomach/chest** Width and depth in attack Pressing the ball in defence **Dribbling with the full instep (reinforce level 2)** Mobility in attack Balance in defence	200 210 211 245 76 77
7	**Heading with the side zone of the forehead** Width and depth in attack Pressing the ball in defence **Kicking the ball with the inside of the instep (reinforce level 3)** Penetration in attack Pressing the player without the ball in defence	202 210 211 224 134 135
8	**The shoulder charge** Width and depth in attack Pressing the ball in defence **Dribbling with the sole of the foot (reinforce level 2)** Mobility in attack Balance in defence	204 210 211 246 76 77
9	**Basic combinations — 2:2** Width and depth in attack Pressing the ball in defence **Kicking the ball with the outside of the instep (reinforce level 3)** Penetration in attack Pressing the player without the ball in defence	206 210 211 225 134 135
10	**Basic combinations — 2:2** Width and depth in attack Pressing the ball in defence **Kicking the ball with the full instep (reinforce level 2)** Mobility in attack Balance in defence	206 210 211 247 76 77

TERM 2

WEEK NO.	TECHNICAL–TACTICAL PROGRAM — LEVEL 4	PAGE NO.
1	**Changing direction and speed** Width and depth in attack Pressing the ball in defence **The wall pass — 1–2 pass (reinforce level 3)** Penetration in attack Pressing the player without the ball in defence	190 210 211 226 134 135
2	**Chipping the ball** Width and depth in attack Pressing the ball in defence **Kicking the ball with the inside of the foot (reinforce level 2)** Mobility in attack Balance in defence	192 210 211 248 76 77
3	**Full volley kick (front side)** Width and depth in attack Pressing the ball in defence **Receiving (amortisation) with the thigh (reinforce level 3)** Penetration in attack Pressing the player without the ball in defence	194 210 211 227 134 135
4	**Half volley kick (front side)** Width and depth in attack Pressing the ball in defence **Receiving (amortisation) with the inside of the foot (reinforce level 2)** Mobility in attack Balance in defence	196 210 211 249 76 77
5	**Heading with the side zone of the forehead** Width and depth in attack Pressing the ball in defence **The wall pass — 1–2 pass (reinforce level 3)** Penetration in attack Pressing the player without the ball in defence	202 210 211 226 134 135

WEEK NO.	TECHNICAL–TACTICAL PROGRAM — LEVEL 4	PAGE NO.
6	**Receiving (amortisation) with the head** Width and depth in attack Pressing the ball in defence **Receiving (amortisation) with the chest (reinforce level 3)** Penetration in attack Pressing the player without the ball in defence	198 210 211 228 134 135
7	**Receiving (trapping) with the stomach/chest** Width and depth in attack Pressing the ball in defence **Receiving (amortisation) with the full instep (reinforce level 2)** Mobility in attack Balance in defence	200 210 211 250 76 77
8	**Heading with the side zone of the forehead** Width and depth in attack Pressing the ball in defence **Receiving (trapping) with the outside of the instep (reinforce level 3)** Penetration in attack Pressing the player without the ball in defence	202 210 211 229 134 135
9	**The shoulder charge** Width and depth in attack Pressing the ball in defence **Receiving (trapping) with the inside of the foot (reinforce level 2)** Mobility in attack Balance in defence	204 210 211 251 76 77
10	**Basic combinations — 2:2** Width and depth in attack Pressing the ball in defence **Heading with the middle zone of the forehead (reinforce level 3)** Penetration in attack Pressing the player without the ball in defence	206 210 211 230 134 135

TERM 3

WEEK NO.	TECHNICAL–TACTICAL PROGRAM — LEVEL 4	PAGE NO.
1	**Changing direction and speed** Width and depth in attack Pressing the ball in defence **Receiving (trapping) with the sole of the foot (reinforce level 2)** Mobility in attack Balance in defence	190 210 211 252 76 77
2	**Chipping the ball** Width and depth in attack Pressing the ball in defence **The sliding–straddle tackle (reinforce level 3)** Penetration in attack Pressing the player without the ball in defence	192 210 211 231 134 135
3	**Full volley kick (front side)** Width and depth in attack Pressing the ball in defence **The delay and basic block tackle (reinforce level 2)** Mobility in attack Balance in defence	194 210 211 253 76 77
4	**Half volley kick (front side)** Width and depth in attack Pressing the ball in defence **Basic combinations — 2:0 (reinforce level 3)** Penetration in attack Pressing the player without the ball in defence	196 210 211 232 134 135
5	**Receiving (amortisation) with the head** Width and depth in attack Pressing the ball in defence **Basic combinations — 1:1 (reinforce level 2)** Mobility in attack Balance in defence	198 210 211 254 76 77

WEEK NO.	TECHNICAL–TACTICAL PROGRAM — LEVEL 4	PAGE NO.
6	**Receiving (trapping) with the stomach/chest** Width and depth in attack Pressing the ball in defence **Basic combinations — 2:1 (reinforce level 3)** Penetration in attack Pressing the player without the ball in defence	200 210 211 233 134 135
7	**Heading with the side zone of the forehead** Width and depth in attack Pressing the ball in defence **The wall pass — 1–2 pass (reinforce level 3)** Penetration in attack Pressing the player without the ball in defence	202 210 211 226 134 135
8	**The shoulder charge** Width and depth in attack Pressing the ball in defence **Basic combinations — 2:0 (reinforce level 3)** Penetration in attack Pressing the player without the ball in defence	204 210 211 232 134 135
9	**Basic combinations — 2:2** Width and depth in attack Pressing the ball in defence **Basic combinations — 2:1 (reinforce level 3)** Penetration in attack Pressing the player without the ball in defence	206 210 211 233 134 135
10	**Heading with the side zone of the forehead** Width and depth in attack Pressing the ball in defence **The wall pass — 1–2 pass (reinforce level 3)** Penetration in attack Pressing the player without the ball in defence	202 210 211 226 134 135

TERM 4

WEEK NO.	TECHNICAL–TACTICAL PROGRAM — LEVEL 4	PAGE NO.
1	Agility in the air and on the ground (reinforce level 3) Small pitch soccer	256 208
2	Agility in the air and on the ground (reinforce level 3) Small pitch soccer	256 208
3	Basketball Small pitch soccer	Ref. Basketball* 208
4	Basketball Small pitch soccer	Ref. Basketball* 208
5	Agility in the air and on the ground (reinforce level 3) Small pitch soccer	256 208
6	Agility in the air and on the ground (reinforce level 3) Small pitch soccer	256 208
7	Volleyball Small pitch soccer	Ref. Volleyball* 208
8	Volleyball Small pitch soccer	Ref. Volleyball* 208
9	Agility in the air and on the ground (reinforce level 3) Small pitch soccer	256 208
10	Agility in the air and on the ground (reinforce level 3) Small pitch soccer	256 208

*For the rules of volleyball and basketball, coaches should refer to the relevant coaching books.

LEVEL 5: 15 TO 16 YEARS

Players in level 5 are 15 to 16 years of age.
    In this level, greater emphasis is placed on the tactical and physical development of the player.
    The program is for 4 terms of the year, with the 4th term comprising recreation and small pitch soccer.

Term 1

TERM 2

Term 3

WEEK NO.	TECHNICAL–TACTICAL PROGRAM — LEVEL 5	PAGE NO.
1	**The overhead (scissors) volley kick** Switch of play Zone and combined zone defence **Heading with the middle zone of the forehead (reinforce level 3)** **The sliding–straddle tackle (reinforce level 3)** Penetration in attack Pressing the player without the ball in defence	278 316 317 354 355 134 135
2	**Kicking with the toe, heel and knee** **The diving header** Switch of play Zone and combined zone defence **Receiving (trapping) with the inside of the foot (reinforce level 2)** **Receiving (trapping) with the sole of the foot (reinforce level 2)** Mobility in attack Balance in defence	280 282 316 317 375 376 76 77
3	**Intercepting the pass** Switch of play Zone and combined zone defence **Basic combinations — 2:2 (reinforce level 4)** Width and depth in attack Pressing the ball in defence	284 316 317 337 210 211
4	**Basic combinations — 3:0** Switch of play Zone and combined zone defence **Basic combinations — 2:0 (reinforce level 3)** Penetration in attack Pressing the player without the ball in defence	286 316 317 356 134 135
5	**Basic combinations — 3:2** Switch of play Zone and combined zone defence **The delay and basic block tackle (reinforce level 2)** Mobility in attack Balance in defence	288 316 317 377 76 77

WEEK NO.	TECHNICAL–TACTICAL PROGRAM — LEVEL 5	PAGE NO.
6	**Team technical–tactical playing patterns — attack** Switch of play Zone and combined zone defence **Chipping the ball (reinforce level 4)** Width and depth in attack Pressing the ball in defence	290 316 317 330 210 211
7	**Team technical–tactical playing patterns — defence** Switch of play Zone and combined zone defence **Basic combinations — 2:1 (reinforce level 3)** Penetration in attack Pressing the player without the ball in defence	296 316 317 357 134 135
8	**Set play — attacking situations** Switch of play Zone and combined zone defence **Basic combinations — 1:1 (reinforce level 2)** Mobility in attack Balance in defence	303 316 317 378 76 77
9	**Set play — defending situations** Switch of play Zone and combined zone defence **The wall pass — 1–2 pass (reinforce level 3)** Penetration in attack Pressing the player without the ball in defence	308 316 317 350 134 135
10	**Basic combinations — 3:2** Switch of play Zone and combined zone defence **Basic combinations — 1:1 (reinforce level 2)** Mobility in attack Balance in defence	288 316 317 378 76 77

Term 4

WEEK NO.	TECHNICAL–TACTICAL PROGRAM — LEVEL 5	PAGE NO.
1	Basketball Small pitch and full pitch soccer	Ref. Basketball* 314
2	Basketball Small pitch and full pitch soccer	Ref. Basketball* 314
3	Agility in the air and on the ground (reinforce level 4) Small pitch and full pitch soccer	380 314
4	Agility in the air and on the ground (reinforce level 4) Small pitch and full pitch soccer	380 314
5	Volleyball Small pitch and full pitch soccer	Ref. Volleyball* 314
6	Volleyball Small pitch and full pitch soccer	Ref. Volleyball* 314
7	Agility in the air and on the ground (reinforce level 4) Small pitch and full pitch soccer	380 314
8	Agility in the air and on the ground (reinforce level 4) Small pitch and full pitch soccer	380 314
9	Basketball Small pitch and full pitch soccer	Ref. Basketball* 314
10	Basketball Small pitch and full pitch soccer	Ref. Basketball* 314

*For the rules of volleyball and basketball, coaches should refer to the relevant coaching books.

LEVEL 6: 17+ YEARS

Players in level 6 are 17 plus years of age.

In level 6, all the soccer development program's technical–tactical elements are to be reinforced, maintaining the level of excellence in execution.

The program is for 4 terms of the year, with the 4th term comprising recreation and small pitch soccer.

Term 1

WEEK NO.	TECHNICAL–TACTICAL PROGRAM — LEVEL 6	PAGE NO.
1	**Basic running and sprinting technique** **Dribbling with the full instep** Switch of play Zone and combined zone defence **The start technique (forward side)** **The wall pass — 1–2 pass** Width and depth in attack Pressing the ball in defence	367 369 316 317 368 350 210 211
2	**Basic combinations — 1:1** **Basic combinations — 2:0** Switch of play Zone and combined zone defence **Basic combinations — 2:1** **Basic combinations — 2:2** Penetration in attack Pressing the player without the ball in defence	378 356 316 317 357 337 134 135
3	**Basic combinations — 3:0** **Basic combinations — 3:2** Switch of play Zone and combined zone defence **Kicking the ball with the inside of the foot** **Receiving (amortisation) with the inside of the foot** Mobility in attack Balance in defence	286 288 316 317 372 373 76 77
4	**Team technical–tactical playing patterns — attack** Switch of play Zone and combined zone defence **Team technical–tactical playing patterns — defence** Width and depth in attack Pressing the ball in defence	290 316 317 296 210 211
5	**Receiving (amortisation) with the full instep** **The delay and basic block tackle** Switch of play Zone and combined zone defence **Dribbling with the sole of the foot** **Receiving (amortisation) with the head** Penetration in attack Pressing the player without the ball in defence	374 377 316 317 370 333 134 135

Term 2

WEEK NO.	TECHNICAL–TACTICAL PROGRAM — LEVEL 6	PAGE NO.
1	**The wall pass — 1–2 pass** Switch of play Zone and combined zone defence **Receiving (trapping) with the outside of the instep** **Heading with the middle zone of the forehead** Penetration in attack Pressing the player without the ball in defence	350 316 317 353 354 134 135
2	**Basic combinations — 1:1** **Basic combinations — 2:0** Switch of play Zone and combined zone defence **Basic combinations — 2:1** **Basic combinations — 2:2** Mobility in attack Balance in defence	378 356 316 317 357 337 76 77
3	**Basic combinations — 3:0** **Basic combinations — 3:2** Switch of play Zone and combined zone defence **Changing direction and speed** **Chipping the ball** Width and depth in attack Pressing the ball in defence	286 288 316 317 329 330 210 211
4	**Full volley kick (front side)** **Half volley kick (front side)** Switch of play Zone and combined zone defence **Team technical–tactical playing patterns — attack** Penetration in attack Pressing the player without the ball in defence	331 332 316 317 290 134 135
5	**The wall pass — 1–2 pass** Switch of play Zone and combined zone defence **Receiving (trapping) with the outside of the instep** **Heading with the middle zone of the forehead** Penetration in attack Pressing the player without the ball in defence	350 316 317 353 354 134 135

TERM 3

WEEK NO.	TECHNICAL–TACTICAL PROGRAM — LEVEL 6	PAGE NO.
1	**Basic combinations — 1:1** **Basic combinations — 2:0** Switch of play Zone and combined zone defence **Basic combinations — 2:1** **Basic combinations — 2:2** Penetration in attack Pressing the player without the ball in defence	378 356 316 317 357 337 134 135
2	**Basic combinations — 3:0** **Basic combinations — 3:2** Switch of play Zone and combined zone defence **The wall pass — 1–2 pass** Mobility in attack Balance in defence	286 288 316 317 350 76 77
3	**Team technical–tactical playing patterns — attack** Switch of play Zone and combined zone defence **Team technical–tactical playing patterns — defence** Width and depth in attack Pressing the ball in defence	290 316 317 296 210 211
4	**Set play — attacking situations** **Set play — defending situations** Switch of play Zone and combined zone defence **Kicking the ball with the inside of the foot** **Receiving (amortisation) with the inside of the foot** Mobility in attack Balance in defence	303 308 316 317 372 373 76 77
5	**Basic combinations — 1:1** **Basic combinations — 2:0** Switch of play Zone and combined zone defence **Basic combinations — 2:1** **Basic combinations — 2:2** Penetration in attack Pressing the player without the ball in defence	378 356 316 317 357 337 134 135

WEEK NO.	*TECHNICAL–TACTICAL PROGRAM — LEVEL 6*	PAGE NO.
6	**Basic combinations — 3:0** **Basic combinations — 3:2** Switch of play Zone and combined zone defence **The wall pass — 1–2 pass** Mobility in attack Balance in defence	286 288 316 317 350 76 77
7	**Team technical–tactical playing patterns — attack** Switch of play Zone and combined zone defence **Team technical–tactical playing patterns — defence** Width and depth in attack Pressing the ball in defence	290 316 317 296 210 211
8	**Dribbling with the inside of the instep** **Kicking the ball with the inside of the instep** Switch of play Zone and combined zone defence **Dribbling with the outside of the instep** **Kicking the ball with the outside of the instep** Penetration in attack Pressing the player without the ball in defence	347 348 316 317 346 349 134 135
9	**Team technical–tactical playing patterns — attack** Switch of play Zone and combined zone defence **Team technical–tactical playing patterns — defence** Width and depth in attack Pressing the ball in defence	290 316 317 296 210 211
10	**Basic combinations — 3:0** **Basic combinations — 3:2** Switch of play Zone and combined zone defence **The wall pass — 1–2 pass** Mobility in attack Balance in defence	286 288 316 317 350 76 77

TERM 4

WEEK NO.	TECHNICAL–TACTICAL PROGRAM — LEVEL 6	PAGE NO.
1	Basketball Small pitch and full pitch soccer	Ref. Basketball* 409
2	Basketball Small pitch and full pitch soccer	Ref. Basketball* 409
3	Agility in the air and on the ground Small pitch and full pitch soccer	380 409
4	Agility in the air and on the ground Small pitch and full pitch soccer	380 409
5	Volleyball Small pitch and full pitch soccer	Ref. Volleyball* 409
6	Volleyball Small pitch and full pitch soccer	Ref. Volleyball* 409
7	Agility in the air and on the ground Small pitch and full pitch soccer	380 409
8	Agility in the air and on the ground Small pitch and full pitch soccer	380 409
9	Basketball Small pitch and full pitch soccer	Ref. Basketball* 409
10	Basketball Small pitch and full pitch soccer	Ref. Basketball* 409

*For the rules of volleyball and basketball, coaches should refer to the relevant coaching books.

Superstar Romario triumphantly holds the World Cup trophy from the World Cup USA '94

Technical-tactical
conditioned games

Technical-tactical element in defence

Balance

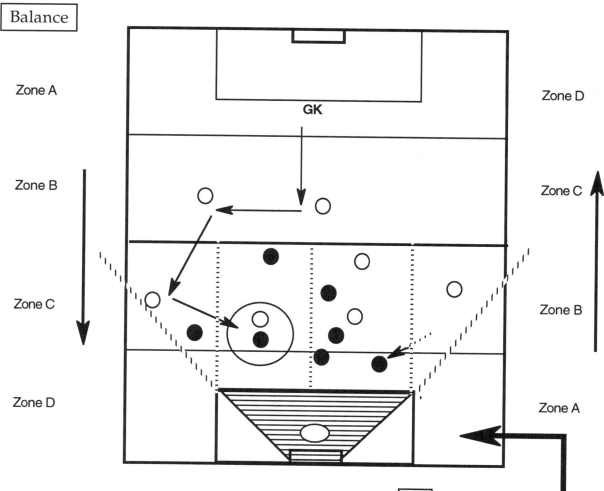

Small pitch game is played with offside rule.

Balance is the ability to limit the creation of space, penetration and passing angles by the attacking team.

A defending team can be in balance in any zone.

This conditioned game starts with the goalkeeper throwing a short pass to a supporting player.

The defending team recovers behind the ball and funnels back into a zone formation in zone B.

Here the defending team members adjust their positions to cut the passing angles and reduce the time and space the attacking players will have on the ball.

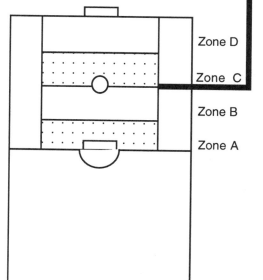

On winning possession in zone A or B the team goes on a counterattack until possession is lost.

The exercise then starts from the other goalkeeper.

Pressing the player

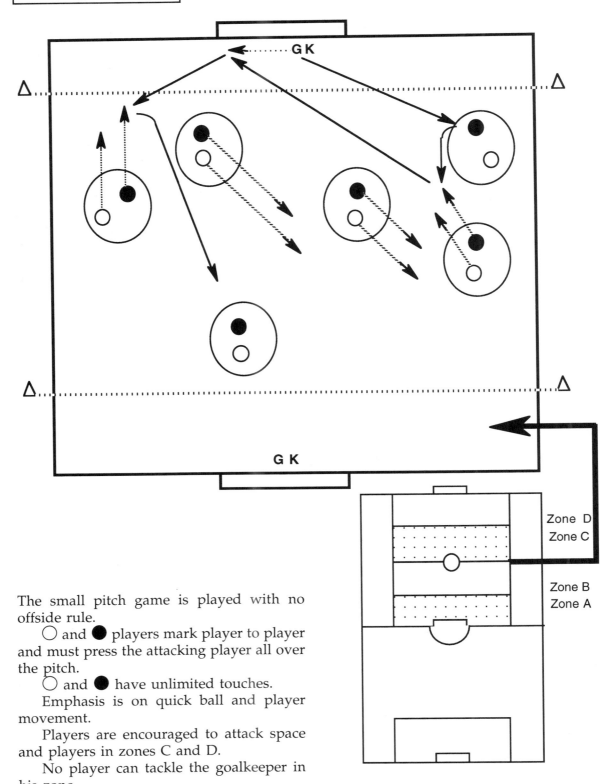

The small pitch game is played with no offside rule.

○ and ● players mark player to player and must press the attacking player all over the pitch.

○ and ● have unlimited touches.

Emphasis is on quick ball and player movement.

Players are encouraged to attack space and players in zones C and D.

No player can tackle the goalkeeper in his zone.

The goalkeeper is limited to 1 touch when the ball is played back from a team member.

When possession is lost the exercise starts from the other goalkeeper.

Pressing the ball

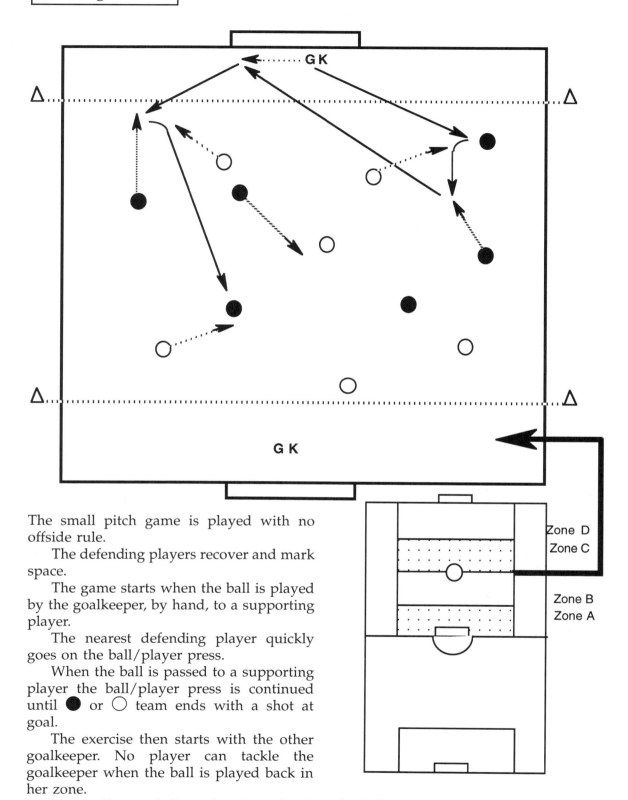

The small pitch game is played with no offside rule.

The defending players recover and mark space.

The game starts when the ball is played by the goalkeeper, by hand, to a supporting player.

The nearest defending player quickly goes on the ball/player press.

When the ball is passed to a supporting player the ball/player press is continued until ● or ○ team ends with a shot at goal.

The exercise then starts with the other goalkeeper. No player can tackle the goalkeeper when the ball is played back in her zone.

The goalkeeper is limited to 1 touch when the ball is played back from a team member.

Emphasis is on the press before the second touch.

Zone-combined zone defence

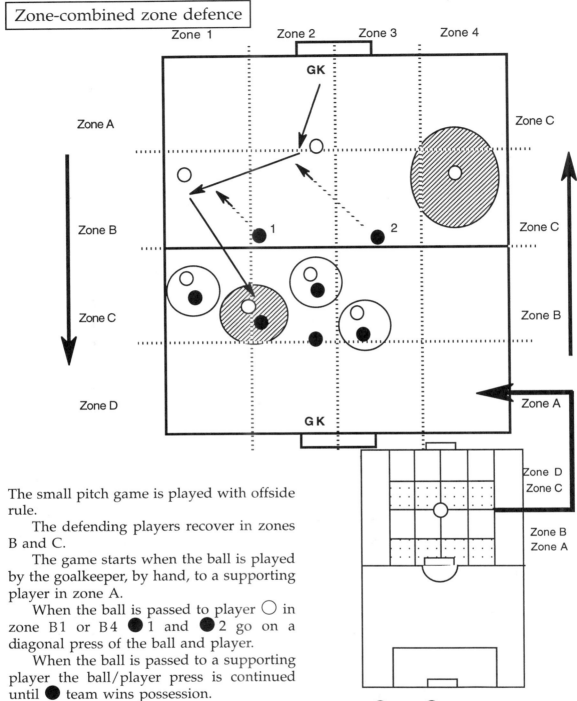

The small pitch game is played with offside rule.

The defending players recover in zones B and C.

The game starts when the ball is played by the goalkeeper, by hand, to a supporting player in zone A.

When the ball is passed to player ◯ in zone B1 or B4 ●1 and ●2 go on a diagonal press of the ball and player.

When the ball is passed to a supporting player the ball/player press is continued until ● team wins possession.

On winning possession the first pass is forward to ●1 or ●2 in zone C.

No ◯ player can tackle ●1 or ●2 on their first touch in zone C. The first touch in zone C by ● must be played back to a supporting player. The whole ● team now is moving out on a counterattack and going for goal. Both ● and ◯ players are now under full pressure.

If zone-combined pressing the player breaks down then pass onto zone-combined pressing the ball.

After a shot at goal the exercise is repeated with the other goalkeeper.

In this conditioned game the ball cannot be played back to the goalkeeper.

Mobility in attack

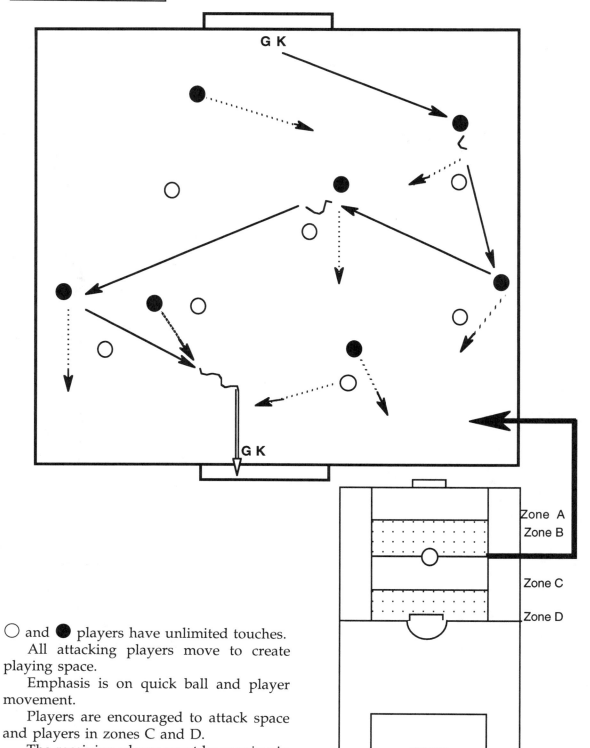

○ and ● players have unlimited touches.

All attacking players move to create playing space.

Emphasis is on quick ball and player movement.

Players are encouraged to attack space and players in zones C and D.

The receiving player must be moving in space while receiving. After the kick, the player with the ball must move into supporting space.

If the player is static after passing the ball or the player receiving is static, a free kick is given to the opponents.

Penetration

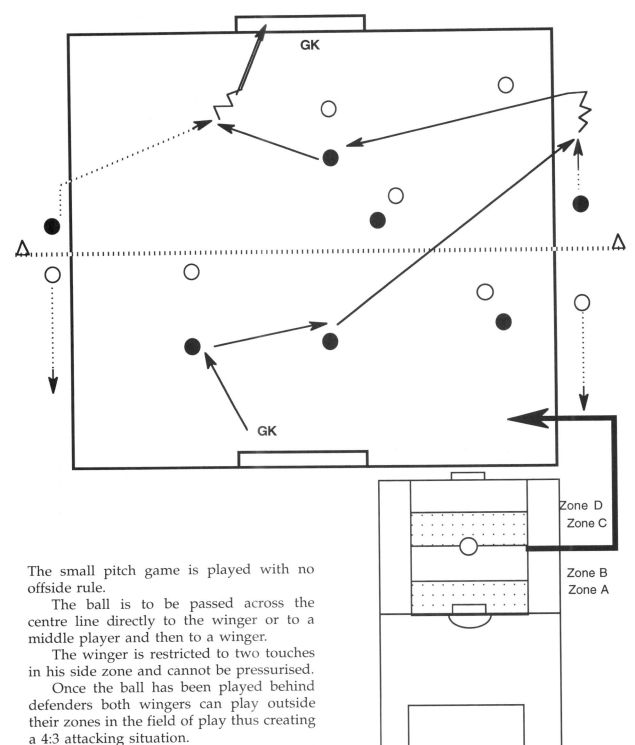

The small pitch game is played with no offside rule.

The ball is to be passed across the centre line directly to the winger or to a middle player and then to a winger.

The winger is restricted to two touches in his side zone and cannot be pressurised.

Once the ball has been played behind defenders both wingers can play outside their zones in the field of play thus creating a 4:3 attacking situation.

In this situation they have unlimited touches and are pressurised by the three defenders.

After a shot at goal or lost possession the exercise commences with the other goalkeeper.

Width and depth in attack

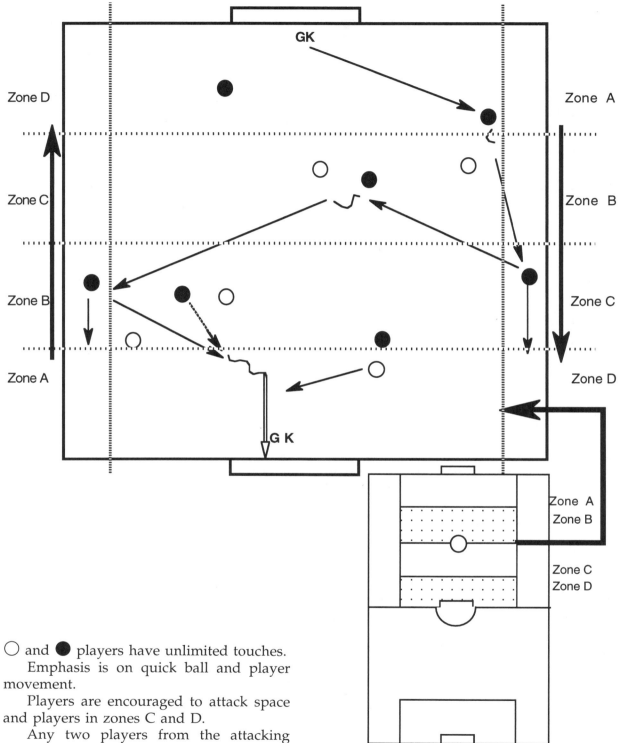

○ and ● players have unlimited touches.

Emphasis is on quick ball and player movement.

Players are encouraged to attack space and players in zones C and D.

Any two players from the attacking team *must* be in the left and right side zones (*width*), with remaining players in zones B, C and D (*depth*) for a goal to count.

If any attacking player is in zone A or all players are in zones C and D then the goal does not count.

Switch of play

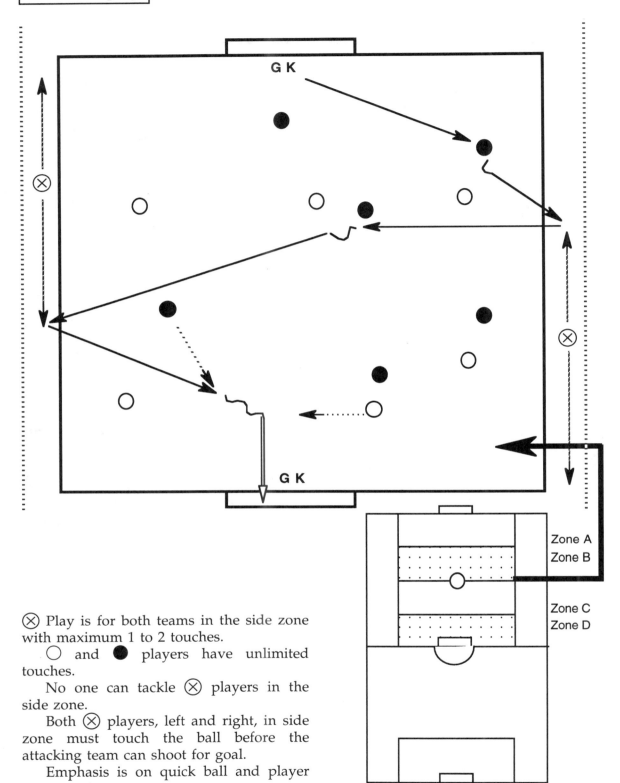

Zone A
Zone B

Zone C
Zone D

⊗ Play is for both teams in the side zone with maximum 1 to 2 touches.

○ and ● players have unlimited touches.

No one can tackle ⊗ players in the side zone.

Both ⊗ players, left and right, in side zone must touch the ball before the attacking team can shoot for goal.

Emphasis is on quick ball and player movement.

When switch is made, side zone players can play ball short or cross the ball into goal area.

Glossary

Accurate hitting the target

Active exercises exercises with player moving

Agility moving the whole body quickly while maintaining balance

Analytic method of coaching the movement is broken up so that 1 particular phase is executed

Arch the back bend the back

Attacking when the team is in possession

Balance in defence limit the creation of space, penetration and passing angles

Basic running jogging

Bend the ball the ball is struck off-centre, making it rotate and swerve in the air

Block tackle the ball is wedged by the defender in the tackle

Central (basic) basic elements of the game to be learnt

Change direction change to a different line of movement

Change places move to a different position

Chest part of body enclosed by the ribs

Chipping the ball kicking with the lower part of the instep below the ball centre

Coach one who instructs

Coaching session conducted by the coach

Combination 1 vs 1 1 player versus another player

Combined method of coaching movement executed as a whole but frozen where the fault occurs and analytic method applied

Controlled systematic development thorough and regular control of the player's planned development

Co-ordination combination and harmonisation of movements

Create produce by force of imagination

Create a basis produce a solid foundation for future development

Deceive mislead the opponent in particular phases of the game

Defending when the team is not in possession

Delay tackle the defending player pulling back a distance before tackling

Diagonal pass cross-wise movement of the ball

Diagonal run cross-wise movement of the player

Disguise conceal

Diving header diving to head the ball when it is between the waist and shoulder

Dribbling running with the ball under close control

Dummy to move with or without the ball to unbalance the opponent

Explosive foot strength great intensity in a very short period of time

Eye on the ball keep watching the ball

Feinting making deceptive body movements to delude the opponent

Field players players not able to touch the ball from the arms to the hands

Filter system separate the players into groups

Flexibility being elastic

Full instep the laces part of the boot

Full pitch soccer playing on a full-sized soccer pitch

Full volley kick kicking with any part of the foot while the ball is in the air

Get in front move forward

Goalkeeper the player in goals able to use his or her hands

Half volley kick kicking with any part the moment the ball hits the ground

Heading the ball striking the ball with the head

Individual corrective TE-TA coaching individual technical–tactical correction of faults

Informal game game without strict laws; casual game

Inside of the foot the large flat area on the inside of the foot

Inside of the instep inner surface from the toe to the ankle joint

Intercepting the pass at the moment the ball is about to be passed, quickly moving to intercept

Juggling the ball keeping a moving ball off the ground with any part of the body except from the arms to the hands

Jumping with 1 foot springing from the ground by the muscle action of 1 leg

Jumping with 2 feet springing from the ground by the muscle action of both legs

Keep the ball low play the ball along the grass surface

Kicking with the toe, heel and knee passing to a supporting player or shooting at goal with the toe, knee and heel

Locked and hard held fast or inactive

Markers cones to define area of coaching

Mobility in attack the ability to move with or without the ball to create playing space

Net a device on the goals for catching the ball

Offside less than 2 opponents between receiver and goal line when ball played forward

Outside of the instep outside surface from the small toe to

the the ankle joint

Overhead scissors (volley) kick kicking the ball over the head

Partner supporting player

Penetration ability to get past or behind defenders, with or without the ball

Playing patterns in attack a model of play to be copied when in possession

Playing patterns in defence a model of play to be copied when not in possession

Practice actual doing of the exercise

Pressing the ball to reduce time and space the attacking player will have to receive the pass, dribble or shoot at goal

Pressing the player without the ball to reduce time and playing space of a player when receiving the ball

Pressure a player reduce the attacking player's time and space

Program a plan of procedure

Psychomotor factor muscle action from conscious mental activity

Receiving (amortising) the ball deadening the ball

Receiving (trapping) the ball forming a wedge to control the ball

Recover behind the ball defend and reduce space for the attacking team

Reduce the space increase pressure on the attacking team

Set play when the referee stops the game it is restarted with a set move

Shot at goal trying to beat the goalkeeper and score a goal

Shoulder charge shoulders make contact as the defender tackles for the ball

Side team

Situational method of coaching teaching movements that meet the conditions of the game

Sliding tackle defender, slightly behind the attacker, slides to the ball

Small pitch soccer playing on a smaller soccer pitch

Small-sided game reduced number of players playing in a game

Space area in which a player can play

Specialisation concentration on a special activity

Speed high frequency of movement

Spin turning around the axis

Static exercise a sustained stretch

Stomach abdomen or belly

Straddle tackle defending player, in front of the attacker, jumps at the ball

Strategy overall plan embracing factors that influence team performance

Support in attack or defence to assist or help team mates when in possession or not in possession

Switch of play the ability to draw defenders out of position and exploit space on the opposite side

System arrangement of players on the field of play

Tactics the art of employing the player's technical and physical skills to accomplish the best possible result

Thigh from the hip to the knee

Tighter allow less playing space

To have balance to be stable

Wall pass — 1–2 pass 2 players passing the ball behind a defender

Weight the pass timing the speed of the pass correctly

Width and depth the ability to create playing space across and along the field of play

Work to produce a desired effect physically or mentally

Zone and combined zone defence ability to recover goalside of the ball, cover an area and press any player entering that zone

Photo acknowledgments

The photographs in this book are from the following sources:
Pages 12, 290, 320, 358, 389, 408—Live Action
Pages 100, 185, 312—Vedat Acikalin/Live Action
Page 338—Sipa-Press/Live Action
Page 41—Jan Collsioo/Allsport/Australian Picture Library
Page 296—Kishimoto/Live Action
Pages 170, 214, 234, 264, 277, 302, 313, 413, 467—Allsport
Pages 13, 49, 80, 91, 138, 147—The Hamlyn Book of World Soccer, Peter Arnold
and Christopher Davis, The Hamlyn Publishing Group Limited, London, 1973

AM8279-TN

82